First Supplement to James E. Walsh's Catalogue of the Fifteenth-Century Printed Books in the Harvard University Library

FIRST SUPPLEMENT

TO

JAMES E. WALSH'S CATALOGUE

OF THE

FIFTEENTH-CENTURY PRINTED BOOKS

IN THE

HARVARD UNIVERSITY LIBRARY

David R. Whitesell

HOUGHTON LIBRARY OF THE HARVARD COLLEGE LIBRARY 2006

Distributed by Harvard University Press
Cambridge, Massachusetts and London, England

A Special Issue of the *Harvard Library Bulletin*
Volume 16: Number 1-2

HARVARD LIBRARY BULLETIN
VOLUME 16: NUMBERS 1-2 (SPRING-SUMMER 2005)
PUBLISHED SEPTEMBER 2006
ISSN 0017-8136

Editor
Wiliam P. Stoneman

Coordinating Editor
Matthew Battles

ADVISORY BOARD

The Harvard Library Bulletin *is published quarterly by Houghton Library of the Harvard College Library. Annual subscription $35 (U.S., Canada, and Mexico), $41 (foreign); single issue $15.*

Editorial correspondence should be addressed to Matthew Battles, Houghton Library, Harvad University, Cambridge, MA 02138, email mbattles@fas.harvard.edu; claims and subscription inquiries should be addressed to Monique Duhaime, Houghton Library, Cambridge, MA 02138, email duhaime@fas.harvard.edu.

Publication of the Bulletin *is made possible by a bequest from George L. Lincoln '95, and by a fund established in memory of William A. Jackson.*

The paper used in this publication meets the minimum requirements of the American National Standard for Information Sciences—Permanence of Paper for Printed Materials, ANSI z39.49-1984.

ISBN for this issue is 0674021452. Distributed by Harvard University Press, Cambridge, Massachusetts and London, England.

Contents

Preface

On Tuesday, 9 December 1997, friends and colleagues of James Edward Walsh gathered in Houghton Library's Edison and Newman Room to celebrate two milestones. The first was Walsh's fifty years of continuous Harvard Library service, impeded not at all by the formality of his "retirement" at approximately the forty-year mark. The second was the publication of the fifth and final volume to Walsh's monumental *A Catalogue of the Fifteenth-Century Printed Books in the Harvard University Library*.[1] Nearly a decade in the writing, Walsh's catalogue fully described the 4,187 incunabula he had located in the nearly one hundred libraries at Harvard; volume five added copious indexes and an invaluable history of the collection.[2] Many of the world's leading incunabulists sent tributes to be read aloud during the reception. Paul Needham, for one, pointed out that Walsh's catalogue "is, for America, unique" in providing full access to the copy-specific features of the nation's third-largest collection of early printed books. He correctly predicted that "we're never going to call it the 'Harvard' catalogue; its name is 'Walsh.'" Fittingly, many of its subjects—the two-thousand-odd incunabula shelved in bookcases lining the Edison and Newman Room—were silent witnesses to the festivities.

James Walsh's reception was one of the first public events hosted by William P. Stoneman, who had recently been appointed Librarian of Houghton Library. Stoneman had come from the Scheide Library at Princeton University, where he curated one of the world's notable collections of fifteenth-century printing. Naturally eager to learn more about Harvard's incunabula, Stoneman quickly discovered that Walsh's book catalogue provided far superior access to Harvard's "fifteeners" than did the Harvard University Library's online catalogue, HOLLIS.

Only a few months previously, the Harvard University Library had celebrated the successful conversion to electronic form of its entire card catalogue, which documented a collection then totalling over thirteen million volumes. With ease of access, however, came significant problems, some inherent to the conversion process, others inevitable in an environment where for decades Harvard's many libraries had followed multiple cataloguing standards. One did not have to search long in HOLLIS to find duplicate records for multiple copies, or even for the same copy, of a single edition, with additional duplicate records for microform surrogates. Some HOLLIS records credited Harvard with owning editions other than the ones actually on its shelves. Sometimes a book had no HOLLIS record at all, in which case it was effectively

---

1   Volumes 1-4: Binghamton, NY: Medieval & Renaissance Texts & Studies, 1991-1996; volume 5: Tempe, Ariz.: Medieval & Renaissance Texts & Studies, 1997. Volumes 2 and 3 were reprinted in 1997.

2   The collection history has been reprinted, with additional illustrations, as: James E. Walsh, "Forming Harvard's Collection of Incunabula," *Harvard Library Bulletin*, n.s., v. 8, no. 3 (Fall 1997): 1-74.

lost. In many instances works by the same author or editions of the same title were entered under variant headings, so that it was impossible to retrieve all through a single search. Hence locating incunabula in HOLLIS, even with Walsh in hand, could be a game of bibliographical hide-and-seek. Perhaps the greatest shortcoming was that the vast majority of incunabula in HOLLIS were significantly undercatalogued, as had been the tradition in most American research libraries until quite recently: relatively few had received full bibliographical or copy-specific descriptions, or adequate subject access.

Early in 1998 Stoneman and Mollie Della Terza, Head of Houghton Library's Department of Technical Services, successfully sought funding from the Harvard College Library for two three-year projects: one to upgrade HOLLIS records for Houghton's incunabula, and another to enhance records for its equally distinguished collection of pre-1641 English ("STC") imprints. It was my privilege to be asked to plan and supervise the incunabula project. Work began on 1 July 1998, with the expert assistance first of Damian G. Konkoly and later of Bridget Balint. For each of Houghton Library's 2,700-odd incunables, duplicate HOLLIS records were eliminated, new records were created where none existed, variant name and title headings were standardized, and substandard records were replaced, where possible, with better records from the OCLC and RLIN databases. Then most of the bibliographical and copy-specific information provided in the Walsh catalogue was added to the online record. By the beginning of 2001, researchers anywhere in the world with Internet access could freely obtain through HOLLIS[3] most of the information to be found in Walsh. Concurrently, as other priorities permitted, I began to enhance each HOLLIS record until it fully met national rare book cataloguing standards. This has been a more laborious process: the standards employed in library cataloguing are far different from those followed by incunabulists, so it was necessary to re-examine each incunable and glean additional information from it. To date approximately 1,200 of Houghton Library's incunabula have been fully recatalogued in HOLLIS.[4]

Meanwhile, Harvard libraries have continued to acquire incunabula since Walsh's 1994 cut-off date, and other incunabula acquired earlier which somehow eluded Walsh's dragnet have been flushed from their hiding places. It was inevitable, too, that the recataloguing process would reveal additional information of note, in particular provenance data, as well as some errors in need of correction. By 1999 it was clear that a Walsh supplement would be desirable; and when James Walsh declined to undertake

3   http://hollisweb.harvard.edu.

4   Houghton is by no means the only Harvard library for which the Walsh catalogue has been a call to action. The Francis A. Countway Library of Medicine has launched a project to recatalogue its incunabula, and the Harvard Law Library has recatalogued its English incunabula. Taking advantage of their temporary relocation to Houghton Library during the recent Andover-Harvard Theological Library renovation, I recatalogued the twenty-six Andover-Harvard incunabula.

it, I agreed to do so. This, then, is the first in what is hoped will be an ongoing series of supplements. In publishing it we seek to honor Walsh's magnificent achievement in the most responsible way possible: by ensuring that scholars worldwide continue to have full and timely information on all fifteenth-century printing in the Harvard University Library.

II

It is necessary to outline carefully what this first supplement includes, and what remains to be described in future supplements. The initial section consists of selected additions and corrections to Walsh catalogue entries, arranged by Walsh number. These are confined largely to copy-specific information for incunabula at Houghton Library, as gathered during the ongoing recataloguing process mentioned above. Included are corrections and clarifications to provenance information, some newly identified provenances, descriptions of additional defects or significant physical features of interest, call number changes and other library housekeeping matters, and additional references to published scholarly work on Harvard incunabula. A few binding descriptions have been revised, not because Walsh got them wrong, but because the anticipated conservation work has yet to be undertaken.[5] *Not* included here are minor corrections such as typographical errors in Walsh entries, and most edition-specific information such as new attributions of author, printer, or publication date, or revised contents notes. This information will continue to change, and change again, as long as scholars remain interested in early printed books, and researchers should consult the bibliographical literature and the *Incunabula Short-Title Catalogue* (ISTC) database[6] for the latest scholarly opinion on such matters.

The following section of "New Entries" consists primarily of incunabula found in or acquired by Harvard libraries in the decade since Walsh completed his survey. A few escaped Walsh's notice because of inadequate record-keeping or miscataloguing. A perfect case in point is the incunable discovered in the Widener Library stacks in 1999 by Kenneth E. Carpenter.[7] Lacking a colophon, it had not unreasonably been catalogued as "N.p., n.d." and had languished on Widener's shelves, unnoticed and unused, for nearly a century. More proudly, we can point to no fewer than forty-six new incunabula purchased by Houghton Library and the Harvard Law Library over the past decade. In Houghton Library's case, this was made possible through the assistance of the Harvard College Library and the generosity of donors who have established several new acquisition funds. Other incunabula have been received as

---

5   A significant weakness of Walsh is that contemporary bindings and their tools were not described more fully, nor were workshop identifications attempted. I have not yet tried to remedy this deficiency.

6   The ISTC database is accessible free of charge at http://www.bl.uk/catalogues/istc/index.html.

7   Entry S1-1043A in this supplement.

gifts, most notably the three English incunabula bequeathed to the Harvard Law Library by Henry N. Ess (J.D. 1944).

For this supplement, the decision was made to include nearly all identifiable fragments of fifteenth-century printing now in the Harvard University Library, a category for which Walsh had provided, without explanation, only highly selective coverage. This decision was not made lightly, as it opened a veritable Pandora's Box of problems for a collection as rich as Harvard's. Should, for instance, one include modern bindings made more appealing by covering the boards with fragmentary incunable leaves, or older bindings incorporating fifteenth-century printed waste as pastedowns, boards, spine liners, or quire guards? Readers may be relieved to learn that binding waste has generally been excluded from this supplement if it remains *in situ*, but fragments removed from bindings have been included.[8] A cursory perusal of this supplement, then, will reveal a preponderance of single leaves and fragments. Some of these are admittedly of little interest, and their inclusion here may seem debatable, even decidedly unhelpful for thereby concealing the more interesting items. Others, however, are of the greatest importance and would merit inclusion no matter how fragmentary. There is no satisfactory way to separate the incunabular wheat and chaff, and the most responsible policy is to be as inclusive as possible.

Hence in this supplement one will find a full accounting, with separate index, of Harvard's holdings of "leaf books" containing original incunable leaves, including several interesting publications not generally recognized as such.[9] Also described are a substantial number of fragments gathered from various sources. Of particular note is the magnificent album of printed waste removed from bindings on books from the library of Hannibal Gamon, which W.H. Allnutt assembled in the late nineteenth century.[10] William A. Jackson acquired the album for Houghton Library in 1963 because most of its fragments belonged to STC imprints, and Katharine F. Pantzer has made a thorough study of these. It was my good fortune to rediscover the album and to identify eleven of its fragments as fifteenth-century printing, including one from a previously unrecorded edition.[11] Another unexpected source has been the single leaves from illustrated incunabula which Philip Hofer caused to have framed and hung in Houghton Library's ground floor corridor, where visitors admired them for decades. Removed during a recent refurbishment and passed along to me for cataloguing, one of these has been identified as a fragment of a previously unrecorded

---

8 But see entries S1-866.8 and S1-1199.2A for mention of some *in situ* binding waste. In principle, any identifiable fragment, no matter where found, would merit inclusion in future supplements unless considered of little interest.

9 Leaf books in Harvard libraries which lack the original specimen leaves have been excluded.

10 This album is shelved under Houghton call number *fEC.A100.B659c. See, e.g., entry S1-372.5 for further information about the album.

11 Entry S1-3931.5.

edition.[12] Another rich mine has been the two large boxes of unidentified fragments that have gradually been added to by generations of despairing cataloguers.[13] I have managed to identify a good number, though a few fragments likely to be fifteenth-century printing still defy precise identification. Other single leaves have been culled from Houghton Library's unclassified accessions.

Two large groups of fragments have been deliberately excluded from this supplement, for it seems more useful to describe these in separate supplements using a modified format appropriate to their contents. The first group consists of the 620 leaves to be found in Houghton Library's copies of the Haebler and Schreiber incunabula leaf portfolios. Between 1927 and 1929, the Munich antiquarian bookseller Weiss & Co. published an ambitious series of eight portfolios, each containing between 55 and 120 single leaves from nearly as many incunabula; the number of copies issued ranged from 50 to 103. Six of the portfolios provide examples of a wide range of fifteenth-century printing types, with commentary by Konrad Haebler.[14] Two portfolios provide examples of leaves bearing woodcuts, from a broad range of illustrated incunabula, with commentary by Wilhelm Ludwig Schreiber.[15] Harvard owns five of the portfolios in a total of seven copies, all housed at Houghton Library.[16] It seemed counterproductive to include these in the present supplement, for their 620 leaves

12   Entry S1-3941.5.

13   These boxes, bearing Houghton call numbers bInc 25.3 and bInc 25.5, have now been merged into one. Similar caches have not been reported by other Harvard libraries, though they may nonetheless exist.

14   The six portfolios edited by Haebler are: 1) *Der deutsche Wiegendruck in Original-Typenbeispielen: 115 Inkunabelproben* (München: Weiss & Co., 1927), and its English issue: 2) *German Incunabula: 110 Original-Leaves* (Munich: Weiss & Co., 1927); 3) *Der italienische Wiegendruck in Original-Typenbeispielen: 120 Inkunabelproben* (München: Weiss & Co., 1927), and its English issue: 4) *Italian Incunabula: 110 Original-Leaves* (Munich: Weiss & Co., 1927); 5) *Der westeuropäische Wiegendruck in Original-Typenbeispielen: 60 Inkunabelproben: niederländischer, französischer, iberischer und englischer Pressen* (München: Weiss & Co., 1928), and its English issue: 6) *West-European Incunabula: 60 Original Leaves from the Presses of the Netherlands, France, Iberia and Great Britain* (Munich: Weiss & Co., 1928). The German and English issues vary somewhat in their contents.

15   The two portfolios edited by Schreiber are: 1) *Der Buchholzschnitt im 15. Jahrhundert in Original-Beispielen: 55 Inkunabelproben deutscher, schweizer, niederländischer, tschechischer und italienischer Pressen* (München: Weiss & Co., 1929), and the English issue: 2) *Woodcuts from Books of the 15th Century Shown in Original Specimens: 55 Leaves Detached from Books Printed in Germany, Switzerland, Bohemia, the Netherlands, and Italy* (Munich: Weiss & Co., 1929). The German and English issues vary substantially in their contents as, indeed, do individual copies of each issue.

16   Houghton Library possesses two copies of *German Incunabula* (call numbers Inc 10000PF and Typ Inc 499.99.446PF), two copies of *Italian Incunabula* (Inc 10001PF and Typ Inc 499.99.447PF), and single copies of *Der Westeuropäische Wiegendruck* (Inc 10003PF), *West-European Incunabula* (Typ 499.99.448PF), and *Woodcuts from Books of the 15th Century* (*93HR-2618PF).

David R. Whitesell xi

would have overwhelmed and obscured the other contents, to the detriment of all. Rather, these have been described in a second supplement, now nearing completion, which will be primarily a checklist and index to all eight Weiss & Co. portfolios, and secondarily a description of the leaves in the Harvard copies.

The second group consists of several hundred fragments in the collection of the Agnes Mongan Center for the Study of Prints, Drawings, and Photographs in the Fogg Art Museum. These are not properly part of the Harvard University Library collections, though Walsh set a precedent of sorts by describing the Fogg's eleven complete incunabula. Virtually all of the Fogg fragments belong to fifteenth-century illustrated books, including at least two blockbook leaves. Hence these are of considerable potential interest, for many of the editions represented are important and rare. A substantial number were the gift of Philip Hofer, who deposited his complete incunabula in Houghton Library while placing most of his fragments in the Fogg's study collections. Another significant group was given by Fogg benefactor and former associate director Paul J. Sachs. Access to the Fogg fragments is far from satisfactory at present: most are listed only in the Mongan Center's card catalogue, with few properly identified by author, text, edition, or leaf; some have been described and illustrated in Harvard's Visual Information Access (VIA) online catalogue.[17] It is hoped that eventually these may be fully described in a third Walsh supplement, the format modified in such a way as to meet the needs of art historians as well as incunabulists.

One of Walsh's objectives was to provide briefer descriptions of "books once thought to be incunabula but now believed or known to be post-1500."[18] In the course of preparing this supplement, it soon became clear that, as with incunable fragments and leaf books, Walsh for some reason omitted numerous post-incunabula meeting his criterion. The universe of books "once thought to be incunabula" by one or more bibliographers is potentially vast, so the decision was made to focus almost exclusively on those post-incunabula cited by Goff. That is, if a Harvard copy of a post-incunabulum is listed in Goff, then it should be described in this supplement if not previously included in Walsh. A search was also made for additional copies of Goff post-incunabula acquired by or identified in a Harvard library since Goff's publication in 1964. But given the richness of Harvard's collections and the difficulties of identifying undated post-incunabula in HOLLIS, there inevitably will be copies I have overlooked. Since post-incunabula often defy precise identification because they are imperfectly described in the literature, I have decided to give full descriptions for those in this supplement. Post-incunabula in Walsh have not been re-described, save for the important group of Florentine Savonarola tracts lumped together in his entry (3035e); these have been re-listed here under entries (S1-3033a-m).

17   Freely accessible over the Internet at http://via.harvard.edu.

18   Volume 1: x.

This supplement, therefore, describes 202 new incunabula at Harvard: 67 complete or nearly complete copies and 135 single leaves or fragments, representing a total of 173 editions, including 110 not in Walsh. To these have been added 69 post-incunabula (including three fragments) meeting the criteria described above. As of 14 October 1994, James Walsh reported that the Harvard collection "comprises 3517 editions in 4187 copies"; ten years later, the count has risen to 3627 editions in 4389 copies.[19]

III

IN COMPILING THIS supplement, I have deliberately adhered as closely as possible to Walsh's editorial model.[20] Entries are arranged in modified Proctor order, that is, geographically by place of publication and by printer. Each entry has been assigned an "S1" prefix (for supplement one), "S" having already been employed for entries in the "Supplement" section of Walsh's fourth volume. In that section (and occasionally elsewhere in volumes 1-4) Walsh adopted the practice of intercalating both added copies and new editions into their proper places in the entry sequence by assigning them numbers with a capital letter suffix. It soon became clear to me that Walsh's system was ill-designed for expansion. At Paul Needham's suggestion, I have therefore numbered the entries in this supplement as follows: added copies receive a capital letter suffix to the Walsh entry number, while new editions receive a dot number. Entry numbers for books considered to be post-incunabula follow Walsh's practice, i.e. they have a lower-case letter suffix and are enclosed in parentheses.

As in Walsh, "the author or title entry follows the form found in incunabula catalogues such as those of the British Library, Goff, and the *Gesamtkatalog der Wiegendrucke…*; the author and anonymous title index contains cross-references to variant forms and ascriptions…. Undated books are assigned an unbracketed date, usually with a question mark or 'ca.' Next comes a statement of format and the number of leaves contained in a perfect copy of the book; if the leaves are numbered the foliation is recorded as found, with a list of misnumberings, omissions, or repetitions; if the leaves are unnumbered the number is given in square brackets. Blank leaves are always recorded. If the book contains illustrative matter of any kind, the abbreviation 'ill.' indicates the fact. A leaf measurement in millimeters ends this section." However, the number of leaves and their foliation are generally not provided if 1) the Harvard copy is a single leaf or fragment, or 2) the copy described in this supplement is an added copy for which such information has already been furnished in Walsh.

If "no satisfactory description exists in one of the standard incunabula

---

19   Volume 4: [vii]. Walsh's totals include some single leaves and fragmentary copies, though I have not attempted a count of these; nor have I counted the number of post-incunabula described by Walsh.

20   See v. 1: [ix]-xi, from which the quotations in this section are taken.

catalogues," a fuller description is given,[21] with "details of collation, number of lines, type measurement and identification, etc., added. When required, a separate paragraph of general information applicable to all copies lists contents, the names of editors or translators, and mentions variants when they occur and are known. Copy-specific details follow: a description of illumination and/or rubrication, binding, MS marginalia and ownership inscriptions, bookplates or labels, and, finally, any imperfections, including missing blank leaves."

"References to standard catalogues are set off in another paragraph. These include Hain, Proctor, BMC, Pellechet, Polain, GW, Goff, CIBN, and Sack, in that order," to which have been added references to BSB-Ink, ISTC, and other pertinent catalogues. So as not to repeat information previously given in Walsh, references have been omitted if the copy described in this supplement is an added copy. "A final paragraph gives date and source of acquisition, whether by gift or purchase, and the shelf-number for books in Houghton. Books in other libraries are simply recorded under the name of the library."

The apparatus also follows the Walsh model, but with a few deliberate changes. Only those sources first cited in this supplement are included in the list of "References"; for full citations of other references, see the comprehensive list in Walsh.[22] With one exception, the indexes cover only entries in this supplement and are not intended to be cumulative. To these have been added a new "Leaf Book Index," which includes the few previously described in Walsh in addition to those found in this supplement. Readers should be advised that Walsh interpreted provenance in the broadest possible sense, hence his "Provenance Index" lists many persons who in fact never owned the incunables attributed to them. Most of these pseudo-owners were donors of money or book funds used to acquire specific incunabula, as Walsh's entries (though not his index) usually make clear. Despite requests to "purify" this supplement's provenance index, I have elected to continue Walsh's practice, if only to maintain consistency of method. As in Walsh, concordances are provided between supplement ("HUL") entry numbers and Hain, Proctor, GW, and Goff numbers, with the important departure that entry numbers for copies previously described in Walsh are repeated here. Seven fascicles of the *Gesamtkatalog* have been published since the appearance of Walsh's GW concordance. In order to bring it fully up to date, all new GW numbers for incunabula described by Walsh have been added to the GW concordance appended to this supplement.

I owe a great debt to William P. Stoneman and Mollie Della Terza, not only for making this supplement possible, but for supporting my work even as its scope

---

21 Because of typographical limitations, transcriptions in this supplement sometimes employ bracketed expansions in place of the contractions actually found in the original.

22 Volume 5: [77]-105.

widened and deadlines retreated. Stoneman's reinvigoration of Houghton Library's incunabula acquisitions program has made this supplement far more substantive than it otherwise would have been. He also contributed new provenance information and, in furnishing me with the ISTC database on CD-ROM, greatly facilitated my work. Other Houghton colleagues, notably Roger E. Stoddard, Hope Mayo, and William H. Bond have offered moral and material support. I am especially indebted to former incunabula cataloguing project assistant Damian G. Konkoly for his perceptiveness, dedication in hunting for overlooked incunabula, and collegiality—our working relationship remains the highlight of my Houghton years.

Other Harvard Library colleagues have graciously shared information and provided access to incunabula in their care: Kenneth E. Carpenter; Elizabeth Vernon in the Judaica Division of Widener Library; David Ferris, Mary Person, and David Warrington at the Harvard Law Library; Thomas A. Horrocks at the Francis A. Countway Library of Medicine, and especially Jack Eckert for many kindnesses; Russell Pollard at the Andover-Harvard Theological Library; Karen Bailey at Baker Library; Suzanne G. Kemple at Hilles Library; Linda Lott at Dumbarton Oaks Research Library; and Ilaria Della Monica at the Biblioteca Berenson, I Tatti.

Outside Harvard, Stephen Tabor of the Huntington Library and John Bidwell of the Pierpont Morgan Library have been exemplary in answering my frequent queries concerning incunabula in their care. Others who have generously offered assistance include Walter Kofler; John Goldfinch of the British Library; Cristina Dondi and Kristian Jensen of the Bodleian Library; Jonathan Harrison of the Library at St. John's College, Cambridge University; Jane Rodgers Siegel of the Rare Book and Manuscript Library, Columbia University; Georgianna Ziegler of the Folger Shakespeare Library; Daniel De Simone of the Rosenwald Collection, Library of Congress; Valérie Neveu of the Bibliothèque Universitaire d'Angers; Ingrid Bouwens of the Museum Meermanno-Westreenianum; William J. Sheehan, C.S.B. of the Bibliotheca Apostolica Vaticana; and the staff of the Bibliotheca Bodmeriana. I have also benefitted from Peter Amelung's detailed reviews of Walsh; many of his provenance corrections were received by James Walsh in time to update the cumulative index in volume 5, and others are incorporated here.[23] No one has been more helpful than Paul Needham of the Scheide Library, Princeton University, at various times my teacher and colleague, and always freely sharing of his incomparable expertise in early printing, binding, and especially provenance. Although this supplement falls well shy of his standards, it is nonetheless the better for his interest and support. All errors are exclusively my own.

---

23   Amelung's reviews, which contain much useful information not reflected in this supplement, are available online at: http://www.bsz-bw.de/depot/media/3400000/3421000/3421308/97_0042.html, and http://www.bsz-bw.de/depot/media/3400000/3421000/3421308/00_0008.html.

It was on or about 9 December 2003 that failing health brought to a close James Walsh's unprecedented fifty-sx-year tenure at Houghton Library. Until that time he was my closest and most valued collaborator: reviewing my incunabula cataloguing, cheerfully examining once again books he had handled many times previously, and providing much information for supplement entries. By then he had approved a late draft of this supplement, though it remained "in progress" at the time of his death on 13 November 2004. In the following month alone Houghton Library acquired eight new incunabula at auction, and another was discovered at the Countway Library; the latest addition arrived only a week ago. All of these are recorded here; and by the time this supplement is finally fixed in print, the next will be well under way. What a magnificent gift James Walsh has left Harvard, and perhaps we can show no greater appreciation than to keep the collection constantly growing, its catalogue perpetually unfinished.

David R. Whitesell
Rare Book Cataloguer, Houghton Library
1 March 2005

ADDITIONS AND CORRECTIONS TO WALSH ENTRIES

Walsh No.

(vol. 1)

1	Sold by Sir George Holford to A.S.W. Rosenbach in 1925. See Leslie A. Morris, *Rosenbach Abroad* (Philadelphia, 1988): p. 21, no. 7.
3	The decoration in the Widener copy of the Gutenberg Bible was applied in Utrecht in the early 1460's. See Gisela Gerritsen-Geywitz, "Zur Frühgeschichte der Harvarder Gutenberg-Bibel," *Gutenberg-Jahrbuch* (2000): 64-72.
6	Paul Needham has identified the four Harvard leaves as follows: v. 1, leaves 89 (10_1; Judges), 96 (10_8; Ruth), 111-112 ($12_{5,6}$; Samuel). In other words the leaves, now disjunct, once constituted two bifolia; and as Walsh pointed out, the rubrication suggests all came from the same copy. Needham has found that the rubrication also matches that of a leaf (v. 1, leaf 210 (22_4)) at Columbia University, as well as a bifolium at Cornell University (v. 1, leaves 108, 115 ($12_{2,9}$)) acquired in 1876 from the bookseller Henry Stevens. It would appear that all of these leaves once belonged to the imperfect copy Stevens displayed at the 1877 Caxton Celebration (no. 618 in *Catalogue of the loan collection of antiquities, curiosities, and appliances connected with the art of printing* (London, 1877).
7	From the library of John Eliot Hodgkin, with his collation mark and "Adnotatio" on rear flyleaf.
19	From the library of Adolphus Williamson Green, presented to the Harvard College Library by his daughter.
58	Walsh lists ten incunabula and one post-incunable (Walsh 58, 731, 732, 1305, 1783, 1792, 1807, 2239, 2653, 3052, and (3631b)) in the collections of Hilles Library, which closed in June 2005. The Hilles rare book holdings are being transferred to other Harvard libraries, but the ultimate location of the 11 Walsh items has yet to be determined.
69	This copy lacks not only the 20 leaves ([1], [131]-[148], [212]) mentioned in Walsh, but also leaves [276]-[514].
70	Sold by Sir George Holford to A.S.W. Rosenbach in 1925. See Leslie A. Morris, *Rosenbach Abroad* (Philadelphia, 1988): p. 28, no. 105.
95	Following its secularization in 1803, the library of the Carthusians at Buxheim became the property, first of Johann Friedrich, Graf von Ostein, then of Friedrich Karl, Graf von Waldbott-Bassenheim. The library was sold at auction in Munich, in September 1883, by Carl Förster at the direction of Hugo, Graf von Waldbott-Bassenheim.

118	For additional provenance information, see 95 above.
128	A misplaced heading wrongly assigns this edition to Heinrich Knoblochtzer (first press) instead of Georg Husner (first press); the index entries are correct.
139	For additional provenance information, see 95 above.
141	Formerly classified as Inc 25.1PF; now classified as pInc 299.
154-156	A misplaced heading assigns this edition to the Printer of the 1483 Vitas Patrum instead of the Printer of the 1481 Legenda Aurea; the index entries are correct.
159	Blind impressions of bearer type are visible on several leaves.
182	For additional provenance information, see 95 above.
199	The printed booklabel is that of the Franciscan Conventuals of Maihingen.
216	The first of three works bound in the volume (Petrus Comestor, *Historia scholastica* (Strassburg, Georg Husner, 16 November 1503; see (S1-304a) below) bears an early MS inscription on the title page, "Johannes Zyssenheim poss.", which presumably applies to all three works.
238	For additional provenance information, see 95 above.
240	For additional provenance information, see 95 above.
255	The oval stamp is that of the Franciscan Conventuals of Maihingen.
270	Blind impressions of four to five lines of bearer type are visible at top and bottom of blank l9v and leaf l10.
293-294	In each copy, one line of blind bearer type is visible at the foot of leaf a1.
324	The oval stamp on leaves [a]4, [a]8, and [c]2 is that of Indiana Asbury University.
325	From the library of Richard Heber, with subsequent purchase inscription, "V Gand 8br. 1835 … heber N. 75." (lot 75 in the Heber sale held by Ch. Citerne in Ghent beginning 26 October 1835). The Houghton Library copy of the sale catalogue, which is annotated with buyers's names and prices, identifies the purchaser as [François Joseph] "Vergauwen".
335	This copy is no. 37 in H.P. Kraus, *Catalogue 19* (1940), his first American catalogue.
446	For additional provenance information, see 3900 below, with which this is bound.
467	Blind impressions of several lines of bearer type are visible at the foot of the title page.

469 From the library of Count Paul Riant.

485 From the library of Count Paul Riant, with his signed note on front flyleaf, "Acheté 36 francs à Paris chez Tross, Le 24 novembre 1868."

496 Paul Needham has identified the binding tools as those of Kyriss shop 49 (Augsburg, Ambrosius Keller).

500 Bound for Charles Spencer, 3rd Earl of Sunderland, with the Sunderland shelf marks on front flyleaf, "C5:17" (in ink), "41.b.16" (in pencil).

501 Formerly classified as Inc 1533; now classified as Inc 1533 (A).

523 For additional provenance information, see 95 above.

545 Leaf 5_{8+1}v contains printed text on the top half only; a series of accidentally inked bearer quads appears on the lower half.

554 Formerly classified as Inc 1636PF; now classified as Inc 1636 (A) PF. As Curt F. Buhler has noted, bearer types are visible on several leaves (see C.F. Buhler, "Remarks on the Printing of the Augsburg Edition (c. 1474), of Bishop Salomon's *Glossae*," in *Homage to a Bookman: Essays on Manuscripts, Books and Printing Written for Hans P. Kraus* (Berlin, 1967), 133-[35]). These are sometimes partly inked in error, e.g., lines 2-12 from leaf 29_7v column 1 appear at the foot of leaf 29_3r column 2. A "Qu" ligature is frequently positioned as a bearer type at the outer corners of blank spaces, e.g., leaves 8_1r, 28_4v, and 29_8r. Its use on 29_8r exacerbated the shortages faced by the printer in setting the text of 29_1v, in which blank spaces are left for many of the Qu ligatures; in this copy, these spaces have been filled in in contemporary MS. The same bearers also appear in the second Harvard copy (see entry S1-554A).

556 For additional provenance information, see 95 above.

563-565 The blind bearer impressions described in BMC—four lines from 4_5v and three lines from 4_6v appear in blind on 6_8v and 3_1v respectively—are also present in the three Harvard copies; however, another 18 lines on 1_1v and 15 lines on 27_7r also appear in blind, as well as seven lines (lines 23-29 from 38_3r) at the foot of 38_6r.

567 From the library of Ernst II, Duke of Saxe-Gotha, with a crowned initial "E" and date "1798" gilt-stamped on front cover.

568 In the initial space on a2r, there is a faint partly-inked impression of a woodcut initial used as blind bearer type.

606 The bookstamp is that of Isaac C. Bates.

620 Old oval ownership stamp of the Universitätsbibliothek Leipzig, "Bibl. Vnivers. Lips."; with added "Duplum" stamp. Ownership signature of Eadmond Waterton on front flyleaf (lot 250 in the Sotheby sale catalogue, 18 January 1895).

655	Rubricator's (?) MS note on c6r, "[?] In die [?] anno 1500".
692	See also entry S1-866.8 for a single-leaf fragment incorporated into a modern binding.
707	Peter Amelung has identified the binding tools as those of Kyriss shop 111 (Memmingen).
711	Formerly classified as Inc 2061; now classified as bTyp Inc 2061.
731-732	See entry 58 above.
736	For additional provenance information, see 95 above.
751	Formerly classified as Inc 2111; now classified as Inc 2111 pt. 1. Three of the four missing leaves have now been acquired; see entry S1-751A.
759	For additional provenance information, see 95 above.
815	In addition to the accidentally inked bearer impressions noted, blind impressions of bearer type appear at the foot of leaf tt6.
905-908	Page 351 was misprinted (repeating the text of page 350), thereby deleting part or all of entries 905-908. Although an errata leaf was prepared, the full text of entries 905-908 is given here for the benefit of those who do not have it.
905	**Gobius, Johannes:** Scala coeli. 1480.
	f°. [168] leaves; 269 x 195 mm.
	Initials, paragraph marks, capital strokes, and underlinings added in red in quires [a-f], not thereafter. Modern olive morocco by R. Wallis; edges gilt. MS ownership notation on [a]1r, "Monasterij Weingartensis A° 1619. in Veldkirch. In Hofen."
	H 9406*; Pr 2524; BMC 2:526 (IB.9192); Pell 5269; Polain 1661; GW 10945; Goff G-311; Sack 1572; Amelung 41.
	Countway Library (William Norton Bullard Collection)
906	— Another copy. 278 x 195 mm.
	Initials crudely added in brown ink in quires [a-d] only. Half contemporary leather and wooden boards, badly worn and wormed; in a cloth case. MS ownership notation on [a]1r, "Alexander Khistner data est a p[at]re suo Thoma Khistner 1.5.47"; pasted down inside back cover is a letter headed "Andreas Lochner p[rae]p[osi]t[us] in Eberndorff, et Archidiacon[us] Vallis ... Dilecto nobis in xp̄o dño Alexandro Eccl[es]iae beatae Mariae Virginis in Ebernsdorffingē plebano" and dated "Datū in coenobio meo Eberndorff ... tercia die Junij Anno salutis. 1.5.43"; booklabel of Le Comte Ferdinand d'Egger. Imperfect: leaves [v]7, [x]6-7 wanting.
	3 April 1882 – Bought with the Subscription fund. Inc 2524

907   **Pseudo-Albertus Magnus:** Compendium theologicae veritatis. Not after 1481.

f°. [192] leaves (1 and 192 blank); 293 x 210 mm.

Includes Bernoldus de Caesarea, *Distinctiones de tempore et de sanctis quarum declarationes ex Compendio theologicae veritatis capiuntur*, and the *tabula* of Thomas Dorniberg.

Initial spaces not filled in; without rubrication. For binding description see no. 850, Martinus Polonus, *Margarita Decreti, seu Tabula Martiniana* (Speyer, Peter Drach, ca. 1483), with which this is bound, along with *Modus legendi abbreviaturas* (Speyer, Peter Drach, ca. 1484); *Modus legendi abbreviaturas* (Strassburg, the R-Printer, not after 1 November 1478); Pseudo-Albertus Magnus, *De adhaerendo Deo* (Urach, Conrad Fyner, ca. 1481); and Andreas de Escobar, *Modus confitendi* (Strassburg, Printer of Henricus Ariminensis, ca. 1475/78). Imperfect: quires [a-d⁸] only (the work of Bernoldus de Caesarea), all thereafter wanting.

H 437*; Pr 2532; BMC 2:527 (IB.9213); Polain 4446; GW 600; Goff A-235; Sack 64.

17 May 1944 – Received. Law Library

908   **Zeichen der falschen Gulden.** 1482.

f°. broadside; ill.; 220 x 184 mm.

Removed from a binding and mounted on linen in half 19th-century vellum and marbled boards along with a facsimile. Imperfect: most of the first line of text trimmed away.

GW(Einbl) 1569; Goff Z-20; Amelung 50; Schramm 5:19.

16 June 1920 – Bought with the Edward Henry Hall fund. Inc 2539.5

910   The inscription reads "Taxa," not "Täpae"; possibly the same provenance as BSB-Ink A-211 4. Exemplar.

911   Formerly classified as Inc 2548; now classified as Inc 2548 (A).

932   For additional provenance information, see 95 above.

966   For additional provenance information, see 95 above.

979   For additional provenance information, see 95 above.

984   Formerly classified as Inc 2793.5; now classified as Typ Inc 2793.5.

1003   Blind impressions of bearer type, possibly from a2r, are visible on a1r.

1008   Two lines of blind bearer type are visible at the foot of blank leaf E6.

1045   One line of large blind bearer type is visible at the foot of leaf C6.

1050   The text consists of book 17 and a part of book 18 of Priscianus's *Institutio de arte grammaticae*. The Greek portions are omitted.

David R. Whitesell xxi

(1061c)	Formerly classified as Inc 3100; now classified as *GC.W1884.479sb.
1074	17th-century MS inscription on title page: "V: Conventûs Medlingani ord. Praed."
1092-1093	The MS ownership notations read, "… Khelhaimensi" and "… Kelhaym …" respectively, i.e. from the library of the Franciscans at Kelheim.
1119	Peter Amelung has identified the binder, not as Johannes Meifogl of Tübingen, but as Johannes Meifoge of Ellwangen (cf. Kyriss shop 68).
1159	Vol. 1 was formerly bound in doeskin over wooden boards.
1206	The MS pastedowns noted by Walsh as having been removed from the binding of this copy and transferred to Houghton Library are now catalogued as MS Mus 192.
1210	For additional provenance information, see 95 above.
1216	MS inscriptions of the church of the deanery in Tachov, Czechoslovakia: vol.1, leaf gg6v, "Ecclesiae Tachaue"; vol. 2, leaf j1r, "Pro decanatu Tachaw"; vol. 2, leaf QQ5v, "Pro Ecclesia Decanali in Tachau."
1220	For additional provenance information, see 95 above.
1227	This copy is imperfect: leaves AA1 (title), AA8, ²A1 (blank), and ²E8 wanting.
1244	Formerly classified as Inc 7727; now classified as Inc 7727 (A).
1247	Blind impressions of bearer type are visible on several leaves. The bookstamp is that of Isaac C. Bates.
(vol. 2)	
1282	Headlines (on rectos only), and the incipits on leaves 1₁r and (to book 2) on 9₁r, have been added in red in contemporary ms. (now very faint).
1294	Bound for Charles Spencer, 3rd Earl of Sunderland, with the Sunderland shelf marks on front flyleaf, "C2:12" (in ink), "53.e.6" (in pencil).
1305	See entry 58 above.
1589	Armorial bookplate of Maximilian, Emperor of Mexico (with initials "MMI" and motto "Cuidade la justicia") inside front cover.
1619	For additional provenance information, see 95 above.
1698	Blindstamp of the American Antiquarian Society on leaf a2.
1739	The references to leaf "a2r" actually refer to leaf ã2r.
1783	See entry 58 above.
1792	See entry 58 above.
1807	See entry 58 above.

1834   Formerly classified as Inc 4401; now classified as Inc 4401 (A).

1850   Early MS contents note on blank a1r, beneath which, in a later hand, is the addition: "Libri Paraphraseos Themistij [page] 175"; "Themisthius" is written on the bottom edge. Presumably this copy was formerly (but not originally) bound with an unidentified edition of Themistius, *Periphrasis tōn Peri psychēs Aristotelous*.

1884   Formerly classified as Inc 4699; now classified as Inc 4699 (A).

1887   Doge Marco Barbarigo died in 1486 and was succeeded by Agostino Barbarigo, to whom this copy was presumably presented when completed.

1914   A blind impression of bearer type is visible at the foot of leaf m10.

1924   "Tiezman 1743" is presumably the ownership inscription of Theodor Heinrich Tiezmann.

2148   The call number is Inc 4853.5, not Inc 4853.4.

2159   Protzer bequeathed his library to the Hospital of the Holy Ghost in Nördlingen, but the books were divided and placed elsewhere. Those on subjects other than law were housed in the Church of St. George; the non-theological volumes from this group were sold in 1859. See Anthony Hobson, "A German Student in Italy: His Books and Bindings," *Mélanges d'histoire de la reliure offerts à Georges Colin* (Brussels, 1998): 87-99.

2192   MS ownership inscription at foot of leaf 1r, "ad vsu[m] f[rat]ris cherubini de Sorbulo .15.22. I[n] loco sacri Mo[n]t[is] ex Ian[?]."

2202   Long MS inscription above title, dated 24 January 1494, recording the gift of this book by Joannes Vulpius to an unidentified recipient.

2204   19th-century signature of G. Tatti on blank p. [92].

2212   Formerly classified as Inc 5124; now classified as Inc 5124 (A). Contains the complete text (Books I-IV), not Books I and III only.

2229   The MS ownership inscription (partially trimmed) on the title page reads: "Sum Stanislai Sauri." Paul Needham notes that this may be the Stanislaus Saur who was a canon of Breslau in 1506.

2239   See entry 58 above.

2256   For additional provenance information, see 95 above.

2300-2302   For detailed comparisons of the two editions described by Walsh, and a more precise dating of the line-for-line reprint edition (Walsh (2354b)) to between 1504 and 1507, see Michal Spandowski, "Two Editions of Quintilianus (H* 13652)," *Gutenberg-Jarbuch* (2004): 81-92.

2330   The binding's endleaves were removed long ago and are now classified as fMS Lat 119. They consist of two parchment bifolia from a Latin MS of Aristotle, *Physica* (book 4, chapters 5-11) written in England in the second half of the 13th century. For a full description, see Laura Light, *Catalogue of Medieval and Renaissance Manuscripts in the Houghton Library* (Binghamton, NY), 1: 135-136.

2332 The call number is Inc 5323, not Inc 5068.

2340 See 2330 above, with which this is bound.

2347 The MS ownership inscription "Ad vsum Sti. Jannis ad Carbonariam 1580" is presumably that of the Augustinian Canons at Naples (San Giovanni a Carbonara).

2353 Paul Needham has identified the MS ownership inscription as that of Johann Pengl of Weissenburg, who matriculated at the University of Vienna in 1489.

(2354b) See 2300-2302 above.

2376 Later housed in the Church of St. George, Nördlingen; see 2159 above.

2395 An early MS contents list on the title page indicates that this copy was once bound in a tract volume preceding an unidentified edition of Dio Chrysostomus, *De Troia non capta* and one other work.

2397 This copy is disbound, with remains of old blue paper wrappers; in a brown cloth case.

2402 With the notable exception of BSB-Ink (V-141) and Walsh, ISTC and other bibliographies mistakenly call this edition a quarto instead of an octavo.

2441 The work (possibly one of two) formerly bound with this copy may be Walsh 2582 (Aulus Persius Flaccus, *Satirae* (Venice: Johannes Tacuinus, de Tridino, 4 November 1499)): both copies have similar provenance, and some worm holes align.

2462 The work with which this is bound bears two MS ownership inscriptions: 1) on title page, "Liber Antonius dauidis [?]"; 2) on leaf a2r, "Ex libris domus Sti. Antonij in [Isnegem?]".

2502 17th-century ownership notation on title page: "Collegi [?]man".

2510 Later housed in the Church of St. George, Nördlingen; see 2159 above.

2529 It has now been established that this copy was given to the Harvard College Library shortly before the devastating fire of 24 January 1764, in which 90% of the library was lost. This is the only one of seven incunabula to have survived (cf. Walsh 5: 2-3). The volume is one of 42 given byThomas Hollis and received on 24 October 1763, all of which escaped the fire because they had yet to be placed on the shelves. At the foot of H4v, six lines of bearer type have been accidentally inked and printed; the text consists of lines 33-38 from H1r.

2530	This entry is cancelled. See revised entry under S1-2212A.
2551	Blind impressions of bearer type are visible on many leaves. Later housed in the Church of St. George, Nördlingen; see 2159 above.
2567	At the time of acquisition in 1903, this work was bound with two other works, since separated and rebound individually: 1) Gaius Sallustius Crispus, [*Works*] (Venice: Heirs of Giovanni Maria Bonelli, 1573) (Ls 5.115.60F*); 2) Marcus Junianus Justinus, *Historiae Philippicae* (Venice: B. de Zanis, 1503) (Li 12.50F*).
2582	It is possible that this copy was once bound with Walsh 2441 (Lucius Annaeus Seneca, *Tragoediae* (Venice: Lazarus de Soardis, 12 December 1492)): both copies have similar provenance, and some worm holes align.
2591	From the library of Adolphus Williamson Green, presented to the Harvard College Library by his daughter.
2592	The MS ownership notation reads: "P[er]tinet frat[ri] pet[ro] de g'taal xxxiiij Julij a[nn]o d[omin]i 1500."
2605	Blind impressions of bearer type are visible on leaf C2.
2653	See entry 58 above.
2662	A few contemporary MS annotations in Greek. Contemporary MS ownership notation beneath colophon, "Antonij Seripandi et amicoru[m]".
2685-2686	In light of the recent article by Neil Harris, "The Blind Impressions in the Aldine *Hypnerotomachia Poliphili* (1499)," *Gutenberg-Jarbuch* (2004): 93-146, it should be noted that both Harvard copies of this work have been pressed, removing almost all traces of bearer type impressions.
2718	The call number is Inc 5615, not Inc 5616.
2721	This copy is bound in nineteenth-century gray pasteboard, spine lined with marbled paper.

(vol. 3)

2777	Some initials added in red and/or blue, some paragraph marks added in red or blue; mostly without rubrication.
2806	For additional provenance information, see 95 above.
2835	Initials "S.C." written on top edge (apparently from the same library as Walsh 19).
2870	This copy has been rebound in half vellum and tan boards, with the covers and spine of the nineteenth-century binding preserved in a brown cloth case.

David R. Whitesell xxv

2871   The MS textual corrections may be in the hand of Politianus. See Joseph A. Dane, "'Si vis archetypas habere nugas': Authorial Subscriptions in the Houghton Library and Huntington Library Copies of Politian, *Miscellanea* (Florence: Miscomini 1489)," *Harvard Library Bulletin*, n.s. 10, 2 (1999): 12-22. See also Ernest H. Wilkins, "Una copia d'omaggio dei 'Miscellanea,'" *Convivium*, n.s. 1 (1955): 88-90.

2872   The extensive MS marginalia are by Bartolomeo Fonzio. See Lucia A. Ciapponi, "Bartolomeo Fonzio e la prima centuria dei 'Miscellanea' del Poliziano," *Italia medioevale e umanistica* 23 (1980): 165-177.

2915   This copy was mistakenly recorded in Goff under S-170; Harvard does not own a copy of that edition. Walsh correctly describes it as Goff S-169. Goff, under S-171, also credits Harvard with the only recorded copy of another Bartolommeo di Libri edition of this work ("about 1495?"). The copy in question (now Typ 525.10.771 (B)) is in fact one of two Harvard copies of Goff S-172 (described in this supplement under entries (S1-3033h-i)).

(3035e)   This entry is cancelled. The 10 post-incunable Savonarola tracts recorded here by Walsh have been given separate entries in this supplement; see entries (S1-3033a-m).

3040   For additional provenance information, see 95 above.

3052   See entry 58 above.

3068   Later housed in the Church of St. George, Nördlingen; see 2159 above.

3089   16th-century ownership inscription on blank leaf a1r in vol. 1, "Hic: est: Aloisij: Boneti:".

3105   The armorial bookplate is that of J.P.R. Lyell.

3163-3164   In both copies, leaf H3 is missigned "Ziii", with a hand-stamped "H" added at left.

3165   This copy, previously unavailable for inspection, has been located. 340 x 235 mm. The four misprints on ZZ6r have been corrected, but the two hand-stamped corrections present in Walsh 3163 and 3164 (and in the BL copies) are here made in contemporary MS. In this copy, leaf o2 is unsigned, with the signature added in contemporary MS. Leaf H3 is missigned "Ziii", with the hand-stamped correction. Initial spaces not filled in; without rubrication. 18th-century diced calf, rebacked. Royal Society "ex dono Henr. Howard Norfolciensis" bookstamp on [alpha]1v. Ballard 659.

3316   This copy has been rebound in modern half calf and gray boards. The extensive contemporary MS marginalia were mostly bleached away at an earlier time.

3328   This copy is actually bound in 19th-century half calf and decorated boards, rebacked.

3369   Laid in is a printed document ([1] p.) in Italian, ca. 1780, completed in MS with the name of Primicerio Malvezzi, who may have owned this copy.

(vol. 4)

(3631b)   See entry 58 above.

3653   Through the kind offices of Cristina Dondi and Father William J. Sheehan, this edition has been identified as that of 19 April 1499, printed by Pigouchet for Simon Vostre. The only other known copy (a complete copy reported subsequent to publication of Walsh's description) is in the Vatican Library; see William J. Sheehan, *Incunabula Bibliothecae apostolicae vaticanae* (Città del Vaticano, 1997), H-150 and ISTC ih00399400. Walsh's entry may now be completed with a transcription of the colophon, as it appears in the Vatican Library copy: m4v, line 8, COLOPHON: Ces prefentes heures a lusage de Rom ‖ me fuerent acheuees le xix. iour de Auril. ‖ Lan mil. CCCC. iiiixx. [et] xix. pour Si= ‖ mon voftre Libraire demourant a Paris ‖ en la rue neuue ntẽ dame a lenseigne sainct ‖ Iehan leuangelifte. Formerly classified as Typ Inc 8191.5; now classified as Typ Inc 8197.5.

3654   From the library of Francis Calley Gray.

3748   Formerly classified as pTyp Inc 8531.5; now classified as pInc 8531.5.

3755   The woodcut of the earth on leaf c5r has been crudely hand-colored.

3783   This copy has been given a conservation binding of Japanese paper over boards; the spine and covers of the 19th-century binding have been preserved and are shelved with the book in a tan cloth case.

3790   Formerly classified as PA 6755 .Azx 1493; now classified as TS 239.255.

3801   For a checklist of other extant incunabula known to have been owned in 1501 by the Benedictines of St. Emmeram, Regensburg, see Bettina Wagner, "'Libri impressi Bibliothecae Monasterii Sancti Emmerammi': The Incunable Collection of St Emmeram, Regensburg, and Its Catalogue of 1501," *Incunabula and Their Readers: Printing, Selling and Using Books in the Fifteenth Century*, ed. by Kristian Jensen (London, 2003): 179-205.

3861   According to unpublished research by Valérie Neveu of the Bibliothèque Universitaire d'Angers on the variant states of Le Forestier's devices, this edition can be dated more precisely to ca. 1500.

3892-3893   For additional provenance information, see 3900 below, with which these two works are bound.

3900   The title page to this copy, now preserved at the Stadsbibliotheek Haarlem, is in an album compiled by Jacobus Koning (cf. the article by Jaspers cited in Walsh). Presumably this copy, and the three other incunabula bound with it in the 18th century, were also once owned by Koning. Later this volume was acquired by Richard Heber: although there are no visible ownership marks, it matches the description of lot 684 in pt. 13 of the sale catalogue of Heber's library (sale conducted by Benjamin Wheatley, February 1837). Two of the incunabula (Walsh 446 and 3892) in this sammelband have the later ownership signature of C. De Poer [Kennedy?] M.A. Harvard received this volume by exchange from W.A. Gough in 1934.

3929   A contemporary MS correction similar to that on a4v has also been made to the colophon on l1or. Capital strokes added in yellow. This copy displays considerable offsetting on nearly every page.

3941   ISTC (record no. ih00427000) describes this edition as follows: "The first quire identical with Camp-Kron I 990a; quires a-c different from this and from Camp 994; quires d-h, A-M identical with Camp 994." Cristina Dondi of the Bodleian Library Incunable Project has examined this copy and notes that, despite the title, the text is in fact that of the use of Rome, not of Utrecht.

3945   In this copy, the woodcuts (but not the genealogical table) have been hand-colored.

3960   This work is incorrectly described as a translation by Miguel Pérez into the Valencian dialect. It is actually a translation into Latin by Guarinus Veronensis. The Harvard copy remains unique, no other copy having been reported to ISTC (which assigns this work to the Valencia press of "Nicolaus Spindeler?, about 1500").

3990   Formerly classified as STC 4853; now classified as bSTC 4853.

3994   This copy has an impression of a printing type (text type) lying flat on the forme on leaf ²B7r. A few 16th-century MS annotations in English and Latin. Two-line Latin MS epigram on ²T7v signed "PB"; two-line English MS verse on ²T8v with initials "TW". 16th-century signatures (?) of Sir James Clark, Susanna Clarke, William Jackson, Robarte Jacksonne, Dorothy Savile, and [?] Coppersmythe.

4003   A note in this copy by David Constable states that he obtained it from "John B. Inglis Esq. of Mark Lane London."

4004   This copy was owned by William Davenport Talbot and was inherited by his son, the noted photographic pioneer William Henry Fox Talbot.

	Fox Talbot mutilated this copy by removing leaf r6, trimming away the margins, and using the piece as a photographic subject, per the explanatory note of Fox Talbot's son Charles (quoted in Walsh).
4005	Some early MS marginalia throughout. From the collection of Francis Hargrave, purchased by the British Museum in 1813, with his annotations on A2r.
4015	George Dunn's notes in the book indicate that this copy was once bound preceding two other works: 1) *Natura brevium* (London: Richard Pynson, ca. 1506; STC 18387), and 2) Sir Thomas Littleton, *Tenores novelli* (London: Richard Pynson, ca. 1502; STC 15722.5). Dunn had acquired that copy of the *Natura brevium*, also bound in 19th-century red morocco, in February 1897, nearly seven years before acquiring its former mate; it is also now in the Harvard Law Library.
Heb-34	Bound in half modern crimson morocco and red cloth.
S-195A	For additional provenance information, see 95 above.
S-207A	For additional provenance information, see 95 above.
S-748A	Paul Needham has identified the MS ownership inscription as that of Johann Pengl of Weissenburg, who matriculated at the University of Vienna in 1489.
S-1229A	For additional provenance information, see 95 above.
S-1342A	The presentation inscription from "D. D." is probably by David Douglas.
S-2563A	This copy, previously unavailable for inspection, has been located. 292 x 198 mm. Initial spaces, with guide-letters, not filled in; without rubrication. Modern gray boards. A few contemporary MS marginalia.

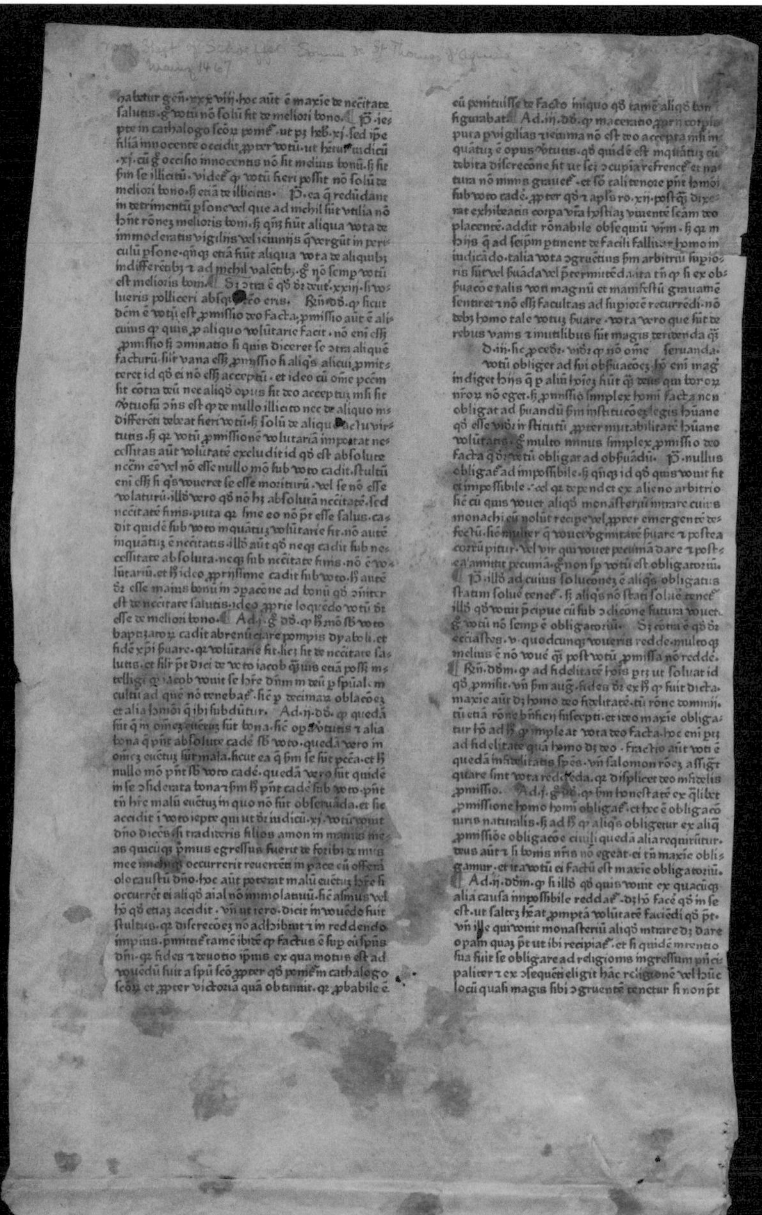

Figure 1. S1-6.3: THOMAS AQUINAS *Summae theologicae secundae partis pars secunda*
(Mainz: Peter Schoeffer, 6 March 1467). Waste leaf (131 verso) on vellum.
(pInc 83, Houghton Library, Harvard College Library)

New Entries

GERMANY

Mainz

PETER SCHOEFFER

S1-6.3 **Thomas Aquinas:** Summae theologicae secundae partis pars secunda. 6 March 1467.

f°. A single leaf only. 370 x 223 mm.

A waste leaf, printed on vellum on one side only. The leaf contains the text of leaf 13₁ verso (portion of Quaestio 88), apparently without setting variants from the published text. Initial letter added in blue, paragraph marks added in alternating red and blue. Removed from a binding: margins unevenly trimmed, some small holes, soiled and stained, the rubrication partly washed away. "21" added in pencil at lower right. An accompanying clipped catalogue description in French (no. 1548, annotated by E.B. Krumbhaar in pencil, "La Licorne, 6/36" [i.e. the Parisian bookshop A la Licorne]) describes two proof leaves from this edition, each printed on vellum on one side only, offered singly at 400 fr. or 750 fr. for the pair. Presumably Krumbhaar acquired only this leaf; the present location of the other leaf is not known.

H 1459*; Pr 83; BMC 1:24 (IC.122); Pell 1049 (+ var.); Goff T-209; BSB-Ink T-287; CIBN T-175.

17 November 1955 – Gift of E.B. Krumbhaar. pInc 83

S1-24A **Gart der Gesundheit.** 28 March 1485.

f°. Two leaves only; ill.

Edited by Johannes von Cuba.

In: Claus Nissen, *Herbals of Five Centuries: 50 Original Leaves from German, French, Dutch, English, Italian, and Swiss Herbals, With an Introduction and Bibliography* (Zurich: L'Art ancien, 1958).

David R. Whitesell 1

The unsigned leaves are: 1) chapter ccccx, "Urtica nesseln", containing a near full-page woodcut on recto with contemporary hand coloring, and initial letter added in red (239 x 173 mm); and 2) chapter liiij, "Buglossa ochsen zunge", containing a near full-page woodcut on recto with contemporary hand coloring, and initial letter, paragraph marks, and capital strokes added in red (265 x 200 mm). No. 12 of 100 copies. Tipped into a cream paper mat; in a cloth case. "[T]hree antiquarian booksellers have combined and pooled their stocks of incomplete herbals .... The greater part of the particularly rare early herbals comes from the library of Dr. Karl Becher, Karlsbad" (Editorial Preface, p. IX).

Countway Library

S1-24B — Two leaves only; ill.

In: Claus Nissen, *Herbals of Five Centuries* ... (Zurich: L'Art ancien, 1958).

The unsigned leaves are: 1) chapter xix, "Azarum hazelwortz", containing a near full-page woodcut on recto with contemporary hand coloring, and initial letter added in red (240 x 170 mm); and 2) chapters cclxxiiij-cclxxv, containing a near full-page woodcut on verso with contemporary hand coloring, initial letters added in red or blue, and paragraph marks and capital strokes added in red (265 x 200 mm). No. 66 of 100 copies. Tipped into a cream paper mat; in a cloth case. Possibly from an imperfect copy formerly owned by Dr. Karl Becher, Karlsbad.

Dumbarton Oaks Garden Library

S1-24.7 **Langer, Johannes:** De censibus. After 25 August 1489.

4°. [26] leaves (26 blank); 215 x 154 mm.

Initial spaces, some with guide-letters, not filled in; without rubrication. 19th-century vellum-backed boards covered with 2 vellum leaves from a 15th-century scientific manuscript in Latin. A few contemporary MS marginalia. No. 508 in the Christie's South Kensington sale catalogue, 18 November 2003 (unnamed, but library of Percy Barnevik).

HC 9892*=H 9893; Pr 128; BMC 1:36 (IA.253); Polain 2439; Goff L-58; CIBN L-40; BSB-Ink L-59.

10 December 2003 – Bought with the Bayard Livingston Kilgour & Kate Gray Kilgour fund. Inc 128

PRINTER OF THE
'DARMSTADT' PROGNOSTICATION

S1-30.7   **Urdemann, Heinrich:** Dialogus inter Hugonem, Catonem, et Oliverium super libertate ecclesiastica. After 14 June 1477?

4°. [20] leaves (1 blank); 203 x 146 mm.

Initial space not filled in; without rubrication. Recent half vellum, incorporating a MS fragment from a 15th-century Latin Missal. No. 214 in the Christie's South Kensington sale catalogue, 7 December 2004 (unnamed, but library of Percy Barnevik).

HC 6140*; Pr 153; BMC 1:42 (IA.317); Pell 4217; Polain 1271; Goff D-162; CIBN U-30; Sack 3605; BSB-Ink U-77.

2 February 2005 – Bought with the Edward and Bertha C. Rose Acquisition fund. Inc 153

JACOB MEYDENBACH

S1-40A   **Hortus sanitatis.** 23 June 1491.

f°. A single leaf only; ill.; 309 x 213 mm.

In: Claus Nissen, *Herbals of Five Centuries: 50 Original Leaves from German, French, Dutch, English, Italian, and Swiss Herbals, With an Introduction and Bibliography* (Zurich: L'Art ancien, 1958).

The leaf is E3, containing chapters lix-lxxi from *De herbis*. Initial letters and paragraph marks added in red or blue; capital strokes and underlinings added in red; woodcuts uncolored. No. 12 of 100 copies. Tipped into a cream paper mat; in a cloth case. Possibly from an imperfect copy formerly owned by Dr. Karl Becher, Karlsbad.

Countway Library

S1-40B   — Single leaf only; ill.; 306 x 213 mm.

In: Claus Nissen, *Herbals of Five Centuries* ... (Zurich: L'Art ancien, 1958).

The leaf is I1, containing chapters cxxiij-cxxiiij from *De herbis*. Initial letter added in blue; paragraph marks added in red or blue; capital strokes and underlinings added in red. No. 66 of 100 copies. Tipped into a cream paper mat; in a cloth case. Possibly from an imperfect copy formerly owned by Dr. Karl Becher, Karlsbad.

Dumbarton Oaks Garden Library

S1-40C — Single leaf only; ill.; 308 x 212 mm.

In: Claus Nissen, *Tierbücher aus fünf Jahrhunderten: sechzig originalgraphische Tafeln aus deutschen, französischen, niederländischen, englischen, italienischen und schweizerischen Prachtwerken, 1491-1966, mit einer Einführung in die Geschichte der Zoologie* (Zurich: L'Art ancien, 1968).

The leaf is aa6, containing chapters xix-xxj from *De piscibus*. Initials added in alternating red and blue; paragraph marks, capital strokes, and underlining added in red; woodcuts uncolored. No. 28 of 100 copies of the German issue. Tipped into a cream paper mat; in a cloth case. This leaf is Tafel 1. Tafel 2 of the portfolio (missing in the Harvard copy) is a leaf from Goff H-489 (cf. (S1-216c-e) below for other leaves); the remaining portfolio leaves are post-1500.

Museum of Comparative Zoology Library

Strassburg

JOHANN MENTELIN

S1-54.5 **Augustinus, Aurelius, Saint:** Epistolae. Not after 1471.

f°. Two leaves only. 392 x 292 mm.

The leaves are disjunct and apparently come from the same copy. Capital strokes added in red. Acquired by E.B. Krumbhaar six years apart (one in 1928, one in 1934), but from the same source ("McLeish").

H 1966*=1967; Pr 208; BMC 1:55 (IC.535-36); Pell 1481; GW 2905; Goff A-1267; CIBN A-708; Sack 365; Schorbach 22; BSB-Ink A-887.

17 November 1955 – Gift of E.B. Krumbhaar. pInc 208

THE R-PRINTER
(ADOLPH RUSCH)

S1-71.3   **Biblia Latina.** ca. 1473.

f°. A single leaf only. 390 x 262 mm.

The leaf contains Revelation 14-18. Initials, paragraph marks, capital strokes, and headlines added in red. Old repair conceals some text on verso.

HC 3034*; Pr 234; BMC 1:60 (IC.618-19); Pell 2279; GW 4209; Goff B-534; CIBN B-371; BSB-Ink B-414.

17 November 1955 – Gift of E.B. Krumbhaar. pInc 234

S1-79.7   **Vincentius Bellovacensis:** Speculum doctrinale. Between 1477 and 11 February 1478.

f°. A single leaf only. 429 x 300 mm.

The leaf is 47_6, containing chapters CXV-CXXI of Book 16. Without rubrication. A specimen leaf distributed by the Gesellschaft für Typenkunde des XV. Jahrhunderts, with its printed caption label tipped at foot of recto.

C 6242; Pr 253; BL IC.679a; Polain 3938; Goff V-278; CIBN V-184 (A); Sack 3669; BSB-Ink V-198.

9 January 1914 – Bought with the Charles Minot fund. pInc 253

PRINTER OF HENRICUS
ARIMINENSIS (GEORG REYSER?)

S1-112.5   **Legrand, Jacobus:** Sophologium. ca. 1476.

f°. Two leaves only. 307 x 217 mm.

A single bifolium (leaves $22_{4,5}$), containing Book 3, Tract 4, Chapters 2-4. Initials added in red or blue, capital strokes and underlinings in red. MS content headlines added on versos.

HC 10469*; Pr 329; BMC 1:81 (IB.908); Polain 2461; Goff M-42; CIBN L-101; Sack 2229; BSB-Ink M-22; Ohly 31.

9 November 1984 – Bequest of Philip Hofer. bTyp Inc 329

GEORG HUSNER
(FIRST PRESS)

S1-125.5 **Marchesinus, Johannes:** Mammotrectus super Bibliam. ca. 1476.

f°. A single leaf only. 261 x 206 mm.

In: Type Facsimile Society, *Publications of the Society for the Year 1906* (Oxford: Horace Hart, [1906?]).

The leaf is unsigned; modern letterpress caption added at foot on recto. Initials, paragraph marks, and capital strokes added in red. "The original leaf which accompanies the present issue is the gift of Dr. Voulliéme to the Society" (descriptive letterpress, p. 25). Blue cloth; the leaf is inlaid and bound in.

HC 10551*; BL IB.1039; Polain 4550; Goff M-237; CIBN M-122; Sack 2336; BSB-Ink M-157.

18 January 1939 – Bought with the Charles Eliot Norton fund. B 5429.00F*
v. 2

ADOLPH RUSCH

S1-141A **Biblia Latina.** Before 25 March 1481.

f°. A single leaf only. 478 x 333 mm.

In: *Monumenta Germaniae et Italiae Typographica: deutsche und italienische Inkunabeln in getreuen Nachbildungen* (Berlin: Reichsdruckerei, 1892-1913). The Houghton Library copy contains six other original incunable leaves, all described in this supplement: S1-516.8, S1-664.5, S1-670B, S1-840A, S1-955.7, S1-1729A.

The leaf is from vol. 4, signed a3, containing the end of 2 Thessalonians and beginning of 1 Timothy; modern letterpress caption added at foot on recto. Initials and paragraph marks added in red and blue, capital strokes in red. Drab board portfolio with cloth ties; the leaf is laid in.

6 July 1896 – Bought with the Charles Minot fund. B 4528.92PF* v. 5

S1-141B — Single leaf only. 439 x 314 mm.

In: Otto F. Ege, *Original Leaves from Famous Bibles: Nine Centuries, 1121-1935 A.D.* ([New York: Philip C. Duschnes, 1945?]).

The leaf is "c8" from vol. 2, containing the beginning of 2 Samuel. Initial letter, paragraph marks, and capital strokes added in red. Rust buckram portfolio; the leaf is matted and laid in.

December 1967 – Gift of Paul Gerard Ecker. Typ 970.45.2100PF

MARTIN SCHOTT

S1-149.9 **Schottus, Petrus:** Lucubratiunculae. 2 October 1498.

4°. [1], CLXXXVII, [4] leaves ([CLXXXXI] blank; XXIX misnumbered XIXX); 213 x 150 mm.

Edited by Jacobus Wimpheling.

Colophon with added red penwork flourish, woodcut device partly colored in red. Recent half dark green morocco and gray boards, by Sangorski & Sutcliffe. Contemporary MS inscription on leaf I7v, "Ego Beatus Volck Argentin[us] depositus sum a d[omi]no baccalaureo Nicolao Textoris spirense Anno d[omi]ni 1499 in festo sancti Thome de Aquino ordinis predicatoru[m]"; with Volck's MS marginalia in Latin in text and on the blank leaf. Circular stamp of a Jesuit library (effaced) on title page. Ownership signature of Heneage Wynne Finch, dated 1936. From the Broxbourne Library of Albert Ehrman, with his armorial bookplate, Broxbourne Library booklabel, and "AE" stamp with added "2072" (no. 594 in pt. 2 of the Sotheby sale catalogue of his library, 8 May 1978); the library of George Abrams, with his booklabel (no. 112 in the Sotheby sale catalogue of his library, 16 November 1989); and the Bibliotheca Philosophica Hermetica of J.R. Ritman, with its bookplate (no. 92 in the Sotheby sale catalogue of its holdings, 5 December 2001).

HC(+Add) 14524*; Pr 409; BMC 1:96 (IA.1214-15); Goff S-321; CIBN S-166; BSB-Ink S-210.

3 January 2002 – Bought with the Margaret F. Cowett fund. Inc 409

PRINTER OF THE 1483 VITAS PATRUM

S1-157A **Pseudo-Petrus de Palude:** Sermones Thesauri novi de tempore. 1483.

f°. A single leaf only. 300 x 207 mm.

The leaf is 8₆, containing portions of sermons 17-18. Initial letter, capital strokes, and underlinings added in red. A specimen leaf distributed by the Gesellschaft für Typenkunde des XV. Jahrhunderts, with its printed caption label tipped at foot of recto.

9 January 1914 – Bought with the Charles Minot fund. bInc 419

JOHANN (REINHARD) GRÜNINGER

S1-166A **Gart der Gesundheit.** ca. 1489.

f°. A single leaf only; ill.; 262 x 190 mm.

Edited by Johannes von Cuba.

In: Claus Nissen, *Herbals of Five Centuries: 50 Original Leaves from German, French, Dutch, English, Italian, and Swiss Herbals, With an Introduction and Bibliography* (Zurich: L'Art ancien, 1958).

The unsigned leaf contains chapters cccciii-ccccv. Woodcuts on recto and verso with contemporary hand coloring; without rubrication. No. 12 of 100 copies. Tipped into a cream paper mat; in a cloth case. Possibly from an imperfect copy formerly owned by Dr. Karl Becher, Karlsbad.

HC 8946*; Goff G-108; Schr 4336.

Countway Library

S1-166B — Single leaf only; ill.; 262 x 190 mm.

In: Claus Nissen, *Herbals of Five Centuries* ... (Zurich: L'Art ancien, 1958).

The leaf is c2, containing chapters xxv-xxvi. Woodcuts on recto and verso with contemporary hand coloring; without rubrication. No. 66 of 100 copies. Tipped into a cream paper mat; in a cloth case. Possibly from an imperfect copy formerly owned by Dr. Karl Becher, Karlsbad.

Dumbarton Oaks Garden Library

S1-171.5   **Salicetus, Nicolaus:** Antidotarius animae. 4 March 1493.

8°. CXLVI (i.e. CXLIV) leaves (LXXXI-LXXXII omitted; LXXXVI and XCIIII misnumbered LXXXV and XCIII); 151 x 102 mm.

Full-page xylographic white-on-black title. There is also a variant issue (Goff S-40) with the title in white against a black and red background.

Some large Maiblumen initials added in red and blue, smaller initials in red or blue, some with penwork marginal extensions and flourishes; paragraph marks, underlinings, and some capital strokes added in red. Contemporary blind-stamped sheep over wooden boards; marks of center and corner bosses, no longer present; brass clasp plate on back cover; latch on front, clasp and thong no longer present; endleaves renewed. Booklabel of Helmut N. Friedlaender (no. 112 in pt. 1 of the Christie's New York sale catalogue of his library, 23 April 2001); no. 176 in Christie's London sale catalogue, 20 November 2002 (unnamed, but library of Percy Barnevik).

HC 14161*; Pr 463; BMC 1:108 (IA.1417); Goff S-39.

2 January 2003 – Bought with the Hofer Trust fund. Typ Inc 463

S1-183A   **Horatius Flaccus, Quintus:** Opera. 12 March 1498.

f°. A single leaf only; ill.; 301 x 212 mm.

The leaf is 2F2 (leaf CLXX), with large three-part woodcut on verso of a man reading at a lectern. Initials added in red and blue; paragraph marks, capital strokes, and underlinings added in red.

17 November 1955 – Gift of E.B. Krumbhaar. bInc 485

JOHANN PRÜSS

S1-191.2   **Heldenbuch.** ca. 1479.

f°. [282] leaves; ill.; 267 x 187 mm.

Includes *Rosengarten* and *Laurin* (the *Grosser* and *Kleine Rosengarten*).

Eight leaves only: fol. 57 (6_5), 58 (6_6), 93 (12_1), 97 (12_5), 157 (20_7), 172 (22_8), 176 (23_4), and 243 (33_5). The leaves contain nine half-page woodcuts (Heinzle nos. 40, 41, 69, 73, 115, 116, 129, 132, and 204). Woodcuts colored in ochre, red, pink and gray. 16th-century drawing (132 x 74 mm), in brown ink with ochre and pink coloring, depicting two men in contemporary dress on fol. 58v; brown ink flourishes added to woodcut on recto; without rubrication. The leaves come from an imperfect copy which was dispersed on the antiquarian market beginning in 1954, but whose earlier provenance is not known. Walter Kofler has identified 56 extant leaves from this copy (his "Fragmentgruppe 1954"); see the CD-ROM publication: W. Kofler, *Die Heldenbuch-Inkunabel von 1479: alle Exemplare und Fragmente in 350 Abbildungen* (Göppingen: Kümmerle Verlag, 2003).

H 8419(?); C 2905; GW 12185; CIBN H-6; BSB-Ink H-39; Schäfer 148; Schr 4196; Schramm 20:11 and 27; Heldenbuch (ed. J. Heinzle).

9 November 1984 – Bequest of Philip Hofer. bTyp Inc 511.5

S1-215.2   **Ordo missae secundum morem ecclesiae Ratisponensis.** ca. 1499.

4°. [16] leaves; 199 x 140 mm.

Paul Needham has pointed out several errors in the BMC description of this edition; cf. Sotheby's, *Incunables from the Schøyen Collection* (sale, New York, 12 December 1991), lot 32. A more accurate description can be found in GW's draft entry (M28328), available online at: http://www.gesamtkatalogderwiegendrucke.de/. As is true of the Schøyen copy (now at the Pierpont Morgan Library), the Harvard copy clearly shows that the black printing preceded the red printing. BSB-Ink suggests a date of after 1500.

Woodcut Maiblumen and Lombard initials, titles, and rubrics printed in red; without hand rubrication. MS ownership notations on title page, "Nestereos anno & 15·95", "Nestereos annos viuas 15·945.", "[s?] Nestereos", and "Nestereos Annos Anno Dñi Millesimo Quingentesimo Quinto". MS notation at top of a2r, "Mñij Mettensis." Modern half vellum. No. 533 in the Christie's South Kensington sale catalogue, 18 November 2003 (unnamed, but library of Percy Barnevik).

Pr 572A; BMC 1:127 (IA.1747); BSB-Ink O-62.

10 December 2003 – Bought with the Bayard Livingston Kilgour & Kate Gray Kilgour fund. Inc 572A

(S1-216c)   **Hortus sanitatis.** ca. 1507.

f°. A single leaf only; ill.; 293 x 205 mm.

In: Ellen Shaffer, *The Garden of Health: An Account of Two Herbals, the Gart der Gesundheit and the Hortus Sanitatis* ([San Francisco]: The Book

Club of California, 1957).

The leaf is z1. Woodcuts uncolored; without rubrication. Half linen and illustrated rose boards; leaf hinged onto the leaf following the title page.

1957 – Bought with the Horace Davis fund. Typ 970.57.7850F

(S1-216d) — Single leaf only; ill.; 301 x 208 mm.

In: Claus Nissen, *Herbals of Five Centuries: 50 Original Leaves from German, French, Dutch, English, Italian, and Swiss Herbals, With an Introduction and Bibliography* (Zurich: L'Art ancien, 1958).

The leaf is f3, containing chapters xci-xciii from *De herbis*. Woodcuts uncolored; without rubrication. No. 12 of 100 copies. Tipped into a cream paper mat; in a cloth case. Possibly from an imperfect copy formerly owned by Dr. Karl Becher, Karlsbad.

Countway Library

(S1-216e) — Single leaf only; ill.; 300 x 207 mm.

In: Claus Nissen, *Herbals of Five Centuries* ... (Zurich: L'Art ancien, 1958).

The leaf is d4, containing chapters lix-lx from *De herbis*. Woodcuts uncolored; without rubrication. No. 66 of 100 copies. Tipped into a cream paper mat; in a cloth case. Possibly from an imperfect copy formerly owned by Dr. Karl Becher, Karlsbad.

Dumbarton Oaks Garden Library

PRINTER OF THE 1483
JORDANUS DE QUEDLINBURG (GEORG HUSNER)

S1-216.5 **Pseudo-Hugo de Prato Florido:** Sermones dominicales super Evangelia et Epistolas. Not after 1482.

f°. [369] leaves (1 blank); 297 x 215 mm.

Initial space to the prologue on 2,r contains a miniature of a Carmelite friar praying alongside St. Vitus, with initial added in blue above; initial space to sermon 1 in right-hand column contains a foliate initial in green on a pink ground with liquid gold tracery, with a foliate marginal extension in pink, green, blue, and liquid gold down the center margin and branching out across the entire lower margin. Initials, paragraph marks, capital strokes, and underlinings added in red. Blind impressions of bearer type visible at top and bottom of blank outer column of final leaf; "unee" in early gothic type stamped in red on verso of final leaf. Contemporary blind-stamped calf over unbevelled wooden boards; brass clasp plates on back cover, latches on front cover; one clasp with pigskin thong remains; edges stained yellow; rebacked, corners renewed. Contemporary purchase inscription in red ink added by the owner and rubricator on recto of final leaf, "Frate[r] Vitus Wolfframi de nouaciui[ta]te sub salczpurctz ordinis fr[atru]m glo[rio]sissime dei genit[ric]is Ma[r]ie de mo[n]te Carmeli, co[m]p[ar]auit hu[n]c libr[um] suo de pat[ri]monio, dei ob honore[m], suu[m] studiu[m], ast alior[um] om[niu]m eo vti volentiu[m] Anno d[omi]ni .1483. Sa[n]cte Vite duc nos ad gaudia vite Amen"; "Sancte Vite duc nos ad gaudia vite" added in red preceding sermon 8; "S[an]cte Vite ora p[ro] me .1483." added in red preceding sermon 86; with his MS marginalia throughout. 17th-century ownership inscription at top of 1₂r, "Carmel: Bamb:" From the library of Ned J. Nakles (no. 15 in the Christie's New York sale catalogue, 17 April 2000). No. 100 in the Christie's South Kensington sale catalogue, 7 December 2004 (unnamed, but library of Percy Barnevik). Wanting the blank leaf.

HC 9003*; Pr 633A; BMC 1:130 (IB.1938); Polain 2018; Goff H-509; CIBN H-308; BSB-Ink H-416.

2 February 2005 – Bought with the Edward and Bertha C. Rose Acquisition fund. Inc 633A

S1-218A   **Balbus, Johannes:** Catholicon. Not after 1483.

f°. A single leaf only. 384 x 279 mm.

The leaf contains Orbis-Ordo. Paragraph marks, capital strokes, and underlinings added in red. A specimen leaf distributed by the Gesellschaft für Typenkunde des XV. Jahrhunderts, with its printed caption label tipped at foot of recto.

9 January 1914 – Bought with the Charles Minot fund. pInc 632

S1-258.5   **Pseudo-Textoris, Guillelmus:** Sermo de passione Christi. 11 February 1496.

4°. [184] leaves (171 and 183-84 blank); 202 x 138 mm.

Includes Johannes Kannemann, *De passione Christi secundum quattuor evangelistas*; *Passio sive sermo in diebus Parasceves*; Pseudo-Anselmus, *Dialogus de passione Christi*; and Pseudo-Bernardus Claravallensis [Oglerius de Tridino], *De planctu Beatae Mariae Virginis*.

Initials, paragraph marks, capital strokes, and underlinings added in red. Contemporary blind-stamped pigskin over beech boards; brass clasp plate on front cover, latch on back, clasp with pigskin thong; title in ink on lower edges; spine liners cut from an 11th-century Latin devotional MS; liner underneath rear pastedown from a 12th-century Latin sermon MS in German proto-gothic minuscule. Blind bearers (type, large initials?, and what appear to be metal plates) are visible on the title page (a1), colophon page ([et]2), and blank leaves. Extensive contemporary MS annotations in Latin in several hands; partly foliated, and some quire marks added in MS. Bookstamp of the Buxheim library in lower margin of a2r and paper label at spine foot with shelf mark, "M.192."; paper label pasted to rear pastedown with "38" in MS; later owned by Johann Friedrich, Graf von Ostein and Friedrich Karl, Graf von Waldbott-Bassenheim; pencil inscription on rear flyleaf, "HEH Dupl."; pencil signature of Ellen Shaffer on front pastedown; booklabel of Helmut N. Friedlaender (no. 25 in pt. 1 of the Christie's New York sale catalogue of his library, 23 April 2001); no. 35 in Christie's London sale catalogue, 20 November 2002 (unnamed, but library of Percy Barnevik).

H 1140* (Anselmus & Bernardus); H 2909 (Bernardus); C 5778; Pr 641; BMC 1:145 (IA.1969); Polain 3676; Goff T-122; CIBN T-95; BSB-Ink B-513.

2 January 2003 – Bought with the Carl Tilden Keller and Henry Saltonstall Howe funds. Inc 641

GEORG HUSNER
(SECOND PRESS)

(S1-304a)   **Petrus Comestor:** Historia scholastica. 16 November 1503.

f°. [208] leaves (208 blank); 275 x 200 mm.

The copy described by Pellechet lacked the clearly dated colophon leaf. Printer assignment from Proctor.

Large initial, with guide-letter, at the beginning of each book not filled in; other initials, paragraph marks, capital strokes, and underlinings added in red. Contemporary blind-stamped calf, badly flaked, over wooden boards; brass clasp plates on back cover, latches on front; one clasp with leather thong remains. Early MS inscription on title page, "Johannes Zyssenheim poss." Gilt blue leather booklabel of Count Paul Riant. Bound with Magnus Aurelius Cassiodorus, *Historia ecclesiastica tripartita* (Strassburg, Johann Prüss, after 1500?; Walsh 216) and Eusebius, *Ecclesiastica historia* (Hagenau: Heinrich Gran for Johann Rynmann, 1506).

Pr (MDI-MDXX) 10001; BM STC(G) p. 687; Pell 3878; Goff P-467.

28 December 1899 – Gift of J. Randolph Coolidge and Archibald Cary Coolidge. Inc 583

UNASSIGNED

(S1-310a)   **Locher, Jacobus:** Ludicrum drama de sene amatore. ca. 1503.

[For transcriptions see Hain; but in this copy there is no line division on a1r between "drama:" and "plautino".] 4°. a⁴; [4] leaves; ill.; 197 x 143 mm. a3r: 40 lines, 157 x 95 mm. Types: 140G (approx.), title and heading on a2r; 93G, verses; 78G, text. Woodcut; woodcut initial.

For place of publication and dating see BSB-Ink.

Without rubrication. Modern vellum. Bookstamp of the Rathsschulbibliothek Zwickau in lower margin of a1r.

H 10158*; Goff L-262 (Ingolstadt, ca. 1505); IGI 3:236; BSB-Ink L-203; Schr 4514.

April 1959 – Gift of Christian A. Zabriskie. *GC5.L7884.505l

Cologne

ULRICH ZELL

S1-315.5   **Pseudo-Augustinus:** Sermo super orationem dominicam. ca. 1467.

4°. [10] leaves (1 blank); 210 x 144 mm.

Includes *Expositio super symbolum* and *De ebrietate*. *De ebrietate* consists of extracts from sermon 46 of Caesarius Arelatensis; see CIBN.

Imperfect: a single bifolium ($1_{4.7}$) only. Initial letter in blue with penwork infill and marginal extensions added on 1_4r; paragraph marks, underlinings, and capital strokes added in red. Disbound; original quire guard of vellum MS waste preserved.

HC 1988=H 1991*; Pr 811; BMC 1:181 (IA.2740); Pell 1500; Polain 410; GW 2995; Goff A-1302; CIBN A-751; Voull 206.

29 March 1918 – Bought with the Charles Eliot Norton fund. bInc 811

S1-316.5   **Pius II, Pope:** Epistola ad Mahumetem. ca. 1469/72.

4°. [54] leaves (1 blank); 192 x 133 mm.

This copy conforms to CIBN variant B, with the reading "concitauerit In | " on 1_4v, line 27, except that 1_2r, line 3 has the reading "conpoffuit", not "compoffuit". Large initial in red and blue and paragraph mark in red on 1_2r. Some early MS marginalia, a few trimmed by the binder. MS inscription on front pastedown, "Emptus. xiiii β. vi δ". 16th-century blind-stamped dark brown calf over wooden boards, gilt fleurons at corners of the inner panel, arms of Benoît Le Court stamped in silver in center of each cover; the edges of each tract have been colored alternately yellow, red, purple, or uncolored. The second item in a tract volume also containing Pseudo-Phalaris, *Epistolae* (Paris: Pierre Vidoue for Regnault Chaudière, 25 May 1521); Francis I, King of France, *Exemplum variarum litterarum missarum a sanctissimo patre nostro Papa* (Paris: Pierre Vidoue, ca. 1523); Laudivius Zacchia, Vezzanensis, *Epistolae magni Turci* (Lyons: Jean Marion for Romain Morin, 30 March 1520); Desiderius Erasmus, *Epistolae aliquot* (Louvain: Thierry Martens, December 1520); Desiderius Erasmus, *Aliquot epistolae* (Louvain: Thierry Martens, 17 April 1517); Heinrich Auerbach, *Duae epistole* (Leipzig: Melchior Lotter, 1520). Blank leaf not present, lower blank margin of 7_6 has been cut away.

C 39; Pr 818; BMC 1:186 (IA.2759); Pell 111; Polain 3160; Goff P-698; Voull 962; CIBN P-391.

16 July 2004 – Bought with the Amy Lowell and Bayard Livingston Kilgour & Kate Gray Kilgour funds. Inc 818

S1-343.5   **Albertus Magnus:** Sermones de tempore et de sanctis. ca. 1475.

f°. A single leaf only. 285 x 208 mm.

Initial letters not filled in; capital strokes added in red. A specimen leaf distributed by the Gesellschaft für Typenkunde des XV. Jahrhunderts, with its printed caption label tipped at foot of recto.

H 469a; C 203; BL IB.2983; Pell 307; GW 773; Goff A-329; CIBN A-178; BSB-Ink A-214; Voull 47.

9 January 1914 – Bought with the Charles Minot fund. bInc 887.1

JOHANN KOELHOFF THE ELDER

S1-372.5   **Pius II, Pope:** Epistolae familiares. 1478.

f°. [252] leaves (1 blank); 281 x 202 mm.

Imperfect: 16 leaves (g2-9, h2-9) only; g3, 5, 7, 9, h2, 5, 7-8 wanting 1-2 cm. portion of outer margin. Initials and paragraph marks added in red.

Tipped onto fol. 31 of an album of printed fragments removed from bindings (presumably Oxford bindings of the late 16th–early 17th centuries) of books in the library at Lanhydrock House, Cornwall. Hannibal Gamon traditionally has been credited with forming the library, though Mark Purcell has shown that its history is more complicated than once believed; cf. Mark Purcell, "The Library at Lanhydrock," *The Book Collector*, vol. 54, no.2 (2005): 195-227. It is no longer possible to determine precisely the early provenance of these fragments, and this supplement's "Provenance Index" lists only Gamon, John Robartes, 1st Earl of Radnor, and the 7th Viscount Clifden as former owners. The fragments were arranged and mounted by W.H. Allnutt of the Bodleian Library in the 1880s or 1890s (cf. N.R. Ker, *Fragments of Medieval Manuscripts Used as Pastedowns in Oxford Bindings* (Oxford, 1954), p. xvi). From the library of the Viscount Clifden (lot 288 in the Sotheby sale, 2 July 1963). Late 19th-century half tan sheep and brown cloth.

HC 150*; Pr 1037; BMC 1:222 (IB.3510); Pell 91; Polain 3166; Voull 966; CIBN P-410; Sack 2884; BSB-Ink P-518.

October 1963 – Bought with the Susan A.E. Morse fund. *fEC.A100. B659c

S1-373.5   **Salguis, Raymundus de:** Ars inveniendi themata. 1482.

f°. [56] leaves (1 and 56 blank); 293 x 206 mm.

This copy has several variant readings from those given in Hain: on a2r, "materia" and "Themata" (Hain: "materie" and "themata"); on g5v, "Mcccclxxxij." (Hain: "Mcccclyyyij."). These readings agree with Voulliéme's transcription. Initial letters, paragraph marks, capital strokes, and underlinings added in red; traces of MS quiring. Buff boards. "W.868" in MS inside front cover; bookplate removed. Imperfect: worming; two holes in g5 with some text loss; blank leaves not present.

HC 14135*; Pr 1053; Polain 4697; Voull 1060; CIBN S-14; Sack 3120; BSB-Ink S-12.

June 2000 – Bought. Law Library

JOHANN GULDENSCHAFF

S1-415.3 **Concilium Basiliense:** Decretum de conceptione Beatae Mariae Virginis. ca. 1478.

4°. [6] leaves; 200 x 140 mm.

Includes Pseudo-Anselmus, *Epistola de sancta conceptione virginis celebranda*. GW describes this as the final gathering of a Guldenschaff edition of Johannes Gerson, *De conceptione Virginia Mariae sermo* (Goff S-200), with which this is sometimes found.

Initial, paragraph marks, and underlinings added in red on four of 12 pages only. 19th-century brown diced sheep, gilt, edges gilt. Bookplate of William Blades; ownership stamps of the William Blades Library, St. Bride Foundation; unidentified owner's inscription at end, "… it was last purchased in the year 1956 from a bookseller at Amsterdam". Rectangular booklabel removed from front flyleaf. No. 75 in the Christie's South Kensington sale catalogue, 7 December 2004 (unnamed, but library of Percy Barnevik).

C 1763; Pr 1219; BMC 1:254 (IA.4276); Pell 3967; GW 10841 (II); Goff G-217; Voull 347.

2 February 2005 – Bought with the Edward and Bertha C. Rose Acquisition fund. Inc 1219

S1-418.8 **Petrus de Harentals:** Collectarius super librum Psalmorum. 1 March 1483.

f°. A single leaf only. 290 x 206 mm.

The leaf is unsigned; foliated "21" in MS. Initial, paragraph marks, capital strokes, and underlinings added in red. A specimen leaf distributed by the Gesellschaft für Typenkunde des XV. Jahrhunderts, with its printed caption label tipped at foot of recto.

HC(+Add) 8365; Polain 3104; Goff P-472; Voull 919; CIBN P-233; Schr 4926; Schramm 8:19.

9 January 1914 – Bought with the Charles Minot fund. bInc 1209.1

LUDWIG VON RENCHEN

S1-424.5 **Jacobus de Voragine:** Legenda aurea [Low German]. 21 July-31 October 1485.

f°. A single leaf only; ill.; 260 x 189 mm.

The leaf is 8_2 from pt. 1 (leaf lij), containing the beginning of the legend of St. John the Evangelist. Woodcut (77 x 69 mm) depicting the vision of St. John the Evangelist on recto. Initial and capital strokes added in red.

C 6507=4626=3527; Pr 1262-63; BMC 1:266 (IB.4455-56); Polain 2223; Goff J-171; Voull 626; CIBN J-108; BSB-Ink I-105; Schr 4321; Schramm 8:25.

9 November 1984 – Bequest of Philip Hofer. bTyp Inc 1262

HEINRICH QUENTELL
(SECOND PRESS)

S1-427.5 **Ferrerius, Vincentius:** Sermones de tempore. Pars hiemalis. 1485.

f°. A single leaf only. 287 x 212 mm.

The leaf is unsigned; wormed, with minor loss. Without rubrication. A specimen leaf distributed by the Gesellschaft für Typenkunde des XV. Jahrhunderts, with its printed caption label tipped at foot of recto.

HC(Add) 7001*; BL IB.4523; Polain 3951; Goff F-129; GW 9835; Voull 412; BSB-Ink F-85.

9 January 1914 – Bought with the Charles Minot fund. bInc 1285.3

S1-439.5   **Manuale parochialium sacerdotum.** ca. 1492.

4°. [10] leaves (10 blank); ill.; 178 x 138 mm.

Initial spaces not filled in; without rubrication. Recent gray speckled boards, with binder's ticket of Gust. Hedberg, Stockholm. Bookplate of Victor v. Stedingk. No. 516 in the Christie's South Kensington sale catalogue, 18 November 2003 (unnamed, but library of Percy Barnevik). Blank leaf not present.

H 10729; Pr 1413; Polain 2599 bis; Goff M-221; BSB-Ink M-140; Schr 4561; Schramm 8:21.

10 December 2003 – Bought with the Bayard Livingston Kilgour & Kate Gray Kilgour fund. Inc 1413

S1-457.2   **Albertanus Causidicus Brixiensis:** De arte loquendi et tacendi. 1497.

4°. [12] leaves (12 blank); 194 x 140 mm.

Blind impressions of bearer type (not from this edition) are visible on A1 and B6. Initials, paragraph marks, capital strokes, and underlinings added in red. Modern dark brown calf. No. 2 in the Christie's South Kensington sale catalogue, 7 December 2004 (unnamed, but library of Percy Barnevik).

HC 412*; Pr 1340; BMC 1:287 (IA.4661); GW 563; Goff A-209; Voull 37; BSB-Ink A-120.

2 February 2005 – Bought with the Edward and Bertha C. Rose Acquisition fund. Inc 1340

MARTIN VON WERDEN

(S1-478a)   **Sacranus, Johannes:** Errores atrocissimorum Ruthenorum. After 1507.

[For transcriptions see Hain.] 4°. [1⁴]; [4] leaves; ill.; 190 x 143 mm. 1,r: 39 lines, 156 x 101 mm. Types: 2:150G, title; 3:80G, text. Woodcut; Lombards.

The text consists of an extract (Tract 1, Chapter 2) from Sacranus's *Elucidarium errorum ritus Ruthenici*. For printer assignment and date, see Sack.

Paragraph marks, underlinings, and highlights to the title-page woodcut added in red. Modern vellum.

H 6677*; IGI 5:5; Sack 3119a (1); Schr 5175.

10 October 1949 – Gift of Imrie de Vegh. *ZPC5.Sa146.506eb

CORNELIS DE ZIERIKZEE

(S1-491d) **Pseudo-Albertus Magnus:** Liber aggregationis. ca. 1502.

4°. [24] leaves; ill.; 194 x 140 mm.

Includes Pseudo-Albertus Magnus, *De mirabilibus mundi* and *Parvum regimen sanitatis.* For dating see BSB-Ink.

Initial, capital stroke, and underlining added in red on title page. Modern blind-stamped brown calf.

HC 528*; Pr 1494; BMC 1:310 (IA.5195); GW 655; Goff A-265; BSB-Ink A-181; Schr 3064.

Dumbarton Oaks Garden Library

Augsburg

GÜNTHER ZAINER

S1-502A **Isidorus Hispalensis:** De responsione mundi et de astrorum ordinatione. 7 December 1472.

f°. Another copy. 300 x 202 mm.

Large initial on [a]1r added in red and blue; initials added in red or blue; paragraph marks, capital strokes, and underlinings added in red. Modern gray speckled boards.

1 January 1991 – Gift of David P. Wheatland. Inc 1533 (B)

S1-516.8 **Rainerius de Pisis:** Pantheologia. 1474.

f°. A single leaf only. 393 x 272 mm.

In: *Monumenta Germaniae et Italiae Typographica: deutsche und italienische Inkunabeln in getreuen Nachbildungen* (Berlin: Reichsdruckerei, 1892-1913).

The leaf contains portions of chapters 2-4 of *Esse Dei*. Modern letterpress caption added at foot on recto. Initials added in red and blue, paragraph marks and capital strokes in red. Drab board portfolio with cloth ties; the leaf is laid in.

H 13016*; Pr 1543; BMC 2:321 (IC.5473); Goff R-6; Sack 3007; BSB-Ink R-2.

9 March 1903 – Bought with the Charles Minot fund. B 4528.92PF* v. 7

S1-518.5 **Biblia** [German]. Not after 1474.

f°. [2], CCCCXXj (i.e. CCCCXXij), Cx leaves; ill.

BMC (reprint) notes a copy said to have been presented by Zainer in 1474.

Imperfect: 25 woodcut historiated initials only (Schramm vol. 2, Abb. 625-628, 632-633, 636-651, 653-655). Each initial is trimmed to ca. 89 x 72 mm., with later hand coloring. Tipped into four cream paper mats in groups of six or seven.

H 3133*; Pr 1577; BMC 2:323 (IC.5571); Pell 2372; GW 4298; Goff B-627; CIBN B-439; Sack 674-75; BSB-Ink B-485; Schr 3456; Schramm 2:19.

9 November 1984 – Bequest of Philip Hofer. pTyp Inc 1577

JOHANN BÄMLER

S1-547.5 **Quadragesimale viatoris.** 1479.

4°. A single leaf only. 192 x 131 mm.

In: Type Facsimile Society, *Publications of the Society for the Year 1904* (Oxford: Horace Hart, [1904?]).

The leaf is unsigned; modern letterpress caption added at foot on recto. Without rubrication. "The three original leaves which accompany the present issue are the gift of Dr. [Konrad] Burger to the Society" (descriptive letterpress, p. 21). Blue cloth; the leaf is inlaid and bound in.

C 5003; Pr 1624; BMC 2:336 (IA.5696); Goff Q-2; BSB-Ink Q-2.

18 January 1939 – Bought with the Charles Eliot Norton fund. B 5429.00F* v. 1

ULRICH & AFRA,
MONASTERY OF SS.

S1-554A **Pseudo-Salomo III, episcopus Constantiensis:** Glossae. ca. 1474.

f°. Another copy. 402 x 268 mm.

For comments on the bearer types visible in this and other copies, see the note to 554 above. First three woodcut initials hand-colored in red; capital strokes and underlinings added in red to leaves 1₂r, 2₇v, 2₈r only; initial spaces not filled in. The spaces on 29₁v have been left unfilled. Leaves 15₂₋₇ and 27₂₋₉ were supplied, apparently at the time of binding, from a shorter, red-rubricated, and unannotated copy; nearly all rubrication on these leaves has been overpainted recently in white. Extensive contemporary MS annotations in red and black, including some brackets with human profiles, added prior to binding. The binder mistakenly trimmed off the outer 20 mm. of many annotations. Approximately 65 of these were painstakingly salvaged, trimmed to size, and mounted back in place on fore-edge tabs; the fore-edge square of the covers is unusually deep (25 mm) so as to accommodate the tabs. Contemporary South German blind-stamped tawed deerskin over thick oak boards; two brass clasps on front cover, clasp plates on back cover, clasps and deerskin thongs; title in MS on vellum label on front cover. Illuminated arms of the Planta (?) family at foot of leaf 1₂r; 19ᵗʰ-century MS title and oval green stamp (effaced) on blank leaf 1₁r; booklabel of Helmut N. Friedlaender (no. 111 in pt. 1 of the Christie's New York sale catalogue of his library, 23 April 2001); no. 177 in Christie's London sale catalogue, 20 November 2002 (unnamed, but library of Percy Barnevik).

2 January 2003 – Bought with the Bayard Livingston Kilgour & Kate Gray Kilgour fund. Inc 1636PF (B)

ANTON SORG

S1-560.5 **Speculum humanae salvationis** [German]. 9 August 1476.

f°. A single leaf only; ill.; 264 x 186 mm.

The leaf is 7₂. With two half-page woodcuts: King David serenading Saul's daughter (recto); the death of Absalom (verso). Lombard outline initials and woodcut on verso heightened in red, capital strokes added in red.

H 14942*; Goff S-663; Sack 3265; BSB-Ink S-510; Schr 5275; Schramm 4:1 and 50.

9 November 1984 – Bequest of Philip Hofer. bTyp Inc 1646.1

S1-561A   **Ambrosius, Saint:** Expositio in evangelium S. Lucae. 1476.

f°. A single leaf only. 271 x 185 mm.

In: Type Facsimile Society, *Publications of the Society for the Year 1904* (Oxford: Horace Hart, 1904?).

The leaf is 6_{10}; modern letterpress caption added at foot on recto. Without rubrication. "The three original leaves which accompany the present issue are the gift of Dr. [Konrad] Burger to the Society" (descriptive letterpress, p. 21). Blue cloth; the leaf is inlaid and bound in.

18 January 1939 – Bought with the Charles Eliot Norton fund. B 5429.00F* v. 1

JOHANN SCHÖNSPERGER

S1-596.2   **Gart der Gesundheit.** 22 August 1485.

f°. A single leaf only; ill.; 279 x 201 mm.

Edited by Johannes von Cuba.

In: Claus Nissen, *Herbals of Five Centuries: 50 Original Leaves from German, French, Dutch, English, Italian, and Swiss Herbals, With an Introduction and Bibliography* (Zurich: L'Art ancien, 1958).

The leaf is y5, containing on the verso chapter ccc, "Polegium poleÿ". Half-page woodcut on verso with contemporary hand coloring; without rubrication. Contemporary MS annotation in German. No. 12 of 100 copies. Tipped into a cream paper mat; in a cloth case. Possibly from an imperfect copy formerly owned by Dr. Karl Becher, Karlsbad.

H 8949*; Pr 1763; BMC 2:365 (IB.6287); Polain 4445; Goff G-98; Schr 4333.

Countway Library

S1-596.2A   — Single leaf only; ill.; 280 x 202 mm.

In: Claus Nissen, *Herbals of Five Centuries* ... (Zurich: L'Art ancien, 1958).

The leaf is X3, containing on the recto chapter ccncciij, "Tereniabin". Half-page woodcut on recto with contemporary hand coloring; without rubrication. No. 66 of 100 copies. Tipped into a cream paper mat; in a cloth case. Possibly from an imperfect copy formerly owned by Dr. Karl Becher, Karlsbad.

Dumbarton Oaks Garden Library

S1-596.4 **Gart der Gesundheit.** ca. 1485/86.

f°. 2 leaves; ill.; 299 x 217 mm. 31+ lines, 145 mm. wide. Type: 1:120G. Initial spaces.

Edited by Johannes von Cuba.

Proof (waste?) sheets, removed from a binding. The leaves, each printed on one side only, contain the following: 1) chapter ccxxxvj, "Linum" (chapter heading + 28 lines of text preceded by three-line initial space, and direction line with signature "Biij=", without woodcut illustration), unwatermarked; 2) chapter ccxlvj, "Licium" (chapter heading + 31 lines of text preceded by three-line initial space and with large woodcut inset at lower right, unsigned), with bull's head watermark. The text is set in Johann Schönsperger's type 1, with alternative forms of capital D, I, and S present (in use 1482-1488 per BMC). Although this font was not unique to Schönsperger's press, the attribution is strengthened by the woodcut, which is the identical block used in Schönsperger's edition of 22 August 1485.

John Bidwell has kindly compared photocopies of these leaves with their respective pages in the Pierpont Morgan Library copy of the 22 August 1485 Schönsperger edition and reports that the text, type, and woodcut are the same. However, the setting is different and chapter ccxxxvj falls on B2v instead of B3r (with chapter ccxlvj on B7r). While the Houghton leaves may possibly be proof sheets for the 1485 edition, it seems more likely that they belong to another, unrecorded and presumably uncompleted edition. Schönsperger would seem to have had good reason not only to reprint the 22 August 1485 edition, but to abort it as well. Certainly the *Gart der Gesundheit* proved profitable, for the 1485 edition was soon followed by a second dated 5 June 1486 and five more by 1499. Schönsperger's market, however, was quickly challenged by Johann Grüninger's competing edition (Goff G-99, undated but ca. 1485-86) which, by compressing the text into 147 fewer leaves, would have been far less expensive. All subsequent Schönsperger editions adopted

Grüninger's two-column format, with the woodcuts in reduced size and the length cut from 370 to 258 leaves. Having initiated a close reprint of his 1485 edition, then, only to learn of Grüninger's more compact and less expensive edition, Schönsperger may have concluded that his best option was to scrap the reprint, recut the blocks in reduced size, and begin a new reprint copying Grüninger's format. B2v and B7r constitute a single folio forme in the 22 August 1485 edition. It is possible that the two Houghton proof sheets once formed a single bifolium containing B3r and B6v.

Initial spaces not filled in; without hand-coloring or rubrication. Edges trimmed, repaired tears and marginal restorations, with slight text loss. Circular "HD" stamp of Helmuth Domizlaff on each leaf. Some early MS annotations in Latin on verso of the leaf containing chapter ccxlvj.

20 November 1990 – Bought with the Duplicates fund. bInc 1763.5

S1-601.7   **Schedel, Hartmann:** Liber chronicarum. 1 February 1497.

f°. A single leaf only; ill.; 312 x 210 mm.

In: Ellen Shaffer, *The Nuremberg Chronicle: A Pictorial World History from the Creation to 1493* (Los Angeles: Dawson's Book Shop, 1950).

The leaf is H3 (fol. Clxv). Without rubrication. Illustrated blue cloth; the leaf is tipped in at front.

HCR 14509; Pr 1786; BMC 2:370 (IB.6361); Polain 3470; Goff S-308; CIBN S-162; Sack 3183; BSB-Ink S-196; Schr 5204; Schramm 17:9.

9 November 1984 – Bequest of Philip Hofer. *93HR-6430F

S1-608.5   **Gart der Gesundheit.** 13 May 1499.

f°. A single leaf only; ill.; 238 x 166 mm.

Edited by Johannes von Cuba.

In: Claus Nissen, *Herbals of Five Centuries: 50 Original Leaves from German, French, Dutch, English, Italian, and Swiss Herbals, With an Introduction and Bibliography* (Zurich: L'Art ancien, 1958).

The leaf is C2, containing chapters cccxci-cccxcv. Woodcut on verso with contemporary hand coloring; without rubrication. No. 12 of 100 copies. Tipped into a cream paper mat; in a cloth case. Possibly from an imperfect copy formerly owned by Dr. Karl Becher, Karlsbad.

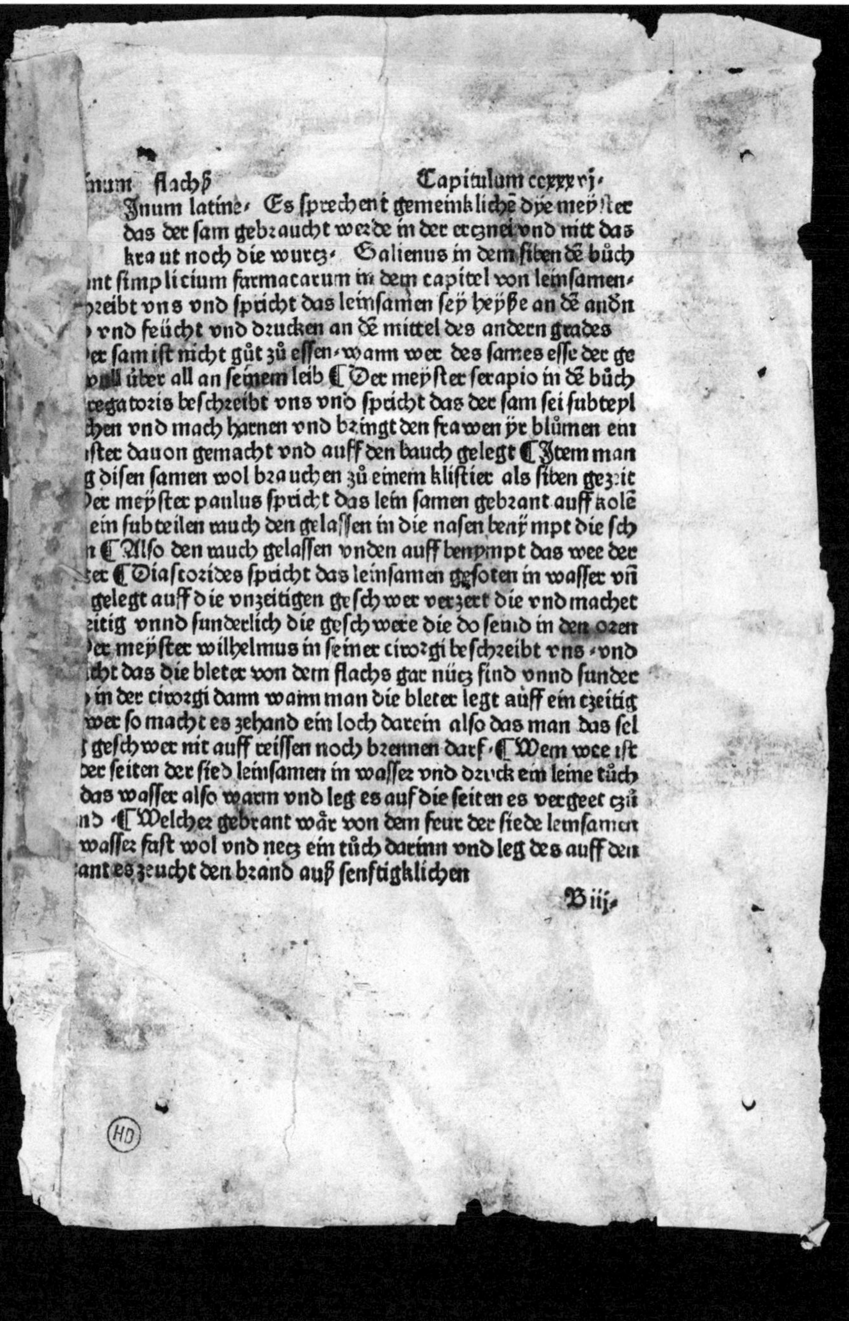
inum flachs Capitulum ccxxxvj·
Linum latine· Es sprechent gemeinkliche dye meyster
das der sam gebraucht werde in der ertznei vnd nitt das
kraut noch die wurtz· Galienus in dem siben dē büch
nt simplicium farmacarum in dem capitel von leinsamen·
reibt vns vnd spricht das leinsamen sey heysse an dē andn
vnd feücht vnd drucken an dē mittel des andern grades
er sam ist nicht gůt zů essen·wann wer des sames esse der ge
oll über all an seinem leib ¶ Der meyster serapio in dē büch
regatoris beschreibt vns vnd spricht das der sam sei subtepl
chen vnd mach harnen vnd bringt den frawen yr blůmen ein
ster dauon gemacht vnd auff den bauch gelegt ¶ Item man
g disen samen wol brauchen zů einem klistier als siben gezeit
er meyster paulus spricht das lein samen gebrant auff kolē
ein subteilen rauch den gelassen in die nasen benympt die sch
n ¶ Also den rauch gelassen vnden auff benympt das wee der
er ¶ Diascorides spricht das leinsamen gesoten in wasser vñ
gelegt auff die vnzeitigen geschwer verzert die vnd machet
eitig vnnd sunderlich die geschwere die do seind in den oren
er meyster wilhelmus in seiner cirorgi beschreibt vns·vnd
icht das die bleter von dem flachs gar nütz sind vnnd sunder
in der cirorgi dann wann man die bleter legt auff ein tzeitig
wer so macht es zehand ein loch darein also das man das sel
geschwer nit auff reissen noch brennen darf·¶ Wem wee ist
der seiten der sied leinsamen in wasser vnd druck ein leine tůch
das wasser also warm vnd leg es auf die seiten es vergeet zů
nd ·¶ Welcher gebrant wär von dem feur der siede leinsamen
wasser fast wol vnd netz ein tůch darinn vnd leg des auff den
ant es zeucht den brand auß senftigklichen
Biij·

Figure 2. S-596.4: *Gart der Gesundheit* (Augsburg: Johann Schönsperger, ca. 1485/86). Waste leaf. (bInc 1763.5, Houghton Library, Harvard College Library)

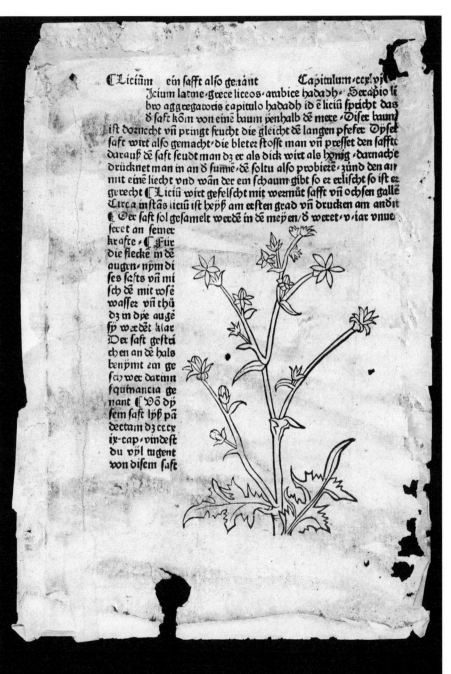

Licium ein safft also genänt   Capitulum cexlvj

Icium latine grece liceos ambice hadadh Serapio li
bro aggregatoris capitulo hadadh id e liciu spricht das
o safft kom von eim baum yenhalb dz mere Diser baum
ist dornecht vn pringt frucht die gleicht dz langen pfefer Dyser
safft wirt also gemacht die bleter stosst man vn presset den saffte
darauß dz safft seudt man dz er als dick wirt als honig darnache
drucknet man in an o summe dz soltu also probiere zund den air
mit eim liecht vnd wän der em schaum gibt so er erlischt so ist er
gerecht Liciu wirt geselscht mit wermut safft vn ochsen galle
Circa instäs liciu ist heyß am ersten grad vn drucken am andit
Der safft sol gesamelt werdz in dz meyen/ o weret v iar vnue
seret an seiner
krafte Für
die flecke m dz
augen nym di
ses safts vn mi
sch dz mit rose
wasser vn thu
dz in dye auge
sy werdet klar
Der safft gestri
chen an dz hals
benymt em ge
sy wer darmn
squinancia ge
nant Dö dy
sem safft lyß pa
dectam dz cecx
ix cap vindest
du vyl tugent
von disem safft

Figure 3. S-596.4: *Gart der Gesundheit* (Augsburg: Johann Schönsperger, ca. 1485/86). Waste leaf with
woodcut illustration. (bInc 1763.5, Houghton Library, Harvard College Library)

H 8956; Goff G-107; Sack 1898; Schr 4344.

Countway Library

S1-608.5A   — Single leaf only; ill.; 244 x 175 mm.

In: Claus Nissen, *Herbals of Five Centuries* ... (Zurich: L'Art ancien, 1958).

The unsigned leaf contains chapters xv-xvi. Woodcuts on recto and verso with contemporary hand coloring; without rubrication. No. 66 of 100 copies. Tipped into a cream paper mat; in a cloth case. Possibly from an imperfect copy formerly owned by Dr. Karl Becher, Karlsbad.

Dumbarton Oaks Garden Library

S1-609A   **Eike von Repgow:** Sachsenspiegel, pt. 2 (Weichbild, Lehnrecht, and Remissorium of Dietrich von Bocksdorf). 9 October 1499.

f°. A single leaf only. 306 x 210 mm.

The leaf is i2 (leaf l [i.e. 50] from the *Weichbild*). Without rubrication. A specimen leaf distributed by the Gesellschaft für Typenkunde des XV. Jahrhunderts, with its printed caption label tipped at foot of recto.

9 January 1914 – Bought with the Charles Minot fund. bInc 1801

JOHANN FROSCHAUER

(S1-658c)   **Dialogus inter clericum et militem super dignitate papali et regia.** ca. 1505?

4°. [12] leaves; 191 x 137 mm.

Includes *Compendium de vita antichristi*. Printer assignment from Proctor; for dating see ISTC, which notes that the text is set in Froschauer's type 6, not found in imprints dated before 1503.

Initial spaces, with guide-letters, not filled in; without rubrication. Half tan cloth and marbled boards.

HC 6112*; Pr 1852; BM STC(G) p. 213; Polain 1322; GW 7:col. 382; Goff D-158; Sack 1237a; BSB-Ink D-112.

30 January 1920 – Bought with the John Harvey Treat fund. *MLC. A100D.1505

JOHANN OTMAR

(S1-658d) **Pelbartus de Themeswar:** Sermones Pomerii de sanctis. Not before 1502.

f°. [310] leaves (6, 310 blank); ill.; 287 x 209 mm.

Dated to between 1502 and 1504 by D.E. Rhodes; see his article, "An Unidentified 'Incunable' Printed at Augsburg Not Before 1502," *The Library*, 5th ser., 13 (1958): 54-56.

Initials and a few paragraph marks and underlinings added in red. A few early MS marginalia. 16th-century blind-stamped pigskin over reverse-bevelled wooden boards; brass clasp plates on back cover, latches, clasps, and thongs gone; quire containing the index to the second part bound as the second quire rather than at end. Early MS inscription on verso of last leaf, "Frater Martinus [K?]oler"; MS inscriptions at top and bottom of aa2r, the bottom one within a red scroll, have been erased; initials "C. S. P." and "1578" stamped on front cover, MS title with "1578" on top edges; MS inscription at top of title page, "Canoniae S. Martini in Dietramszell 1642.", with its inventory "No. 559" at foot and repeated on front pastedown. No. 162 in the Christie's South Kensington sale catalogue, 7 December 2004 (unnamed, but library of Percy Barnevik).

H 12553*; BM STC(G) p. 680; Goff P-253; CIBN 2: p. 371; BSB-Ink (P-129); Schr 4904a.

2 February 2005 – Bought with the Edward and Bertha C. Rose Acquisition fund. Typ 520.02.825F

(S1-658e) **Epistola cuiusdam puellae Romanae.** ca. 1510.

[For transcriptions see Hain.] 4°. a⁴; [4] leaves; 201 x 141 mm. a2r: 28 lines, 149 x 97 mm. Type: 107G.

Printer assignment from Goff. BM STC(G) dates this edition to ca. 1510; BSB-Ink gives a date of ca. 1505.

Without rubrication. Red cloth.

H 6620*; Pr p. 802; BM STC(G) p. 274; GW 8:col. 54; Goff E-48; BSB-Ink E-72.

4 May 1905 – From the library of Charles Eliot Norton. *GC5.A100.505e

Nuremberg

JOHANN SENSENSCHMIDT

S1-664.5   **Corpus iuris civilis. Codex Justinianus.** 24 June 1475.

f°. A single leaf only. 408 x 285 mm.

With the *glossa ordinaria* of Accursius. Printed by Sensenschmidt with Andreas Frisner.

In: *Monumenta Germaniae et Italiae Typographica: deutsche und italienische Inkunabeln in getreuen Nachbildungen* (Berlin: Reichsdruckerei, 1892-1913).

The leaf is foliated "334" in MS; modern letterpress caption added at foot on recto. Some initials and capital strokes added in red. Drab board portfolio with cloth ties; the leaf is laid in.

H 9599*; Pr 2198; BMC 2:406 (IC.7844); Polain 2379-79A; GW 7723; Goff J-575; BSB-Ink C-561; Schr 4406; Schramm 18:14.

6 July 1896 – Bought with the Charles Minot fund. B 4528.92PF* v. 5

ANTON KOBERGER

S1-670A   **Rainerius de Pisis:** Pantheologia. 3 August 1474.

f°. A single leaf only. 443 x 317 mm.

The leaf contains the beginning of "Adulatio". Large initial added in red and blue with red and green penwork, initials and paragraph marks added in red and blue, capital strokes in red.

28 May 1943 – Gift of Denman W. Ross. pInc 1967

S1-670B   — Single leaf only. 482 x 342 mm.

In: *Monumenta Germaniae et Italiae Typographica: deutsche und italienische Inkunabeln in getreuen Nachbildungen* (Berlin: Reichsdruckerei, 1892-1913).

The leaf contains chapters lvi-lxix, with headline "PRO" in MS, and modern letterpress caption added at foot on recto. Headlines, initials, and paragraph marks added in red and blue, capital strokes in red. Drab board portfolio with cloth ties; the leaf is laid in.

21 April 1893 – Bought with the Charles Minot fund. B 4528.92PF* v. 1

S1-672.5   **Rainerius de Pisis:** Pantheologia. 12 February 1477.

f°. Two fragments only. 199 x 199 mm. and 200 x 165 mm.

The fragments constitute the upper left and lower right corners of leaf 78₃. Initial letters added in red or blue, paragraph marks and capital strokes in red.

Tipped onto fol. 44 of an album of printed fragments removed from bindings (presumably Oxford bindings of the late 16th–early 17th centuries) of books in the library formed by Hannibal Gamon Jr., later removed to Lanhydrock House, Cornwall. For additional provenance information, see S1-372.5. Late 19th-century half tan sheep and brown cloth.

HC 13018*; Pr 1972; BMC 2:413 (IC.7137); Polain 3314; Goff R-8; CIBN R-6; BSB-Ink R-5.

October 1963 – Bought with the Susan A.E. Morse fund. *fEC.A100. B659c

S1-692A   **Biblia** [German]. 17 February 1483.

f°. A single leaf only; ill.; 373 x 264 mm.

In: Otto F. Ege, *Original Leaves from Famous Bibles: Nine Centuries, 1121-1935 A.D.: Sixty Leaves* ... ([New York: Philip C. Duschnes, 1938]).

The leaf is 15₈ from vol. 2 (leaf CCCCXIIII), containing the end of Ezekiel and beginning of Daniel; without woodcut ill. Large initial added in colors on recto; paragraph marks, capital strokes, and underlinings added in red. Tan buckram portfolio; the leaf is matted and laid in.

April 1965 – Gift of William Bentinck-Smith. B 4406.657.2PF*

S1-714A   **Petrus Lombardus:** Sententiarum libri IV. After 2 March 1491.

f°. 4 leaves only. 302 x 210 mm.

The leaves are all from vol. 1: x6, y1-3 (Distinctio 31-32). Initials added in red. Tipped onto fol. 80 of an album of printed fragments removed from bindings (presumably Oxford bindings of the late 16th–early 17th centuries) of books in the library formed by Hannibal Gamon Jr., later removed to Lanhydrock House, Cornwall. For additional provenance information, see S1-372.5. Late 19th-century half tan sheep and brown cloth. Worming and marginal restorations, with significant text loss.

October 1963 – Bought with the Susan A.E. Morse fund. *fEC.A100. B659c

S1-732A   **Schedel, Hartmann:** Liber chronicarum. 12 July 1493.

f°. A single leaf only; 460 x 312 mm.

In: Henry Lewis Bullen, *The Nuremberg Chronicle, or, The Book of Chronicles from the Beginning of the World* ... (San Francisco: The Book Club of California, 1930).

The leaf is fol. CCXCII (without woodcut ill.). Without rubrication. No. 278 of 300 copies. Half brown sheep and marbled boards; the leaf is tipped in at front.

1952 – Bequest of Rosamond B. Loring. *52L-129PF

S1-732B   — Single leaf only; ill.; 460 x 310 mm.

In: Henry Lewis Bullen, *The Nuremberg Chronicle* ... (San Francisco: The Book Club of California, 1930).

The leaf is fol. CLIIII (with woodcut ill.). Without rubrication; woodcuts uncolored. No. 96 of 300 copies. Half brown sheep and marbled boards; the leaf is tipped in at front.

3 November 1930 – Bought with the Susan Greene Dexter fund. Typ 970N.30.244PF

S1-732C   — Single leaf only; ill.; 418 x 284 mm.

In: Otto F. Ege, *Original Leaves from Famous Books: Eight Centuries, 1240 A.D.-1923 A.D.* ([New York: Philip C. Duschnes, 1949]).

The leaf is fol. CXLVII (with woodcut ill.). Without rubrication; woodcuts uncolored. Rust buckram portfolio; the leaf is matted and laid in.

April 1965 – Gift of William Bentinck-Smith. B 4406.657PF*

S1-751A   **Alexander Carpentarius:** Destructorium vitiorum. 20 September 1496.

f°. Three leaves only. 276 x 200 mm.

Imperfect: leaves a2, 7-8 only (i.e. three of the four leaves wanting from Walsh 751). Initial spaces, with guide-letters, not filled in; without rubrication. Disbound.

10 November 1994 – Gift of James and Devon Gray. Inc 2111 pt. 2

S1-754.5   **Biblia Latina.** 6 September 1497.

f°. A single leaf only. 373 x 264 mm.

With the commentaries of Nicolaus de Lyra and Guillelmus Brito, additions by Paulus Burgensis and Matthias Doering, and Nicolaus de Lyra's *Contra perfidiam Iudaeorum.*

In: Otto F. Ege, *Original Leaves from Famous Bibles: Nine Centuries, 1121-1935 A.D.: Sixty Leaves* ... ([New York: Philip C. Duschnes, 1938]).

The leaf is Dv4 (vol. 2, leaf CLVI), containing Psalms 63-65. Initial letters added in red or blue, capital strokes and underlinings in red. Tan buckram portfolio; the leaf is matted and laid in.

HC 3171*; Pr 2115; BMC 2:443 (IB.7535); Polain 680; GW 4294; Goff B-619; CIBN B-434; Sack 672; BSB-Ink B-477; Schr 3476; Schramm 17:10.

April 1965 – Gift of William Bentinck-Smith. B 4406.657.2PF*

S1-754.5A   — Single leaf only. 340 x 237 mm.

In: Otto F. Ege, *Original Leaves from Famous Bibles: Nine Centuries, 1121-1935 A.D.* ([New York: Philip C. Duschnes, 1945?]).

The leaf is Ef6 (vol. 2, leaf CCXXX), containing Psalms 136-137. Initial letters added in red or blue, underlinings in red. Rust buckram portfolio; the leaf is matted and laid in.

December 1967 – Gift of Paul Gerard Ecker. Typ 970.45.2100PF

(S1-764a)   **Biblia Latina.** 24 March 1501.

f°. [450] leaves; 307 x 212 mm.

The colophon date has been interpreted as 24 March 1500, which GW corrects to 1501.

David R. Whitesell 33

Large Maiblumen initial added in red and blue on a1r; initials and some underlinings added in alternating red and blue. Contemporary blind-stamped pigskin over wooden boards; rebacked in 18th-century brown calf, gilt; clasp plates, clasps, and thongs no longer present; title in MS on front cover.

C 1033; Pr (MDI-MDXX) 10958; BM STC(G) p. 85; GW 4:col. 133; Goff B-605.

23 October 1920 – Bought with the Charles Eliot Norton fund. Bi 35.01.2F*

(S1-764b) — Another copy. 303 x 208 mm.

Initial spaces, with guide-letters, not filled in; without rubrication. Contemporary blind-stamped half pigskin over wooden boards; brass latches on front cover, clasp plates on back cover, 1 clasp and thong present; title in MS on fore-edges. MS marginalia throughout. MS ownership inscription on title page, "Conuentij Bambergensis ordinis Praedicatoru[m]"; ownership inscription of Zacharias Baur, dated 1747; another inscription of Fr. Thaddeus [St?]engel; another illegible inscription. Signature on front endleaf of Johannes Aldenberger, with scored inscription beneath, "Nicolaus Eck me Iure possidet".

Andover-Harvard Theological Library

FRIEDRICH CREUSSNER

S1-766.5   **Sixtus IV, Pope:** De sanguine Christi et De potentia Dei. 1474.

f°. [98] leaves (88, 89 blank); 284 x 210 mm.

Second issue, dated 1474; the first issue (Goff S-580) is dated 1473. Includes Johannes Philippus de Lignamine, *Epistola ad Sixtum IV.*

Maiblumen initials in red on 1_1r and 11_2r, other initials and paragraph marks added in alternating red and blue, capital strokes and underlinings in red. MS quiring (1-11) visible at lower inner corner of the recto of the first leaf in each gathering. Modern blind-stamped dark brown calf antique. Some contemporary MS marginalia. Blue oval stamp, "Bibliotheca Mellicensis", on verso of last leaf. No. 192 in the Christie's South Kensington sale catalogue, 7 December 2004 (unnamed, but library of Percy Barnevik). Blank leaf 89 not present.

HC 14798*; Pr 2128 (1473); BL IB.7587, for the 1473 issue cf. BMC 2:446 (IB.7586); Polain 3552 (1473); Goff S-581; CIBN S-296; BSB-Ink S-444.

2 February 2005 – Bought with the Edward and Bertha C. Rose Acquisition fund. Inc 2128.5

PETER WAGNER

S1-804.5   **Barbarus, Hermolaus:** Oratio ad Fridericum III Imperatorem et Maximilianum I Regem Romanorum. After 2 April 1490.

4°. [14] leaves; 211 x 151 mm.

Edited by Petrus Danhauser. Includes Ludovicus Brunus, *De Maximiliani coronatione gratulatio*; Antonius Graziadei, *Responsio extemporanea*; and an exchange of letters between Barbarus and Johannes Carondeletus.

Without rubrication. Modern boards covered with a vellum waste leaf from a 17th-century MS document in French. No. 430 in the Christie's South Kensington sale catalogue, 18 November 2003 (unnamed, but library of Percy Barnevik).

H 2419*; Pr 2245; BMC 2:463 (IA.7983); Polain 493; GW 3346; Goff B-106; CIBN B-76; BSB-Ink B-63.

10 December 2003 – Bought with the Bayard Livingston Kilgour & Kate Gray Kilgour fund. Inc 2245

GEORG STUCHS

S1-813.8   **Breviarium Lincopense.** 16 April 1493.

8°. A single leaf only. 154 x 123 mm.

In: G. E. Klemming, *Sveriges äldre liturgiska literatur: bibliografi* (Stockholm: Kongl. Boktryckeriet, P. A. Norstedt & Söner, 1879). The "Klemming Leaf Book," issued in 50 copies, is considered to be the first incunable leaf book. All copies include a selection of incunable and post-incunable leaves from books printed either in Sweden or for the Swedish market. The leaves are from copies which, in Paul Needham's words, "were dismembered to provide wrappers for archivalia of the [Swedish] Royal Chamber and other state offices." Klemming recognized the wrappers's significance in 1860; he then proceeded to disbind and assemble the fragments. Copies vary in the number of original leaves bound in: the Harvard copy contains eight incunable leaves (all described in this supplement) and three post-incunable leaves. The Klemming Leaf Book is discussed in detail by Paul Needham in: Sotheby's, *Incunables from the Schøyen Collection* (sale, New York, 12 December 1991), lot 40.

The leaf is A4 (leaf [264]), from the *Proprium de sanctis*. Lombard initials and rubrics printed in red. Half brown cloth and printed gray boards; the leaf is inlaid and bound in following p. 20. MS presentation inscription from Klemming to the Copenhagen bookseller Herman Lynge on front cover; bookplate of Frederik Heyman with motto, "Utile dulci".

HC(+Add) 3852; Pr 2271; BMC 2:467 note (C.18.c.13); GW 5373; Goff B-1164; Schramm 18:21; Bohatta(KLD) 131; Bohatta(LB) 273; Collijn 1:128.

20 March 1902 – Bought with the Emil Christian Hammer fund. Inc 9828.50

S1-818.5 **Breviarium Scarense.** 24 April 1498.

8°. A single leaf only. 170 x 123 mm.

In: G. E. Klemming, *Sveriges äldre liturgiska literatur: bibliografi* (Stockholm: Kongl. Boktryckeriet, P. A. Norstedt & Söner, 1879).

The leaf is O8 (leaf CCXCVIII), from the *Proprium de sanctis*. Lombard initials and rubrics printed in red; a two-line initial has been cut out from the left column of O8v. Half brown cloth and printed gray boards; the leaf is inlaid and bound in following p. 28. For provenance and other information, see S1-813.8, with which this is bound.

HC(+Add) 3938; Pr 2282; BMC 2:467 (C.18.c.13); GW 5458; Goff B-1179; Schr 3625; Bohatta(LB) 493; Collijn 1:169.

20 March 1902 – Bought with the Emil Christian Hammer fund. Inc 9828.50

CASPAR HOCHFEDER

(S1-829a) **Etzlaub, Erhard:** Der Romweg. ca. 1650-1670.

1°. broadside map; 412 x 312 mm. (image: 405 x 290 mm)

One of nine extant impressions of this woodcut map; two others from a variant woodblock are also known. The earliest impression, in the Bayerische Staatsbibliothek, is accompanied by a broadside letterpress register printed in Hochfeder's types, though the map is generally attributed to the press of Georg Glogkendon. The map has been variously dated from 1492-1501; Campbell suggests "1500?", while BSB-Ink proposes ca. 1496-1498. The eight other copies have been shown, on the basis of woodblock wear, to be later impressions (cf. Tony Campbell, "The Woodcut Map Considered as a Physical Object: a New Look at Erhard Etzlaub's *Rom Weg* Map of c.1500," *Imago Mundi* 30 (1978): 78-91; the Harvard copy is reproduced in fig. 2 and 3c.). Campbell considers the Harvard exemplar to be the most recent impression, which he dates to the second half of the 16th century on the basis of the twin-tower watermark's similarity to Briquet no. 15925-15950. However, the watermark, with initials "[M?] L" in the base, more closely resembles Piccard 3:61-94 (Michel I. Löhlein, Ölschwang, ca. 1649-1670), hence this impression might more accurately be dated to Germany, ca. 1650-1670.

Without hand-coloring. Margins trimmed. From the map collection formed by Franz, Ritter von Hauslab; later acquired by Johann II, Prince of Liechtenstein.

GW(Einbl) 813; BSB-Ink E-104; Schramm 18:720; Campbell 6.

April 1952 – Gift of Stephen W. Phillips and Curt H. Reisinger. *51-2477PF (horz)

Speyer

PRINTER OF *GESTA CHRISTI*

S1-833.8   **Turrecremata, Johannes de:** Meditationes seu Contemplationes devotissimae. 24 December 1472.

f°. [16] leaves; 285 x 210 mm.

Initials, paragraph marks, capital strokes, and underlinings added in red; some textual corrections (primarily double hyphens) added in brown ink. Modern red morocco. No. 561 in the Christie's South Kensington sale catalogue, 18 November 2003 (unnamed, but library of Percy Barnevik).

HC 15723*=H 15720; Pr 2317; BMC 2:482 (IB.8422); Polain 3865; Goff T-535; CIBN T-387; BSB-Ink T-559.

10 December 2003 – Bought with the Bayard Livingston Kilgour & Kate Gray Kilgour fund. Inc 2317

PETER DRACH

S1-835.8 **Antoninus Florentinus:** Summa theologica pars secunda. 20 August 1477.

f°. [344] leaves (1, 344 blank).

Imperfect: 17 fragments only, each consisting of the top or bottom half of a leaf and measuring ca. 168 x 236 mm., removed from a binding. One initial added in red, other initial spaces not filled in; capital strokes and underlinings added in red. Stains and soiling, some minor text loss. In a case.

H 1256*; C 515; Pell 889; GW 2197; Goff A-869; Sack 241; BSB-Ink A-605.

29 March 1918 – Bought with the Charles Eliot Norton fund. Inc 2328.1

S1-840A **Dominicus de Sancto Geminiano:** Super sexto Decretalium. Not after 1479.

f°. A single leaf only. 372 x 270 mm.

In: *Monumenta Germaniae et Italiae Typographica: deutsche und italienische Inkunabeln in getreuen Nachbildungen* (Berlin: Reichsdruckerei, 1892-1913).

The leaf is from vol. 2; modern letterpress caption added at foot on recto. Initial spaces not filled in; without rubrication. Drab board portfolio with cloth ties; the leaf is laid in.

9 March 1903 – Bought with the Charles Minot fund. B 4528.92PF* v. 7

S1-841A **Gambilionibus, Angelus de:** Lectura super Institutionibus. 22 February 1480.

f°. A single leaf only. 402 x 290 mm.

Initial and paragraph marks added in red. A specimen leaf distributed by the Gesellschaft für Typenkunde des XV. Jahrhunderts, with its printed caption label tipped at foot of recto.

9 January 1914 – Bought with the Charles Minot fund. pInc 2336

S1-866.6 **Gebote:** Die zehn Gebote [German]. ca. 1500.

1°. broadside. 395 x 309 mm.

Without rubrication. Printed on a full sheet of Chancery paper, with bull's head watermark. Deckle trimmed away at top and bottom (i.e. short edges of the sheet).

GW(Einbl) 654; GW 10567; Goff G-114; Brüggemann (facsim.) 473.

4 February 1998 – Bought with the Hermon Dunlap Smith fund. pInc 2399.5

JOHANN & CONRAD HIST

S1-866.8 **Gerson, Johannes:** De custodia linguae et corde bene ruminanda. ca. 1483.

4°. [8] leaves (1, 8 blank); 202 x 140 mm.

GW calls for [6] leaves. However, this copy may be unique in preserving the original blank leaves 1 and 8, demonstrating that this tract was printed from two full sheets of Chancery paper, with the blank outer bifolium 1.8 providing a protective cover. BSB-Ink dates this edition to ca. 1484.

Initials, paragraph marks, capital strokes, and underlinings added in red. Modern boards covered with a leaf from Koberger's 1483 German Bible (Goff B-632; Walsh 692); the leaf, rubricated in red with verso visible, is fol. cccccxxvii (vol. 2, leaf 30₁, containing Romans XV-XVI). No. 487 in the Christie's South Kensington sale catalogue, 18 November 2003 (unnamed, but library of Percy Barnevik).

H 7686*; Pr 2403; BMC 2:502 (IA.8681); Pell 5165; GW 10762; Goff G-220; Sack 1550; BSB-Ink G-192.

10 December 2003 – Bought with the Bayard Livingston Kilgour & Kate Gray Kilgour fund. Inc 2403

CONRAD HIST

S1-869.8 **Wimpheling, Jacobus:** Defensio immunitatis ecclesiasticae. ca. 1495.

4°. [6] leaves (6 blank); 205 x 144 mm.

Dating from Engel-Stalla; Goff dates to 1495-1498.

Initial, paragraph marks, capital strokes, and underlinings added in red. Modern half vellum and tan boards. No. 566 in the Christie's South Kensington sale catalogue, 18 November 2003 (unnamed, but library of Percy Barnevik).

H 6081*; Pr 2447; BMC 2:508 (IA.8835); Polain 4799; Goff W-24; Sack 3740; BSB-Ink W-55; Engel-Stalla col. 1664.

10 December 2003 – Bought with the Bayard Livingston Kilgour & Kate Gray Kilgour fund. Inc 2447

Ulm

JOHANN ZAINER THE ELDER

S1-907A **Pseudo-Albertus Magnus:** Compendium theologicae veritatis. Not after 1481.

f°. A single leaf only. 260 x 182 mm.

In: Peter Amelung, *Peter Amelung's Johann Zainer the Elder & Younger …: Introduction by Bernard M. Rosenthal: With an Original Leaf from Hugo Ripelin's Compendium Theologiae* [sic] *Veritatis (c. 1478-81)* (Los Angeles: Kenneth Karmiole, 1985).

The unsigned leaf contains portions of chapters 4 and 5 from Book 4. Initial space not filled in; without rubrication. One of 159 copies. Original blue cloth; the leaf is laid in.

January 1986 – Bought with the Douglas W. Bryant fund. *93HR-3467F

S1-911A **Imitatio Christi.** 1487.

8°. Another copy. 140 x 91 mm.

Initials on a1r and h1r added in red, blue, and brown; those elsewhere, paragraph marks, and underlinings added in red. 16th-century blind-stamped leather over wooden boards; marks of clasps and bosses, no longer present. MS marginalia, including one leaf of prayers at end. MS inscription on t.p. in red ink, "TE August: me donationis jure possidet. 1646"; bookplate of Walter Arthur Copinger inside front cover along with autograph of Eadmond Waterton (lot 250 in the Sotheby sale catalogue,

18 January 1895). Blank leaves not present.

22 November 1921 – W.A. Copinger Imitatio Christi Collection, presented by James Byrne. Inc 2548 (B)

CONRAD DINCKMUT

S1-916.2 **Seelen-Wurzgarten.** 26 July 1483.

f°. A single leaf only; ill.; 277 x 204 mm.

The leaf is ee4, with full-page woodcut on verso of the ceasarean birth of the Anti-Christ (Schramm vol. 6, Abb. 105). Without rubrication. Tipped into a binding of half blue cloth and marbled boards.

The Countway Library also has a second example of this woodcut, on a leaf trimmed to 216 x 169 mm. and with no text on the reverse side. However, this is clearly a recent impression, probably made from a line block: it is printed on a blank folio leaf removed from a 16th- or 17th-century volume, which has been turned 90° so that the chainlines run horizontally through the image; the leaf also bears a faint oxidized offset image of a two-column printed text. The leaf has been tipped into a wrapper cut from a MS choir book on vellum, with a letterpress label (ca. 1920-1930) inside the front wrapper: "This woodcut beeing [sic] the first obstetric scene in a printed book is taken from the beautiful woodcutbook 'Seelwurzgarten' printed by Conrad Dinkmut, Ulm, 1483". Presumably other examples of this reprint are extant.

C 5345; Pr 2561=1767; BMC 2:533 (IB.9335); Goff S-364; Amelung 97; Schr 5229; Schramm 6:18; Ballard 635.

Countway Library

S1-917.5 **Gart der Gesundheit.** 31 March 1487.

f°. A single leaf only; ill.; 252 x 183 mm.

Edited by Johannes von Cuba.

In: Claus Nissen, *Herbals of Five Centuries: 50 Original Leaves from German, French, Dutch, English, Italian, and Swiss Herbals, With an Introduction and Bibliography* (Zurich: L'Art ancien, 1958).

The leaf is n3, containing chapters clxxvi-clxxviii. Initial letters, paragraph marks, capital strokes, and underlinings added in red;

woodcut on verso uncolored. Some MS annotations in German. No. 12 of 100 copies. Tipped into a cream paper mat; in a cloth case. Possibly from an imperfect copy formerly owned by Dr. Karl Becher, Karlsbad.

H 8952*; BMC 2:535 (IB.9359); Goff G-103; Amelung 115; Schr 4338; Schramm 6:18.

Countway Library

S1-917.5A — Single leaf only; ill.; 252 x 182 mm.

In: Claus Nissen, *Herbals of Five Centuries* ... (Zurich: L'Art ancien, 1958).

The leaf is C3, containing chapters cccxci-cccxcv. Initial letters, paragraph marks, capital strokes, and underlinings added in red; woodcut on verso uncolored. No. 66 of 100 copies. Tipped into a cream paper mat; in a cloth case. Possibly from an imperfect copy formerly owned by Dr. Karl Becher, Karlsbad.

Dumbarton Oaks Garden Library

Lübeck

BARTHOLOMAEUS GHOTAN

S1-946.7 **Missale Aboense**. After 17 August 1488.

f°. A single leaf only. 291 x 191 mm.

In: G. E. Klemming, *Sveriges äldre liturgiska literatur: bibliografi* (Stockholm: Kongl. Boktryckeriet, P. A. Norstedt & Söner, 1879).

The *Missale Aboense* was issued concurrently with a *Missale Dominicanum* (Weale-Bohatta 1820), which shares the same typesetting and differs only in the preliminaries. The Klemming Leaf Book leaves traditionally have been treated as belonging to the *Missale Aboense*, though it is not possible to tell whether they belong to this or to the *Missale Dominicanum*.

The leaf, from the *Proprium de sanctis*, is numbered ".xix." in the direction line (leaf 23$_3$ (173) per Collijn's collation). Printed on vellum. Lombard initials and rubrics printed in red. Initials and one marginal extension added in blue. MS archival title dated 1578, from the leaf's prior use as a document wrapper, on verso. Half brown cloth and printed gray boards; the leaf is inlaid and bound in following p. 12. For provenance and other information, see S1-813.8, with which this is bound.

HC 11253; Pr 2623; BMC 2:553 (C.18.c.13); Goff M-644; Schr 4661; Schramm 12:11; Meyer-Baer 32; Weale-Bohatta 1; Collijn 1:87.

20 March 1902 – Bought with the Emil Christian Hammer fund. Inc 9828.50

STEFFEN ARNDES

S1-952.5   **Graduale Arosiense.** ca. 1493.

f°. A single leaf only; music; 317 x 150 mm.

In: G. E. Klemming, *Sveriges äldre liturgiska literatur: bibliografi* (Stockholm: Kongl. Boktryckeriet, P. A. Norstedt & Söner, 1879).

Paul Needham assigns this edition to "Printer of the Graduale (Bartholomaeus Ghotan or Steffen Arndes?)"; he describes it as "the first Gradual of diocesan use to be printed. The edition survives only from archival wrappers and binder's waste." Cf. Sotheby's, *Incunables from the Schøyen Collection* (sale, New York, 12 December 1991), lot 40(4).

The unsigned leaf contains the beginning of the *Dies irae*. A fragment only, consisting of the inner half of lines 3-10 (of 10). Printed on vellum. Four-line staves printed in red, overprinted in black with music types (c- and f-clefs, ligatured Roman neumes). Initials added in alternating red and blue. Half brown cloth and printed gray boards; the leaf is inlaid and bound in following p. 18. For provenance and other information, see S1-813.8, with which this is bound.

C 2765a; Pr 2644; BL C.18.c.13; GW 10983; Goff G-333; Meyer-Baer 19; Bohatta(LB) 705; Collijn 1:186.

20 March 1902 – Bought with the Emil Christian Hammer fund. Inc 9828.50

Blaubeuren

CONRAD MANCZ

S1-953.8   **Donatus, Aelius:** Ars minor. ca. 1475.

f°. [16?] leaves; 277 x 200 mm. 30 lines, 180 x 127 mm. Type: 1:120G. Initial spaces.

One proof (waste?) sheet only of an unrecorded edition, removed from a binding. The leaf is printed on one side only, containing text beginning in chapter 16, line 48, of Paul Schwenke's edition (see his *Donat- und Kalender-Type: Nachtrag und Übersicht* (Mainz: Gutenberg-Gesellschaft, 1903): 37-49) and ending in chapter 17, line 11, with minor variants. This page presumably would have constituted leaf 6r of an edition extending to approximately 16 leaves. The text is set in an early state of Conrad Mancz's type 1 (cf. BMC 2:564): capital S is present only in its first form ("rounded S rather too small for [the font]"); lower case t is present in two forms, with the earlier form ("with a very long sharp tip") predominating.

Four-line initial space not filled in; without rubrication. Unwatermarked. Wormed with slight text loss. Some contemporary MS annotations at bottom and recent MS notes in pencil, including "E[in]bl[att]dr[uck]. 100" on recto and verso.

23 July 1992 – Bought with the Susan A.E. Morse fund. bInc 2659.1

Rostock

FRATRES DOMUS HORTI VIRIDIS AD S. MICHAELEM

S1-955.7   **Bernardus Claravallensis:** Sermones super Cantica canticorum. 28 July 1481.

f°. A single leaf only. 252 x 181 mm.

In: *Monumenta Germaniae et Italiae Typographica: deutsche und italienische Inkunabeln in getreuen Nachbildungen* (Berlin: Reichsdruckerei, 1892-1913).

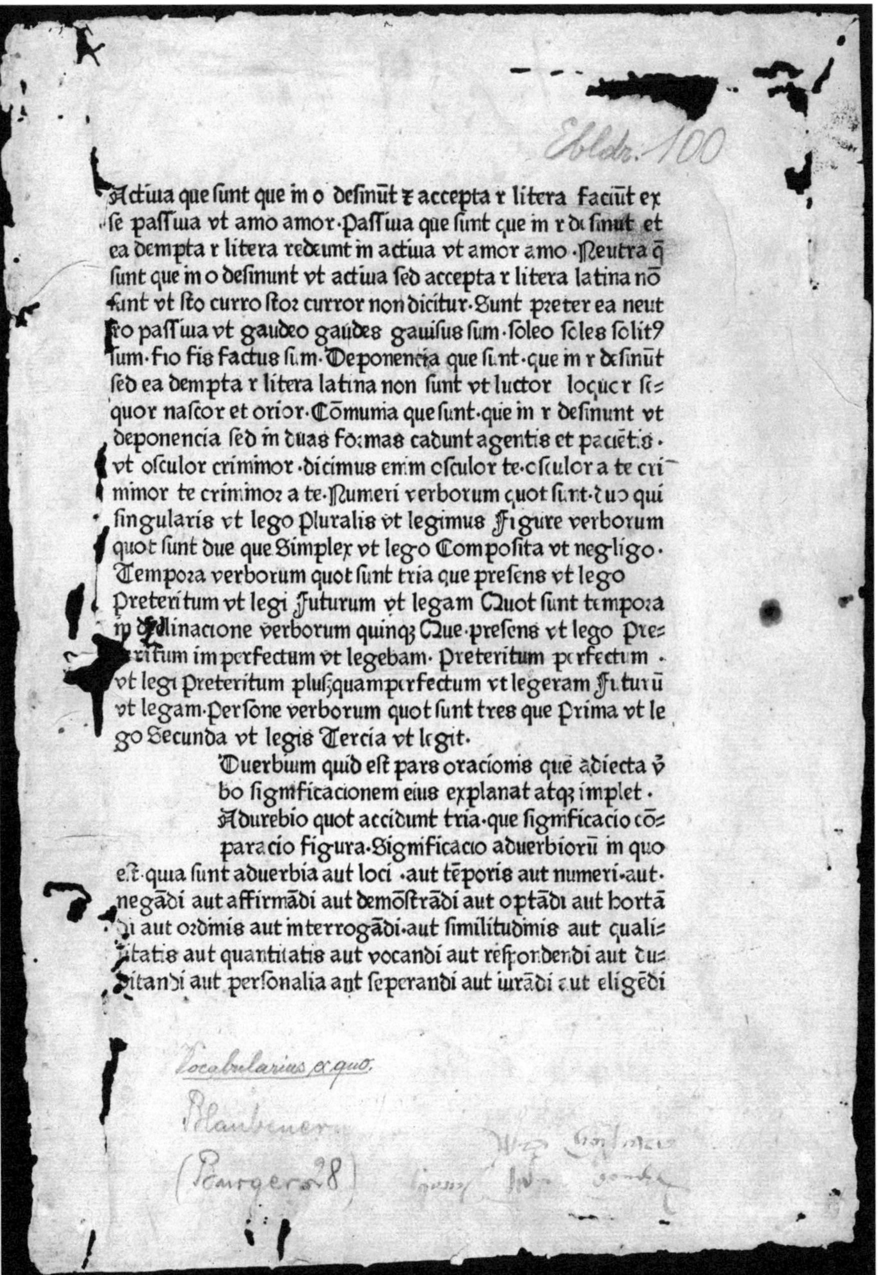

Actiua que sunt que in o desinūt ꝯ accepta r litera faciūt ex
se passiua vt amo amor·Passiua que sunt cue in r di sinut et
ea dempta r litera redeunt in actiua vt amor amo ·Neutra q̄
sunt que in o desinunt vt actiua sed accepta r litera latina nō
sunt vt sto curro stor curror non dicitur·Sunt preter ea neut
ro passiua vt gaudeo gaudes gauisus sum·soleo soles solit?
ſum·fio fis factus sum·Deponencia que sunt·que in r desinūt
sed ea dempta r litera latina non sunt vt luctor loquer se
quor nascor et orior·Comunia que sunt·que in r desinunt vt
deponencia sed in duas formas cadunt agentis et pacietis·
vt osculor crimmor·dicimus enim osculor te·osculor a te cri
minor te criminor a te·Numeri verborum cuot sunt·duo qui
singularis vt lego pluralis vt legimus Figure verborum
quot sunt due que Simplex vt lego Composita vt negligo·
Tempora verborum quot sunt tria que presens vt lego
preteritum vt legi futurum vt legam Quot sunt tempora
in ordinacione verborum quinq Que·presens vt lego pre
teritum imperfectum vt legebam· preteritum perfectum ·
vt legi preteritum plusquamperfectum vt legeram futurū
vt legam·Persone verborum quot sunt tres que prima vt le
go Secunda vt legis Tercia vt legit·

        Duerbium quid est pars oracionis que adiecta ꝟ
        bo significacionem eius explanat atꝗ implet·
        Adurebio quot accidunt tria·que significacio co
        paracio figura·Significacio aduerbiorū in quo
        est quia sunt aduerbia aut loci ·aut teporis aut numeri·aut·
negādi aut affirmādi aut demōstrādi aut optādi aut hortā
di aut ordinis aut interrogādi·aut similitudinis aut quali
tatis aut quantitatis aut vocandi aut respondendi aut du
bitandi aut personalia ant seperandi aut iurādi aut eligēdi

Figure 4. S1-953.8: AELIUS DONATUS *Ars minor* (Blaubeuren: Conrad Mancz, ca. 1475). Waste leaf.
(bInc 2659.1, Houghton Library, Harvard College Library)

The leaf contains portions of Sermons LXI-LXII; modern letterpress caption added at foot on recto. Initial space not filled in; without rubrication. Drab board portfolio with cloth ties; the leaf is laid in.

HC 2856; BL IB.10215; Pell 2095; GW 3934; Goff B-427; CIBN B-272; Meltz 4.

6 July 1896 – Bought with the Charles Minot fund. B 4528.92PF* v. 5

Passau

JOHANN PETRI

S1-997A   **Herbarius** [with German synonyms]. 1485.

4°. Single leaf only; ill.; 211 x 155 mm.

In: Claus Nissen, *Herbals of Five Centuries: 50 Original Leaves from German, French, Dutch, English, Italian, and Swiss Herbals, With an Introduction and Bibliography* (Zurich: L'Art ancien, 1958).

The leaf is fol. lxx, "Gramen grasz". Half-page woodcut on recto with contemporary hand coloring; without rubrication. No. 12 of 100 copies. Tipped into a cream paper mat; in a cloth case. Possibly from an imperfect copy formerly owned by Dr. Karl Becher, Karlsbad.

Countway Library

S1-997B   — Single leaf only; ill.; 211 x 155 mm.

In: Claus Nissen, *Herbals of Five Centuries* ... (Zurich: L'Art ancien, 1958).

The leaf is fol. xcvj, "Naturcium aquaticum". Half-page woodcut on recto with contemporary hand-coloring; without rubrication. No. 66 of 100 copies. Tipped into a cream paper mat; in a cloth case. Possibly from an imperfect copy formerly owned by Dr. Karl Becher, Karlsbad.

Dumbarton Oaks Garden Library

Leipzig

GREGORIUS BÖTTIGER

S1-1037.5 **Jacobus de Jüterbog:** De arte bene moriendi. ca. 1492.

4°. A single leaf only. 212 x 156 mm.

The leaf is a proof (waste?) sheet containing the text of leaf A7r; the verso is blank. The chainlines and extant margins suggest that this leaf was cut from a complete sheet containing the outer forme of sheet A1.2.7.8. Stephen Tabor has compared a photocopy of this leaf with the Huntington Library's complete copy and notes no textual variants. Without rubrication. Removed from a binding; stained; small hole affecting several letters in last line.

HC 9339*; Pr 3023; BMC 3:648 (IA.11850); Goff J-28; BSB-Ink I-37.

20 November 1990 – Bought with the Duplicate fund. bInc 3023

S1-1043A **Breitenbach, Johannes de:** Repetitio [capitulorum V]: De statu monachorum et canonicorum regularium. After 22 November 1496.

4°. Another copy. 198 x 136 mm.

Initial spaces, some with guide-letters, not filled in; without rubrication. Early 20th-century half crimson sheep and marbled boards. Blind impressions of bearer type (large initials) are visible on blank leaf E8. From the library of Count Paul Riant.

26 February 1900 – Gift of John Harvey Treat. Inc 3022

Oppenheim

JAKOB KÖBEL

(S1-1100b) **Henricus de Vrimaria:** Passio domini explanata. ca. 1515.

4°. [16] leaves; ill.; 192 x 135 mm.

Printer assignment and date from Benzing.

Without rubrication. Recent calf antique. Gilt leather booklabel of Carl J. Ulmann.

H 7123*; Goff H-51; CIBN 2:6; BSB-Ink H-60; Schr 4201a; Benzing, *Köbel* 39.

1953 – Gift of Harrison D. Horblit. Typ 520.15.450

SWITZERLAND

Basel

MICHAEL WENSSLER

S1-1135.3 **Officium defunctorum (Vesperae defunctorum).** ca. 1486-1488.

a1r-v blank ‖ a2r: [red-printed:] Incipiunt vefp[er]e defunctoru[m] fup[er] p[salmi]s an[tiphona] ‖ [black-printed:] [music: German neumes on 4-line red stave] ‖ (P³)lacebo Euouae [red-printed:] p[salmi]s ‖ (D⁵) [black-printed:] Ilexi quonia[m] exaudiet ‖ ... a6v, line 2 of text: [red-printed:] Ad matuti[n]as. Inuitatorium ‖ [black-printed:] [music, as above] ‖ (R³)egem tui omnia viuu[n]t ‖ ... e3r, line 3 of text: [red-printed:] Ad laudes ‖ [black-printed:] Non e astormen [red-printed:] Antiphona ‖ [black-printed:] [music, as above] ‖ (R³)equiem Euouae [red-printed:] p[salmi]s ‖ ... f2v, line 5 of text: [red-printed:] In depofitione feptimo v[e]l tricefimo. ‖ ... f9v, line 4: [red-printed:] Secuntur pfalmi pro falute viuoru[m]. p[salmi]s ‖ ... f11r, line 13: confequi mereantur. Per chriftum do ‖ minum n[ost]r[u]m. Viuant feliciter. Amen ‖ f11v-12v blank.

4°. a-e⁸ f¹²; [52] leaves (1, 52 blank); 210 x 151 mm. b2v: 19 lines, 148 x 76 mm. Types: 13:156G, text; music font of German neumes and four-line staves. Ranging Lombards (initial set h, GfT 983); two-line Lombards (initial set g, GfT 697); calligraphic Lombards; large Maiblumen metalcut initials (set a). Many initials, some headings, and the staves red-printed.

This edition, unrecorded until its appearance at auction in 1994, is one of at least five liturgical works printed by Wenssler ca. 1486-1490. These include: *Vigiliae defunctorum secundum ordinem Coloniensem* (ISTC iv00273560); *Vigiliae mortuorum secundum chorum ecclesiae Moguntinae* (Oates 2748); and two editions of the *Vigiliae mortuorum* (Sack 3667, and ISTC iv00273521). Dated from the types. Contents include Vespers,

Matins, Lauds, prayers for masses of the dead, and Psalms 54, 57, and 70.

Without rubrication. Contemporary half pigskin over unbevelled beech boards, covers blind-ruled in a single panel with triple-line diagonals and repeated impressions of a thistle stamp (Kyriss shop 64: Jakob Spindler, Basel); traces of a single fore-edge clasp, the clasp plate, latch, clasp and thong now gone; in a half morocco case. The single endleaves at front and back are printer's waste from Wenssler's shop, which bear impressions of pages from this edition (black text only, which was printed before the red text). Offsetting of other black-printed text is visible on d3r, d5r, and on several other leaves. Foliated 1-50 in old MS; early MS marginalia in Latin, including some music. MS ownership inscriptions in Latin of Udalricus Saen, of Tüllingen (near Basel), dated 1576 and 1589, on leaf a1r. Later owned by the Cistercian nuns at Friedenweiler, per early 19th-century MS inscription inside front cover, "Ex Friedenweiler". Oval stamps of the Fürstlich Fürstenbergische Hofbibliothek, Donaueschingen (no. 234 in the Sotheby sale catalogue, 1 July 1994). Purchased by H.P. Kraus (no. 393 in the Sotheby's New York sale catalogue of its stock, 5 December 2003). Blank leaf [52] not present.

Haegen p. 271 (Anhang V, 36); ISTC iv00273515.

16 December 2003 – Bought with the Bayard Livingston Kilgour & Kate Gray Kilgour fund. Typ Inc 7513.5

BERNHARD RICHEL

S1-1141.5 **Melusina** [German translation by Thüring von Ringoltingen]. ca. 1476.

f°. A single leaf only; ill.; 297 x 204 mm.

The unsigned leaf contains text on recto and, on verso, a woodcut of a knight being devoured by a dragon (Schramm vol. 21, Abb. 396). Woodcut uncolored; without rubrication. Owner's blindstamp, "Werther", in upper margin; "No 176" stamped in black with "/4" added in pencil at lower left; 20th-century MS label, also stamped "No 176", hinged at lower left. Acquired by Philip Hofer from Helmuth Domizlaff, June 1963. In a cream board mat.

HC 11063*; GW 12656; Goff M-476; Sack 2433; BSB-Ink C-688; Schr 4627; Schramm 21:11.

9 November 1984 – Bequest of Philip Hofer. pTyp Inc 7531.5

JOHANN AMERBACH

S1-1159A **Johannes de Bromyard:** Summa praedicantium. Not after 1484.

f°. A single leaf only. 367 x 251 mm.

The leaf is 10₅ from vol. 1. Paragraph marks and capital strokes added in red. A specimen leaf distributed by the Gesellschaft für Typenkunde des XV. Jahrhunderts, with its printed caption label tipped at foot of recto.

9 January 1914 – Bought with the Charles Minot fund. bInc 7615

S1-1162A **Petrus Comestor:** Historia scholastica. After 25 November 1486.

f°. A single leaf only. 293 x 206 mm.

The leaf is p2. Initial letters, paragraph marks, capital strokes, and underlinings added in red. A specimen leaf distributed by the Gesellschaft für Typenkunde des XV. Jahrhunderts, with its printed caption label tipped at foot of recto.

9 January 1914 – Bought with the Charles Minot fund. bInc 7572

S1-1163A **Tudeschis, Nicolaus de:** Lectura super quinque libris Decretalium. 1487-88.

f°. A single leaf only. 343 x 242 mm.

In: Donald Jackson, *Johann Amerbach* (Iowa City, Iowa: Prairie Press, 1956).

The leaf is O2 from pt. 5 (Book III). Initials added in red. Leaf laid in a printed blue paper wrapper.

11 September 1961 – Gift of Philip Hofer. Typ 970.56.4652 (A)

S1-1163B — Single leaf only. 343 x 242 mm.

In: Donald Jackson, *Johann Amerbach* (Iowa City, Iowa: Prairie Press, 1956).

The leaf is CC1 from pt. 5 (Book III). Initials added in red. Leaf laid in a printed blue paper wrapper.

1957 – Bought with the Subscription fund. Typ 970.56.4652 (B)

S1-1173A **Cassiodorus, Magnus Aurelius:** Expositio in Psalterium. 1491.

f°. Single leaf only. 289 x 205 mm.

In: *Printed Pages from European Literature: a Portfolio of Original Leaves Taken from Rare and Notable Books and Manuscripts* (New York: Society of Foliophiles, 1925).

The leaf is d3. Initials, paragraph marks, capital strokes, and underlinings added in red. Ownership signature of E.B. Krumbhaar. Brown board portfolio; the leaf is laid in a folder.

17 November 1955 – Gift of E.B. Krumbhaar. *55-544F

S1-1173B — Single leaf only. 189 x 207 mm.

In: *Printed Pages from European Literature …* (New York: Society of Foliophiles, 1925).

The leaf is e1. Initials, paragraph marks, capital strokes, and underlinings added in red. Brown board portfolio; the leaf is laid in a folder.

9 November 1984 – Bequest of Philip Hofer. *93HR-3523F

S1-1173.5 **Alphabetum divini amoris.** Not after 1491.

8°. [32] leaves (32 blank); 142 x 101 mm.

Initials, paragraph marks, capital strokes, and underlinings added in red. Modern boards. No. 414 in the Christie's South Kensington sale catalogue, 18 November 2003 (unnamed, but library of Percy Barnevik). Blank leaf not present.

HC 7633*; Pr 7637; BMC 3:753 (IA.37480); GW 1561; Goff A-528; Sack 129; BSB-Ink A-435.

10 December 2003 – Bought with the Bayard Livingston Kilgour & Kate Gray Kilgour fund. Inc 7637

S1-1199.2 **Biblia Latina.** 1498-1502.

f°. 7 vols. (vol. 1: [464] leaves; vol. 2: [358] leaves; vol. 3: [268] leaves; vol. 4: [322] leaves (322 blank); vol. 5: [264] leaves (264 blank); vol. 6: [400] leaves; vol. 7: [430] leaves); ill.; 345 x 240 mm.

In seven volumes, only the first three of which were printed before 1501. Dedicatory letters in vols. 1 and 7 are dated 29 October 1498 and 7

November 1502 respectively. Printed for Anton Koberger. Includes the Postilla of Hugo de Sancto Caro.

Volume 5 only (Prophets and Maccabees), printed ca. 1501/02. Illuminated initial on a3r, other initials added in alternating red and blue, paragraph marks and capital strokes added in red on title page, some capital strokes elsewhere added in red. Contemporary blind-stamped calf over wooden boards, rebacked; brass latches on front cover, clasp plates, clasps, and thongs gone. MS ownership notation on title page, "Ad vsum fr[atr]um Minorum ad S. Annam Bambergae".

HC 3175; Pr 7613; BMC 3:759 (IB.37901); Pell 2354; Polain 684; GW 4285; Goff B-610; CIBN B-436; Sack 659; BSB-Ink B-481; Schr 3476; Schramm 21:27.

2 October 1837 – Bought ("Cost 50 cents"). Andover-Harvard Theological Library

S1-1199.2A — Another copy. 322 x 201 mm.

Twenty four leaves only from vol. 5 (Prophets and Maccabees), consisting of g1-8, i1-8, k1-6, and p1, 6. Initial letters not filled in; without rubrication. Trimmed, affecting some marginal notes and headlines, a few other imperfections, stains. Removed from the binding of an unidentified Houghton Library volume. [Another fragmentary leaf from this edition was used to cover the 19th-century boards on a copy of Pierre Godefroy, Proverbiorum liber (Paris: Charles Estienne, 1555), shelved in Houghton Library under the call number Prov 190.4*.]

Date of acquisition and source not known. Inc 7613

NICOLAUS KESLER

S1-1202.7 **Sermones Meffret de tempore et de sanctis, siue Hortulus reginae.** Not after 1483.

f°. 3 vols. (vol. 1: [232] leaves (232 blank); vol. 2: [198] leaves (198 blank); vol. 3: [316] leaves (316 blank); 309 x 217 mm.

In three volumes, arranged by Goff as follows: 1) Sermones de tempore, pars hiemalis; 2) Sermones de sanctis; 3) Sermones de tempore, pars aestivalis. Goff's arrangement is followed here, though BSB-Ink sensibly reorders the parts in the sequence 1, 3, 2.

Volumes 1-2 only. Initial spaces, a few with guide-letters, not filled in; a few leaves in vol. 2 with paragraph marks, capital strokes, and underlinings added in red, otherwise without rubrication. Bound in one volume, with vol. 2 preceding vol. 1. Contemporary blind-stamped calf over unbevelled wooden boards; brass clasp plates on back cover, latches on front, one clasp with leather thong remaining. Some contemporary MS marginalia. From the Fürstlich Fürstenbergische Hofbibliothek, Donaueschingen (no. 213 in the Sotheby sale catalogue, 1 July 1994). No. 142 in the Christie's South Kensington sale catalogue, 7 December 2004 (unnamed, but library of Percy Barnevik).

C 3961 (I-II); Polain 2654 (I), 2653 (II); Goff M-440; Sack 2416; BSB-Ink S-303.

2 February 2005 – Bought with the Edward and Bertha C. Rose Acquisition fund. Inc 7653.5

S1-1216.5   **Bernardus Claravallensis:** Epistolae. 1 December 1494.

f°. Two fragments only. 107 x 173 mm.

The two fragments are from leaves LI and LVI (the bifolium i1.6). Initial letters not filled in; without rubrication. Removed, together with fragments from several other early printed books (including STC 13606), from the binding of Houghton Library *NC5.Er153F.1529 (a sammelband containing Desiderius Erasmus, *Dialogus cui titulus Ciceronianus* (Basel: Hieronymus Froben and Johann Herwagen, March 1529), and Philipp Melanchthon, *Eloquentiae encomium* (Cologne: Johannes Soter, 1525)).

HC 2872*; Pr 7686; BMC 3:771 (IB.37646); Pell 2106; Polain 583; GW 3926; Goff B-386; Sack 565; BSB-Ink B-311.

March 1970 – Bought with the Duplicate fund. bInc 7686

JOHANN FROBEN

S1-1227A   **Biblia Latina.** 27 October 1495.

8°. Single leaf only. 157 x 109 mm.

In: Otto F. Ege, *Original Leaves from Famous Bibles: Nine Centuries, 1121-1935 A.D.: Sixty Leaves* ... ([New York: Philip C. Duschnes, 1938]).

The leaf is m4, containing 1 Samuel 1-3. Without rubrication. Tan buckram portfolio; the leaf is matted and laid in.

April 1965 – Gift of William Bentinck-Smith. B 4406.657.2PF*

S1-1227B — Single leaf only. 157 x 111 mm.

In: Otto F. Ege, *Original Leaves from Famous Bibles: Nine Centuries, 1121-1935 A.D.* ([New York: Philip C. Duschnes, 1945?]).

The leaf is i4, containing Deuteronomy 22-26. Without rubrication. Rust buckram portfolio; the leaf is matted and laid in.

December 1967 – Gift of Paul Gerard Ecker. Typ 970.45.2100PF

JACOBUS WOLFF VON PFORZHEIM

S1-1234.3   **Mayronis, Franciscus de:** Sermones de sanctis. 1498.

4°. [10], CCLIX (i.e. CCLVIII) leaves (CCXXXIX omitted; CXLI-CXLIII, CXLVII misnumbered CXLII-CXLIIII, CXLVIII); 199 x 150 mm.

Includes the *Tractatus super Pater Noster, De poenitentia, De articulis fidei, Super Magnificat, De corpore Christi, De donis Spiritus Sancti, De ultimo judicio,* and *Super Missa est* of Mayronis.

Some initials, paragraph marks, and capital strokes added in red on first and last few leaves. 17th-century blind-stamped pigskin over reverse-bevelled wooden boards; edges stained blue; brass clasps with pigskin thongs attach to pins on fore-edge of front cover; initials "F.S.A.L." (i.e. Frater Stephanus [Mösinger] Abbas Langheimensis) stamped on front cover; in a gray board case. 19th-century MS biographical note on Mayronis on verso of leaf [1]; MS inscription, "Basileae 1498" beneath title. Early signature on I1or, "Joannes Degen"; MS inscription on front endleaf, "The gift of Charles Forrest Cutter, of Princeville, Ill., student in Phillips Academy, recd. 30 June, 1868".

H 10532*; Pr 7706; BMC 3:777 (IA.37711); Pell 4910; Polain 1515; Goff M-94; Sack 2409; BSB-Ink F-247.

Andover-Harvard Theological Library

LIENHART YSENHUT

S1-1237.5   **Retza, Franciscus de:** De generatione Christi, sive Defensorium inviolatae castitatis B.V.M. [Latin and German]. ca. 1489-1500.

4°. A single leaf only; ill.; 214 x 145 mm.

The leaf is c8; each side contains a half-page woodcut (Schramm vol. 22, Abb. 303-304). Without rubrication.

HC 6086*; Pr 7717; BMC 3:780 (IA.37865); Pell 4923; Polain 1518; GW 10275; Goff R-153; Sack 1479; BSB-Ink F-253; Schr 4047; Schramm 22:42.

9 November 1984 – Bequest of Philip Hofer. bTyp Inc 7717

MICHAEL FURTER

S1-1244A   **Thomas Aquinas:** Commentaria in omnes Epistolas Sancti Pauli. 16 October 1495.

f°. Another copy. 306 x 213 mm.

Large initial on a2r added in red and blue, with marginal extension; initials added in red or blue, paragraph marks in blue, underlinings in red. 19th-century blind-tooled half brown calf and paper over (original?) wooden boards; brass clasp plates on back cover, latches on front, one clasp preserved; stamp of Buchbinderei J. Nep. Eckert, Vienna. Booklabel of Buchhandlung u. Antiquariat von Bermann & Altmann, Vienna. Bookplate of George Benson Weston, with his signature and purchase inscription on front flyleaf, "Vienna, Dec. 24, 1898," and note on rear flyleaf, "This book, with the St. Augustine and the Dionysius, forms my Christmas present to myself." Leaf a1 remargined, chi1 repaired with slight loss; blank leaf not present.

1963 – Gift of Charles D. Weston. Inc 7727 (B)

S1-1246.5   **Statuta synodalia Eystettensia cum statutis provincialibus Moguntinis.** Not after 1496.

4°. LXXXVII, [9] leaves; ill.; 197 x 138 mm.

Some copies have an extra bifolium inserted; see Hubay.

This copy lacks the extra bifolium described by Hubay. Initial spaces, with guide-letters, not filled in; without rubrication. Old vellum, edges stained blue. MS inscriptions on title page: "Anno 1597. Antonij S[?]urnaub Parochj ad S. Walpurgae. Ex Aulij." at top; "Loci Capucinoru[m] Monachij." at bottom. Small circular stamp in black on a1v, "Vend. Ex Bibl. [last 2 lines illegible]".

H 15031*; Pr 2749; BMC 3:784 (IA.37829); Polain 3600; Goff S-735; Hubay (Eichstätt) 954; CIBN S-424; BSB-Ink S-558; Schr 5302; Schramm 22:46.

July 2003 – Bought. Law Library

JOHANN BERGMANN DE OLPE

S1-1258A   **Brant, Sebastian:** Das Narrenschiff [Latin]. 1 March 1497.

4°. A single leaf only; ill.; 219 x 156 mm.

The leaf is h3 (fol. LIX), containing a woodcut of Samson and Delilah on recto. Without rubrication; woodcut uncolored. Tipped to a sheet of white paper.

9 November 1984 – Bequest of Philip Hofer. pTyp Inc 7776

POLAND

Cracow

CASPAR HOCHFEDER

(S1-1269a)   **Sacranus, Johannes:** Elucidarius errorum ritus Ruthenici. ca. 1506?

4°. xxxiiij, [2] leaves (xxiiij misnumbered xxiij); ill.; 200 x 146 mm.

The printer assignment and date are from Schäfer; ISTC, following Isaac, dates to ca. 1504. Probably printed by Hochfeder for Johann Haller.

Initial spaces, with guide-letters, not filled in; without rubrication. Modern brown morocco, by "WHS[mith & Son]" (i.e. Douglas Cockerell). From the libraries of C.W. Dyson Perrins (no. 697 in pt. 3 of the Sotheby sale catalogue of his library, 10 March 1947); the Broxbourne Library of Albert Ehrman, with his armorial bookplate, Broxbourne Library booklabel, and "AE" stamp with added MS "R453" (no. 123 in pt. 1 of the Sotheby sale catalogue of his library, 14 November 1977); and Otto Schäfer, with his monogram and added MS "1226" (no. 188 in pt. 3 of the Sotheby's New York sale catalogue of his library, 1 November 1995).

C 2346; Pr 9467 (Johann Haller); BMC 3:xl; Isaac 14384; Schäfer 363; Schr 5174; ISTC is00016400.

14 July 2003 – Bought with the Kilgour Belles-Lettres, Osyp Nowycky, and Ukrainian National Home of Lorain Ohio Book funds. *ZPC5. Sa146.506e

ITALY

Rome

CONRADUS SWEYNHEYM
AND ARNOLDUS PANNARTZ
(SECOND PRESS)

S1-1292.5   **Biblia Latina.** Not before 15 March 1471.

f°. [628] leaves (1, 16, 17, 562, 627 and 628 blank); 408 x 290 mm.

Edited by Giovanni Andrea Bussi. Includes Pseudo-Aristeas, *Ad Philocratem de LXX interpretibus* in Latin translation by Matthaeus Palmerius Pisanus.

Imperfect: 86 leaves only from a disbound copy; present are leaves containing the following biblical texts: O.T., Proverbs 11-24; Isaiah 3-6, 33-58; Jeremiah 20-41; Ezekiel 13-17, 40-43; Daniel 2-3; Amos 1-5; O.T. Apocrypha, I Maccabees 12-14; II Maccabees 14-15; N.T., Matthew 21-27; Mark 1-10, 12-15; Luke 1-8; Acts 1-8, 10-12, 14-26; I Corinthians 11-16; II Corinthians 7-13; Hebrews 3-12; James 1-5; and parts of the index from Ge to Za. In addition there are present two leaves in MS facsimile containing parts of the Wisdom of Solomon, Ecclesiasticus, and Ezekiel. Initials added in red and blue, many with marginal extensions. Formerly laid in a 16th-century account book binding of blind-tooled brown goatskin, presumably not the original binding; the binding now shelved separately at *98-302aF.

HC 3051*; Pr 3316; BMC 4:12 (IC.17163); Pell 2282; GW 4210; IGI 1636; Goff B-535; CIBN B-368.

20 November 1997 (13 leaves); 19 November 1998 (73 leaves) – Gift of Elizabeth MacGillivray Voli. Inc 3051PF

S1-1295A **Nicolaus de Lyra:** Postilla super totam Bibliam. 18 November 1471-26 May 1472.

f°. A single leaf only. 372 x 270 mm.

In: Edwin Hall, *Sweynheym & Pannartz and the Origins of Printing in Italy: German Technology and Italian Humanism* (McMinnville, Oregon: Phillip J. Pirages, 1991).

The leaf is from vol. 1. Initial added in red. No. 91 of 275 copies. Laid in a mylar sleeve, in blue cloth tray case.

1 March 1992 – Bought with the Printing & Graphic Arts Book Reserve fund. Typ 970.91.4472F

S1-1295B — Single leaf only. 371 x 267 mm.

In: Edwin Hall, *Sweynheym & Pannartz and the Origins of Printing in Italy* ... (McMinnville, Oregon: Phillip J. Pirages, 1991).

The leaf is from vol. 1. Initial added in blue. No. 137 of 275 copies. Laid in a mylar sleeve, in blue cloth tray case.

Berenson Library, I Tatti

JOHANNES BULLE

S1-1381.5 **Oratio in funere Cardinalis Spoletani.** After 2 April 1479.

4°. [6] leaves; 193 x 137 mm.

Without rubrication. Formerly bound in a tract volume: foliated 406-411 in old MS. Modern half vellum and tan boards. No. 497 in the Christie's South Kensington sale catalogue, 18 November 2003 (unnamed, but library of Percy Barnevik).

HR 12022; Pr 3617; BMC 4:79 (IA.18282); IGI 7010; Goff H-129; CIBN O-33; Sack 2614.

10 December 2003 – Bought with the Bayard Livingston Kilgour & Kate Gray Kilgour fund. Inc 3617

STEPHAN PLANNCK

S1-1392.8   **Terasse, Petrus:** Oratio de divina providentia. After 9 March 1483.

4°. [6] leaves (6 blank); 208 x 136 mm.

Initial space not filled in; without rubrication. Modern half vellum, the boards covered with fragments from an early 16th-century printed book. At one time this was item 29 in a tract volume: foliated 310-315 in MS, with 28 added on first recto and 29 on following rectos. No. 557 in the Christie's South Kensington sale catalogue, 18 November 2003 (unnamed, but library of Percy Barnevik).

HC 15369*; Pr 3636; BMC 4:82 (IA.18337); IGI 9482; Goff T-62; CIBN T-88; BSB-Ink T-82.

10 December 2003 – Bought with the Bayard Livingston Kilgour & Kate Gray Kilgour fund. Inc 3636

S1-1404.8   **Tegliatus, Stephanus:** Oratio coram Innocentio VIII pro die Pentecostes habita. After 3 June 1487.

4°. [6] leaves; 210 x 140 mm.

Initial space not filled in; without rubrication. Modern boards covered in floral-patterned Dutch gilt paper. No. 558 in the Christie's South Kensington sale catalogue, 18 November 2003 (unnamed, but library of Percy Barnevik).

H 15456*; Pr 3676; BMC 4:87 (IA.18450); IGI 9398; Goff T-123; CIBN T-45; Sack 3348; BSB-Ink T-130.

10 December 2003 – Bought with the Bayard Livingston Kilgour & Kate Gray Kilgour fund. Inc 3676

S1-1427.5   **Casus papales, episcopales et abbatiales.** ca. 1492.

4°. [4] leaves; 199 x 135 mm.

This copy varies from the transcription given by GW in that the explicit on 1_4r has the incorrect reading "Episcepales" instead of "Episcopales".

Without rubrication. Recent gray boards. No. 461 in the Christie's South Kensington sale catalogue, 18 November 2003 (unnamed, but library of Percy Barnevik).

GW 6195; IGI 2568; Accurti (1930) 39; Accurti (1936) p. 107.

10 December 2003 – Bought with the Bayard Livingston Kilgour & Kate Gray Kilgour fund. Inc 3751.5

JACOBUS MAZOCHIUS

(S1-1508a) **Sadoletus, Jacobus:** De bello contra Turcos oratio. Not before 1509.

[For transcriptions see Reichling.] 4°. A-K⁴ L⁶; [46] leaves; 209 x 145 mm. A2r: 26 lines, 147 x 88 mm. Type: 113R. Initial space, with guide-letter, on A1r.

For dating and printer assignment, see the note to S-17 in Goff (Suppl.) and Isaac.

Initial space not filled in; without rubrication. Some contemporary MS marginalia. 19ᵗʰ-century vellum. Gilt blue leather booklabel of Count Paul Riant.

R 717; Isaac 12140; IGI 5:5; Goff S-17; CIBN 2:531.

28 December 1899 – Gift of J. Randolph Coolidge and Archibald Cary Coolidge. *IC5.Sa157.509d

Venice

NICOLAUS JENSON

S1-1581A **Biblia Latina.** 1476.

f°. A single leaf only. 304 x 202 mm.

In: Otto F. Ege, *Original Leaves from Famous Bibles: Nine Centuries, 1121-1935 A.D.: Sixty Leaves ...* ([New York: Philip C. Duschnes, 1938]).

The leaf is y6 (leaf [216]), containing Proverbs 16-21. Initial letters added in red or blue. Tan buckram portfolio; the leaf is matted and laid in.

April 1965 – Gift of William Bentinck-Smith. B 4406.657.2PF*

S1-1581B — Single leaf only. 304 x 202 mm.

In: Otto F. Ege, *Original Leaves from Famous Bibles: Nine Centuries, 1121-1935 A.D.* ([New York: Philip C. Duschnes, 1945?]).

The leaf is N2 (leaf [384]), containing 1 Corinthians 1-6. Initial letters added in red or blue. Rust buckram portfolio; the leaf is matted and laid in.

December 1967 – Gift of Paul Gerard Ecker. Typ 970.45.2100PF

S1-1584A **Tudeschis, Nicolaus de:** Lectura super quinque libris Decretalium. 21 July-10 December 1477-not before 1478.

f°. Another copy. 429 x 280 mm.

Parts 1 and 2 only. Initials, paragraph marks, capital strokes, and underlinings added in red. A few contemporary MS annotations. In pt. 1 of this copy, sheet q2.7 is misfolded; the signature 'q2' has been added in red to q7r by the rubricator, even though q2 is properly signed and the register gives the correct incipit. Bound in one volume, in contemporary blindstamped calf over thick beech boards; each cover with similar central diapered panel; decorated with at least 16 different tools; marks of clasp plates, latches, and four corner bosses on each cover, no longer present; clasps and thongs gone; edges stained yellow; minor repairs; in brown cloth case. Possibly bound at the Augustinian monastery at Dürnstein, Lower Austria, though none of the tools are among those found on Dürnstein bindings dated ca. 1479-1481 (cf. Otto Mazal, "Datierte gotische Einbände aus dem Augustiner Chorherrenstift Dürnstein a. d. Donau," *Gutenberg-Jahrbuch* (1961): 286-91). MS inscription recording the presentation of the book by Wenzel Faber to the Augustinian Canons at Dürnstein on recto of front flyleaf, "Hunc libru[m] dedit d[omi]n[us] Doctor Wentzeslaus de Budweis [?] b[ea]te Marie virg[inis] Can[onum] Regula[ru]m In Durnstain"; second inscription in same hand at foot of A6r (pt. 2), "Iste liber est mon[asterii] b[ea]te Marie Virg[inis] Can[onum] Reg[ularu]m Durnstain". Booklabel of E. P. Goldschmidt.

4 January 2002 – Bought with the Osgood Hooker and Margaret F. Cowett funds. Typ Inc 4108PF

S1-1588A **Plutarchus:** Vitae illustrium virorum. 2 January 1478.

f°. A single leaf only. 407 x 261 mm.

In: Henry Lewis Bullen, *Nicolas Jenson, Printer of Venice: His Famous Type Designs and Some Comment Upon the Printing Types of Earlier*

Printers (San Francisco: John Henry Nash, 1926).

The leaf is 004 from vol. 2. Without rubrication. Copy no. 125 of 207 copies. Half vellum and marbled boards; the leaf is tipped in following the colophon leaf.

6 June 1933 – Gift of George Parker Winship. Typ 970.26.2440F

FRANCISCUS RENNER

S1-1604.5 **Antoninus Florentinus:** Summa theologica pars secunda. 1474.

f°. A single leaf only. 276 x 202 mm.

Printed by Renner with Nicolaus de Frankfordia.

Initial added in red and blue, paragraph marks and capital strokes added in red. The leaf is matted in a white paper folder (312 x 235 mm), with letterpress text on p. [1], "To greet you this holiday season from Norman Alexander Hall …"

HCR 1254; Pr 4160; BMC 5:192 (IB.19840); Pell 887; Polain 274; GW 2195; IGI 699; Goff A-867; CIBN A-459.

Date of acquisition and source not known. bInc 4160

S1-1604.5A — Single leaf only. 272 x 197 mm.

Initial and paragraph marks added in red and blue, capital strokes added in red. The leaf is matted in a white paper folder (312 x 235 mm), with letterpress text on p. [1], "To greet you this holiday season from Norman Alexander Hall …"

9 November 1984 – Bequest of Philip Hofer. bTyp Inc 4160

S1-1605.5 **Biblia Latina.** 1475.

f°. A single leaf only. 265 x 194 mm.

Printed by Renner with Nicolaus de Frankfordia.

The leaf contains Deuteronomy 24-28. Initials added in alternating red and blue with contrasting red or blue penwork extensions; capital strokes added in red. Contemporary MS annotations, including profiles of two human heads.

HC 3054*; Pr 4163; BMC 5:193 (IB.19845); Pell 2284; GW 4216; IGI 1642; Goff B-541; CIBN B-377; BSB-Ink B-419.

9 November 1984 – Bequest of Philip Hofer. bTyp Inc 4163

JACOBUS RUBEUS

S1-1657A   **Corpus iuris civilis. Novellae, etc.** 16 January 1477/78.

f°. Another copy. 387 x 265 mm.

Three leaves only, from the *Libri feudorum*: aa6 (lines 1-41), aa7 (wanting portion along lower inner margin), aa8 (lines 42-75). Initials and paragraph marks added in red or blue. Tipped onto fol. 57 of an album of printed fragments removed from bindings (presumably Oxford bindings of the late 16th-early 17th centuries) of books in the library formed by Hannibal Gamon Jr., later removed to Lanhydrock House, Cornwall. For additional provenance information, see S1-372.5. Late 19th-century half tan sheep and brown cloth.

October 1963 – Bought with the Susan A.E. Morse fund. *fEC.A100. B659c

BERNHARD MALER, ERHARD RATDOLT, AND PETER LÖSLEIN

S1-1729A   **Appianus:** Historia Romana [Pt. 1-2]. 1477.

f°. A single leaf only. 286 x 210 mm.

In: *Monumenta Germaniae et Italiae Typographica: deutsche und italienische Inkunabeln in getreuen Nachbildungen* (Berlin: Reichsdruckerei, 1892-1913).

The leaf is i2 from vol. 1; modern letterpress caption added at foot on recto. Without rubrication. Drab board portfolio with cloth ties; the leaf is laid in.

9 March 1903 – Bought with the Charles Minot fund. B 4528.92PF* v. 7

PETRUS DE PLASIIS, CREMONENSIS, DICTUS VERONENSIS

S1-1777A   **Dante Alighieri:** La Commedia. 18 November 1491.

f°. A single leaf only. 298 x 206 mm.

In: Otto F. Ege, *Original Leaves from Famous Books: Eight Centuries, 1240 A.D.-1923 A.D.* ([New York: Philip C. Duschnes, 1949]).

The leaf is K2 (leaf 76). Without rubrication. Rust buckram portfolio; the leaf is matted and laid in.

April 1965 – Gift of William Bentinck-Smith. B 4406.657PF*

ERHARD RATDOLT (SECOND PRESS)

S1-1800A   **Rolewinck, Werner:** Fasciculus temporum. 24 November 1480.

f°. A single leaf only. 273 x 194 mm.

In: Type Facsimile Society, *Publications of the Society for the Year 1904* (Oxford: Horace Hart, [1904?]).

The leaf is 2_2 (leaf 2); modern letterpress caption added at foot on recto. Without rubrication. "The three original leaves which accompany the present issue are the gift of Dr. [Konrad] Burger to the Society" (descriptive letterpress, p. 21). Blue cloth; the leaf is inlaid and bound in.

18 January 1939 – Bought with the Charles Eliot Norton fund. B 5429.00F* v. 1

S1-1818A   **Eusebius Caesariensis:** Chronicon. 13 September 1483.

4°. Another copy. 217 x 165 mm.

Bound in at the end of this copy is an 11-page MS on paper duplicating the contents and layout of final gathering Y^6 in the 13 June 1512 edition of the *Chronicon* printed by Henri Estienne for Josse Bade (Renouard(B) 12.15). The MS updates the text to 1512. Peter Way recently has suggested that this MS continuation probably was written by the compiler, Jehan de Mouveaux, for use as the printer's setting copy. Way marshals evidence from the MS's orthography, contents, paper stock, and script to argue that the printed text was set directly from it. Because the MS almost exactly duplicates the layout and typographical features of the printed text, Way maintains that it represents, not merely a printer's copy, but "a fair, dummy, and mockup copy all in one," or what Frans Janssen has recently termed a "model copy." If so, it joins the famous MS exemplar for the 1493 Nuremberg Chronicle as only the second documented example from an early printing shop. For a full discussion, with illustrations, see Peter Way, "Jehan de Mouveaux's 'Primum Exemplar' (a Model Copy Made for Henri Estienne's 1512 Edition of Eusebius' *Chronicon*)," *Gutenberg-Jahrbuch* (2003): 93-118. The printed edition with which the MS is bound bears contemporary MS foliation in two hands and a few MS signature marks, but no printing shop markings; it is not clear how long the two have been joined.

Without rubrication. Early 19th-century gilt vellum, rebacked; edges gilt over red sprinkling. Effaced 18th-century (?) MS inscription of a Capuchin library at foot of π2r; booklabel of Charles Butler (no. 413 in pt. 1 of the Sotheby sale catalogue of his library, 5 April 1911); from the library of Peter Way. Blank leaf x10 wanting.

23 February 2005 – Bought with the Bayard Livingston Kilgour & Kate Gray Kilgour fund. Typ Inc 4390

S1-1836A   **Prognosticon:** Opusculum repertorii prognosticon in mutationes aeris. Before 4 November 1485.

4°. Another copy. 208 x 158 mm.

Capital strokes, underlinings, and astrological symbols added in red on a few leaves. Contemporary half blind-stamped leather over thick beech boards, rebacked; brass latch on back cover, clasp plate on front cover, clasp with pigskin thong. Booklabel of David P. Wheatland. A few contemporary MS annotations, including an astrological chart; MS notes in German on blank leaf 49v. Inside the back cover is a contemporary MS volvelle for lunar and solar calculations, consisting of 4 parchment discs, in red, brown, and black ink, fastened by a wooden peg to the rear paper pastedown, on which is drawn the zodiac wheel. Imperfect: leaves 48-49 renewed along inner margin, with loss of a few letters.

1 January 1991 – Gift of David P. Wheatland. Inc 4401 (B)

S1-1836B   — Another copy. 218 x 158 mm.

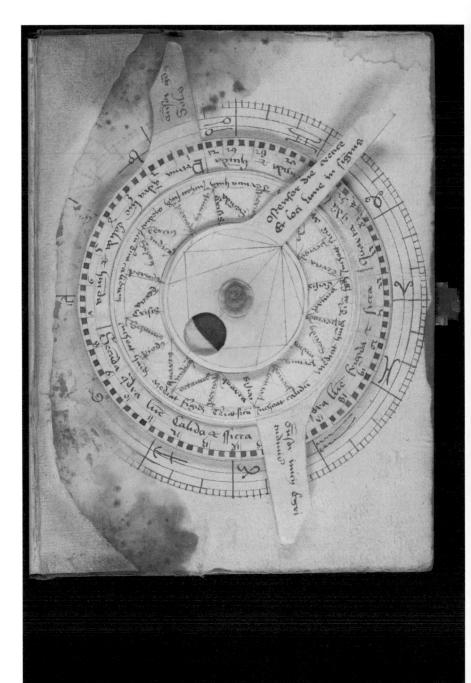

Fig. 5. S1-1836A: *Prognosticon* (Venice: Erhard Ratdolt, before 4 November 1485). Manuscript volvelle. (Inc 4401 (B), Houghton Library, Harvard College Library)

Without rubrication. Modern crimson morocco by Rivière & Son. Bookseller's typescript (carbon) description tipped in at front. Booklabel of Harrison D. Horblit (no. 386 in pt. 2 of the Sotheby sale catalogue of his library, November 1974); booklabel of David P. Wheatland.

1 January 1991 – Gift of David P. Wheatland. Inc 4401 (C)

ANTONIUS DE STRATA, DE CREMONA

S1-1838.8 **Jacobus de Voragine:** Legenda aurea. 1 July 1480.

f°. A single leaf only. 284 x 204 mm.

Printed by Strata in partnership with Marcus Catanellus.

In: Otto F. Ege, *Original Leaves from Famous Books: Eight Centuries, 1240 A.D.-1923 A.D.* ([New York: Philip C. Duschnes, 1949]).

The unsigned leaf is foliated 55 in MS. Paragraph marks added in red, capital strokes in yellow. Rust buckram portfolio; the leaf is matted and laid in.

C 6421; BMC 5:292 (IB.21221); Polain 2193; IGI 5014; Goff J-95; Sack 1976; BSB-Ink I-77; Finzi III:1.

April 1965 – Gift of William Bentinck-Smith. B 4406.657PF*

ANDREAS TORRESANUS, DE ASULA

S1-1884A **Cicero:** Epistolae ad familiares. 31 January 1483/84.

f°. Another copy. 313 x 208 mm.

Large vinework initial on a3r illuminated in gold, blue, red, and green; 15 smaller illuminated initials in text; other initials added in alternating red and blue. Contemporary central Italian binding of brown morocco over reverse-bevelled beech boards; covers uniformly tooled in gilt and blind to a design of two knotwork medallions joined in a "dumb-bell" shape, within concentric frames of repeated tools (stars, scrolls, fronds, and leaves); spine blind-tooled in five compartments, each with hatched circles within a diaper pattern; tawed endbands covered with pink and blue thread; edges plain; star-head nails anchoring four thongs on front cover; marks of four latches on back cover, no longer present; clasps and thongs gone. (See Anthony Hobson, *Humanists and Bookbinders:*

The Origins and Diffusion of the Humanistic Bookbinding 1459-1559 (Cambridge, Eng., 1989), p. 20 for a brief discussion of similar bindings.) Unfinished coat of arms added at foot of a3r: within a circular green wreath with red penwork flourishes, per fess arg and sable, a pale arg in base. Old MS inscription on bare wood inside front cover (i.e. added after original front pastedown had lifted), "Ex Libris Johannis Borgogelli [?]"; recent stamp "0627" in purple on several leaves. Scattered MS marginalia in Latin in several hands. From the library of Michel Wittock (no. 35 in pt. 1 of the Christie's London sale catalogue of his bookbindings, 7 July 2004). Imperfect: leaves a1-2, a8 and blank H10 not present; lower outer corner of p5 torn away with text loss; wormed at beginning and end, affecting a few letters; signature h misbound preceding signature g.

5 August 2004 – Bought with the Amy Lowell fund. Inc 4699 (B)

BAPTISTA DE TORTIS

S1-1934.2 **Avicenna:** Canon [Latin] Lib. III. 11 February 1492/93.

f°. Two leaves only. 373 x 252 mm.

Latin translation by Gerardus Cremonensis, with commentary by Gentilis de Fulgineo; edited by Petrus Rochabonella. For transcriptions and collations of the complete work, see GW.

The disjunct leaves are QQ4-5. Initials and a few paragraph marks added in red. Removed from a binding.

H 2210*; Pell 1667; GW 3124; IGI 1123; Goff A-1427; Sack 416; BSB-Ink A-961.

Date of acquisition and source not known. pInc 4641.5

S1-1934.7 **Duranti, Guillelmus:** Speculum iudiciale. 17 February 1493/94-9 March 1494.

f°. A single leaf only. 427 x 281 mm.

Includes additions by Johannes Andreae and Baldus de Ubaldis; pt. 2 contains the *Inventarium* of Berengarius Fredoli; edited by Bernardinus Landrianus.

The leaf is f6 (leaf 46). Initials, with guide-letters, added in red or blue; underlinings added in red. A specimen leaf distributed by the Gesellschaft für Typenkunde des XV. Jahrhunderts, with its printed caption label tipped at foot of recto.

H 6515*; Pell 4532; IGI 3659; Goff D-452; GW 9159; Sack 1341; BSB-Ink D-367.

9 January 1914 – Bought with the Charles Minot fund. pInc 4645.2

S1-1938.5   **Corpus iuris civilis. Infortiatum.** 4 November 1495.

f°. A single leaf only. 426 x 284 mm.

Includes the *glossa ordinaria* of Accursius and the *Summaria* of Hieronymus Clarius.

In: *Printed Pages from European Literature: a Portfolio of Original Leaves Taken from Rare and Notable Books and Manuscripts* (New York: Society of Foliophiles, 1925).

The leaf is y4 (leaf 172). Without rubrication. Ownership signature of E.B. Krumbhaar. Brown board portfolio; the leaf is laid in a folder.

H 9574*; GW 7692; Sack 1142; BSB-Ink C-622.

17 November 1955 – Gift of E.B. Krumbhaar. *55-544F

S1-1938.5A   — Single leaf only. 426 x 286 mm.

In: *Printed Pages from European Literature …* (New York: Society of Foliophiles, 1925).

The leaf is [con]8 (leaf 200). Without rubrication. Brown board portfolio; the leaf is laid in a folder.

9 November 1984 – Bequest of Philip Hofer. *93HR-3523F

JOHANNES AND GREGORIUS
DE GREGORIIS

S1-1962.2   **Cicero:** Orationes. 8 November 1483.

f°. [252] leaves; 290 x 203 mm.

Printed by Johannes de Gregoriis with Jacobus Britannicus. Edited by Giovanni Andrea Bussi. In some copies, the colophon has the variant reading "Moceuigo" instead of "Mocenigo".

In this copy, the colophon has the reading "Mocenigo". Initial spaces, with guide-letters, not filled in; without rubrication. Old inscription on rear pastedown, "Di Casa Varnacci Marubini"; 19th-century inscription on front pastedown, "Le pagai L[ire] 13..6..8", and paper label with "551" in MS; another inscription on front flyleaf has been torn away. Booklabel of Edith Wharton's library at Sainte-Claire-du-Château, Hyères. 18th-century vellum, MS title on spine, edges speckled red and blue. Imperfect: two leaves at front (table and register) wanting.

HC 5125*; Pr 4503; BMC 5:340 (IB.20943); Pell 3692; GW 6763; IGI 2930; Goff C-545a; Sack 1015; BSB-Ink C-384.

April 2001 – Bequest of Henry N. Ess; transferred from the Law Library. Inc 4503

S1-2033A **Hieronymus, Saint:** Commentaria in Bibliam. 1497-25 August 1498.

f°. Another copy. 341 x 233 mm.

Imperfect; this copy consists of 330 of 845 leaves, i.e. leaves [195]-[524] (quires A-R⁸ S¹⁰ T-BB⁸ CC⁶ DD-HH⁸ DDD-EEE⁸ FFF-HHH⁶ DDDD-GGGG⁶ HHHH⁴ II⁸ KK-LL⁶). Paragraph marks, capital strokes, underlinings, and a few initials added in red; first woodcut initial colored in green, most others colored in red. Contemporary blind-stamped calf over oak boards; brass edge guards; brass clasp plates on back cover, latches, clasps, and thongs gone; marks of corner bosses, no longer present; plain parchment endleaves; in brown buckram case. MS inscription inside front cover: "Monasterij B.M.V. quod est diocaesis Halberstadensis in Huisseburgk"; another inscription has been erased from the front flyleaf.

Andover-Harvard Theological Library

GREGORIUS DE GREGORIIS

(S1-2042b) **Borromaeus, Antonius:** De Christiana religione contra Hebraeos. ca. 1510.

4°. [24] leaves; 193 x 135 mm.

For printer assignment and dating see Hillard.

Without rubrication. Recent half vellum and decorated boards. Bookplate of Lee M. Friedman.

C 1216; Pell 2777; GW 4:col. 573; IGI 1:260; Goff B-1038; CIBN 1:385; Hillard 468.

1957 – Bequest of Lee M. Friedman. *IC5.B6445.5150

BERNARDINUS STAGNINUS, DE TRIDINO

S1-2078.8   **Rhazes, Muhammad:** Liber nonus ad Almansorem. 12 November 1493.

f°. 164 leaves (14 and 62 misnumbered 41 and 80); 344 x 237 mm.

Includes the commentary of Johannes Arculanus. Edited by Hieronymus Turianus and Elyanorus Sanseverinus. Finding himself with too much text for the available space in gathering o, the compositor solved his problem in unusual fashion by widening the text columns rather than by increasing the size of the type-page. On o3r, the margin between the two text columns was almost entirely eliminated, save for a hair space; the margin is slightly wider on o3v-o4v, returning to normal width on o5r. The number of lines per column was increased from 69 to 70 on o3r-o4v, and to 71 on o3r col. 1.

Maiblumen initial on a2r, initials (some with penwork marginal extensions), paragraph marks, capital strokes, and underlinings added in red. Contemporary blind-stamped pigskin over wooden boards; brass clasp plates on back cover, latches on front, clasps with pigskin thongs; MS vellum title label on front cover. Contemporary MS marginalia in Latin.

HC 13899*; BMC 5:367 (IB.22178); Polain 3349; IGI 8348; Goff R-180; BSB-Ink A-665; Ballard 607.

Countway Library

BERNARDINUS RIZUS, NOVARIENSIS

S1-2174.5   **Caracciolus, Robertus:** Sermones quadragesimales [Italian collection]. 19 April 1487.

4°. [114] leaves; 208 x 153 mm.

Initial spaces not filled in; without rubrication. Modern blind-tooled mottled calf. No. 458 in the Christie's South Kensington sale catalogue,

18 November 2003 (unnamed, but library of Percy Barnevik).

GW 6102; IGI 2497; Goff C-156; Accurti (1930) 35.

29 January 2004 – Bought with the Bayard Livingston Kilgour & Kate Gray Kilgour fund. Inc 4945.5

S1-2181.5   **Pseudo-Augustinus:** Sermones ad heremitas. 10 August 1490.

8°. 151, [1] leaves (1, 152 blank); 159 x 108 mm.

Goff, and therefore ISTC (record no. ia01316000), incorrectly describe this edition as a quarto. In some copies, a3 is missigned a2; see GW.

In this copy, a3 is properly signed. Initial spaces, most with guide-letters, not filled in; without rubrication. Contemporary pasteboard covered with a vellum MS fragment, the writing mostly worn away; single endleaves at front and back from an 11th-century liturgical MS in Caroline minuscule, possibly from the same MS as the cover; spine defective at foot, remains of tawed leather ties; in a late 19th-century folding box of half tan calf and marbled boards. Old scored MS ownership notations and cipher "MS" on a2-3; illegible large MS cipher on fore-edge; some later MS marginalia. From the library of Edmund McClure, with his bookplate. No. 426 in the Christie's South Kensington sale catalogue, 18 November 2003 (unnamed, but library of Percy Barnevik). Blank leaves not present.

HC 2003*; Pr 4956; BMC 5:402 (IA.22643); Pell 1514; Polain 4081; GW 3004; IGI 1036; Goff A-1316; CIBN A-757; BSB-Ink A-922.

10 December 2003 – Bought with the Bayard Livingston Kilgour & Kate Gray Kilgour fund. Inc 4956

PRINTER OF CAVICEUS

S1-2192.8   **Caviceus, Jacobus:** Sex urbium dicta ad Maximilianum Romanorum regem. After 16 March 1491.

4°. [6] leaves (6 blank); 214 x 145 mm.

This copy varies from the transcriptions given by BMC and GW: the text incipit on a1r has the reading "parmnem" instead of the correct "parmen".

Without rubrication. Modern blue boards. No. 463 in the Christie's

South Kensington sale catalogue, 18 November 2003 (unnamed, but library of Percy Barnevik).

HC 4805*; Pr 7374 (Italian adespota); BMC 7:1146 (IA.25002); Pell 3455; GW 6433; Goff C-355; Sack 960; BSB-Ink C-204.

10 December 2003 – Bought with the Bayard Livingston Kilgour & Kate Gray Kilgour fund. Inc 5693.5

GUILLELMUS ANIMA MIA, TRIDINENSIS

S1-2199A   **Thomas Aquinas:** Super analytica posteriora et libros de interpretatione Aristotelis. 16 November 1489.

f°. Another copy. 324 x 215 mm.

Initial spaces, most with guide-letters, not filled in; without rubrication. Half vellum and marbled boards. Early MS annotations throughout.

6 May 1918 – Bought with the Constantius fund. Inc 5110.10

JOHANNES AND ALBERTINUS RUBEUS VERCELLENSES

S1-2212A   **Imitatio Christi** [Italian]. 22 March 1488.

4°. Another copy. 208 x 153 mm.

This imperfect copy, wanting the all-important colophon leaf, has caused some bibliographical mischief. When first acquired, it was identified as possibly a copy of Hain 9132, the edition published Venice: Simon Bevilaqua, 30 August 1497. The misidentification is understandable, as the Bevilaqua edition is virtually a page-for-page reprint of Rubeus's edition. The error was codified by Margaret Stillwell in *Incunabula in American Libraries: A Second Census* (New York, 1940), where this copy was dignified as the only American holding of I-50; Goff perpetuated the error in his *Third Census* (New York, 1960), the entry now renumbered as I-54 (still the only American copy). Walsh accordingly described this copy (see 2530) as a Bevilaqua edition. However, he discovered that a copy in the Royal Library at The Hague, with colophon identifiying it as the 30 August 1497 Bevilaqua edition, clearly was not the same edition as that held by Harvard. Pending further investigation, Walsh tentatively concluded that "[t]here are two Bevilaqua editions with the same date." This conclusion was accepted by ISTC, which created a new record (ii00054050) for the Royal Library copy. However, side-by-side comparison of Walsh 2530 with Walsh 2212 (a perfect copy, with colophon leaf k6) proves that they belong to the same edition. To summarize: Walsh 2530 is in fact Goff I-45, not I-54 (for which there now is no copy in America); ISTC record no. ii00054050 should be cancelled and the Royal Library copy returned to no. ii00054000.

Initials added in red or blue. 19th-century marbled boards. Imperfect: leaf k6, containing the colophon, wanting.

22 November 1921 – W.A. Copinger Imitatio Christi Collection, presented by James Byrne. Inc 5124 (B)

(S1-2229a) **Pseudo-Alexander Aphrodisiensis:** Problemata. 26 May 1501.

f°. lxxxii leaves (xix, xxviii, xxxiiii, l misnumbered ix, xviii, xliiii, and lxx); 315 x 210 mm.

Edited by Johannes Calphurnius. Latin translation by Georgius Valla. Includes Pseudo-Aristoteles, *Problemata* (Latin translation of Theodorus Gaza), and Plutarchus, *Problemata* (Latin translation of Johannes Petri Lucensis). The copy described by GW lacks the colophon leaf.

Without rubrication. Half 16th-century blind-stamped pigskin and wooden boards; brass clasp plates on back cover, latches on front, clasps with pigskin thongs. Bound with Strabo's *Geographia* (Venice: Johannes Rubeus Vercellensis, 28 January 1494/95; Walsh 2225). Bookplate of the Bibliotheca Lindesiana (described in the printed catalogue of 1910, vol. 1, col. 136).

Isaac 12384; Pell 438; GW 861; Goff A-387a; CIBN 1:48; Ballard 92.

1948 – Gift of Harrison D. Horblit. Inc 5139.5

(S1-2229b) — Another copy. 299 x 210 mm.

Without rubrication. Buff boards (rebacked). Imperfect: leaves a1, n4 wanting.

Countway Library

(S1-2229c) **Sabellicus, Marcus Antonius:** Opera. 24 December 1502.

f°. 136 (i.e. 138); [72] leaves; 300 x 213 mm.

The first part was assigned by Copinger to Brescia, ca. 1490; the second part has a full imprint.

Initial spaces not filled in; without rubrication. 18th-century vellum. Bookplate of Murray Anthony Potter. Scattered early MS annotations.

C 5196 (I); BL STC(I) p. 188; Polain 3413 (I); IGI 5:3; IBP 4823; Goff S-4.

18 June 1935 – From the library of Murray Anthony Potter. MLs 9.30F*

(S1-2229d) **Claudianus, Claudius:** De raptu Proserpinae. ca. 1505?

f°. [8], LII leaves; 310 x 205 mm.

Includes the commentary of A. Janus Parrhasius. Printer assignment and date from BM STC(I); GW dates this edition to ca. 1510. Printed with Bartholomaeus Rubeus Vercellensis.

Without rubrication. Recent half brown sheep and marbled boards. From the library of Richard Ashhurst Bowie.

CR 1660; R 475; Pr 6091; BM STC(I) p. 186; Pell 3806; GW 6:col. 698; IGI 2:97; Goff C-708; BSB-Ink C-423.

9 November 1908 – Gift of Mrs. E. D. Brandegee. *fOLC.C571A.510

JOHANNES HAMANN

S1-2234.5 **Missale Saresberiense.** 1 September 1494.

f°. [10], CCCXXIIII leaves; ill.

Printed by Hamann for Frederick Egmont and Gerard Barrevelt.

Twenty fragments only, each comprising half of a leaf and measuring ca. 167 x 218 mm., removed from a binding. Included are portions of leaves m5 (CXIII), n2 (CXX), D2 (CCLVIII), D3 (CCLVIIII), D5 (CCLXI), D9 (CCLXV), and D10 (CCLXVI). The two fragments of leaf n2 include, on the recto, a large (93 x 78 mm) red-printed woodcut historiated initial T and most of the full-page woodcut border (cf. Essling, *Les livres à figures vénitiens de la fin du Xve. siècle et du commencement du XVIe.* (Florence, 1907-14), t. 3, pt. 3, p. 189 and p. 8 at end; the border is also reproduced on the cover and title page to each volume and part). The text of n2 (beginning of the *Canon Missae*) is set in a large title font (ca. 270 mm. per 20 lines) identical to that used by the Venetian printers Matteo Capcasa (11:270G) and Paganinus, Jacobus and Hieronymus de

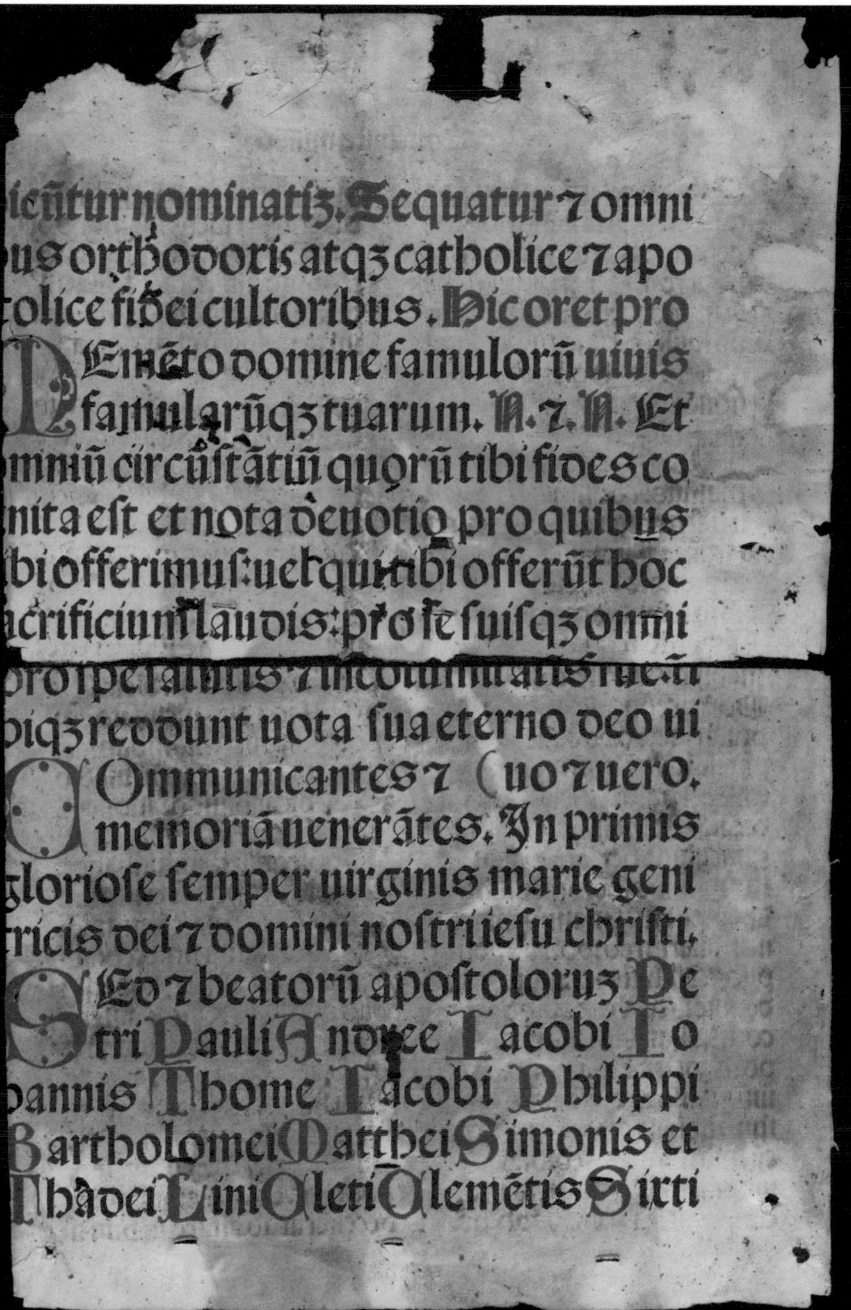

ieūtur nominatiz. Sequatur 7 omni
us orthodoxis atqz catholice 7 apo
tolice fidei cultoribus. Hic oret pro
Emeto domine famuloru uiuis
famularuqz tuarum. N. 7. N. Et
mniu circustatiu quoru tibi fides co
nita est et nota denotio pro quibus
bi offerimus: uel qui tibi offerut hoc
acrificium laudis: pro se suisqz onmi
pro spe salutis 7 incolumitatis sue: ti
biqz reddunt uota sua eterno deo ui
Ommunicantes 7 (uo 7 uero.
memoriā uenerātes. In primis
gloriose semper uirginis marie geni
ricis dei 7 domini nostri iesu christi.
Et 7 beatoru apostoloruz Pe
tri Pauli Andree Iacobi Io
annis Thome Iacobi Philippi
Bartholomei Matthei Simonis et
Thadei Lini Cleti Clemētis Sixti

Figure 6. S1-2234.5: *Missale Saresberiense* (Venice: Johannes Hamann, 1 September 1494). Two fragments of leaf n2 verso displaying type 270G. (Inc 5194, Houghton Library, Harvard College Library)

Paganinis (11:270G). This font, however, apparently is not noted in any published description of this edition, nor is it listed by BMC (5:422-23) among the types employed by Hamann. Woodcut and Lombard initials, rubrics, music staves, and headlines printed in red; woodcut border uncolored. Stains, worming, and other defects, with minor text loss. In a case.

H 11422; Pr 5194; BMC 5:426 (IB.23371); IGI 6651; Weale-Bohatta 1390; Duff 324; STC 16167; Sander 4836.

29 March 1918 – Bought with the Charles Eliot Norton fund. Inc 5194

BONETUS LOCATELLUS

S1-2268.7   **Augustinus, Aurelius, Saint:** De civitate Dei. 9 February 1486/87.

4°. [208] leaves (208 blank); 236 x 175 mm.

Initial spaces, with guide-letters, not filled in; without rubrication. Contemporary blind-stamped brown goatskin over reverse-bevelled beech boards; four brass clasp plates on front cover (two along fore-edge, one each at top and bottom center), four brass latches on back cover, clasp with leather thong preserved at top. Inserted at front and back are two vellum leaves of a 13th- or 14th-century Latin MS.

H 2055*; C 758; BMC 5:436 (IA.22821); Pell 1553; GW 2882; IGI 974; Goff A-1238; BSB-Ink A-860.

1 January 1991 – Gift of David P. Wheatland. Inc 5014.5

PAGANINUS DE PAGANINIS

S1-2359A   **Biblia Latina.** 18 April 1495.

f°. A single leaf only. 354 x 246 mm.

In: Otto F. Ege, *Original Leaves from Famous Bibles: Nine Centuries, 1121-1935 A.D.: Sixty Leaves ...* ([New York: Philip C. Duschnes, 1938]).

The leaf is 3y7 (leaf 461), containing Psalm 44. Without rubrication. Tan buckram portfolio; the leaf is matted and laid in.

April 1965 – Gift of William Bentinck-Smith. B 4406.657.2PF*

S1-2359B — Single leaf only. 354 x 246 mm.

In: Otto F. Ege, *Original Leaves from Famous Bibles: Nine Centuries, 1121-1935 A.D.* ([New York: Philip C. Duschnes, 1945?]).

The leaf is A3 (leaf 497), containing Psalms 79-80. Without rubrication. Rust buckram portfolio; the leaf is matted and laid in.

December 1967 – Gift of Paul Gerard Ecker. Typ 970.45.2100PF

PHILIPPUS PINCIUS

(S1-2473a) **Galenus:** De affectorum locorum notitia. ca. 1520.

a1r, TITLE: GALENI DE AFFE || CTORVM LOCO || RVM NOTITIA || LIBRI · VI · || Guilielmo Copo || Bafileienfi in/ || terprete. || [cross] || a1v: ¶INDEX CAPITVM PRESENTIS OPERIS || … a2r: ¶Galeni de affectorum locorum notitia liber primus Guilielmo Copo Bafileienfi interprete. || (a⁹)On folum recentiores medici, … || … f5v, line 37: fine: orationi quoq[ue] noftræ hic finem imponimus. || ¶Galeni de affectorum || locorum notitia || Finis. || f6r-v blank.

f°. a-c⁶ d-e⁸ f⁶; XXXIX, [1] leaves ([1] blank); 292 x 205 mm. a3r: 61 lines and headline, 256 x 155 mm.; c2r: 58 lines and headline, 253 x 157 mm. Types: 13 mm. roman title font, title and some initials; 136G, title; 84R, text on a2r-c1v; 85R, text on c2r-f5v; 52R, marginal notes on c2v-f5v. Woodcut white-on-black criblé initials on d1r and d8r, woodcut initial on e7r; initial spaces, with guide-letters.

Latin translation by Guilielmus Copus. For dating and printer assignment, see BM STC(I) Suppl.

Initial spaces not filled in; without rubrication. Olive boards. Extensive contemporary MS marginalia in Latin. Inscription cut from title page; partly illegible rectangular red stamp in lower margin of title page, "Bibliotheca W[?]".

H 7428?; Isaac 14068; BM STC(I) p. 287 & Suppl. p. 4; GW 9:col. 261; Goff G-39.

Countway Library

MANFREDUS DE BONELLIS

S1-2482A **Aesopus:** Fabulae [Metrical version "Aesopus moralisatus") by

Anonymus Neveleti (Gualtherus Anglicus?)]. 17 August 1493.

4°. Another copy; ill.; 197 x 147 mm.

Edited, with additions, by Accio Zucco.

A fragment consisting of eight leaves only: a8, b1, 2, 4, 5, 7, 8, c7. Initial spaces, with guide-letters, not filled in; some of the woodcuts have contemporary hand-coloring in red (largely washed away) and green. Disbound; in a case.

9 November 1984 – Bequest of Philip Hofer. Typ Inc 5361.5

SIMON BEVILACQUA
(SECOND PRESS)

S1-2508.5 **Petrus Mantuanus:** Logica. 1 December 1492.

4°. [130] leaves; 214 x 160 mm.

Edited by Johannes Maria Mapellus. Includes Apollinaris Offredus, *De primo et ultimo instanti ad defensionem communis opinionis adversus Petrum Mantuanum.*

Initial spaces not filled in; without rubrication. 18th-century half brown mottled sheep and paste paper boards. Early MS title on bottom edges, "logica petri mantuani". A few contemporary MS marginalia. Early 19th-century bookplate partly removed from front pastedown. No. 538 in the Christie's South Kensington sale catalogue, 18 November 2003 (unnamed, but library of Percy Barnevik).

CR 4725; Polain 4650; IGI 7660; Goff P-501.

29 January 2004 – Bought with the Bayard Livingston Kilgour & Kate Gray Kilgour fund. Inc 5380.5

(S1-2544a) **Petrarca, Francesco:** Bucolicum carmen. 1503.

[For transcriptions see Reichling; but this copy has "buccolico" on A2r.] f°. A-E⁶; [30] leaves; 310 x 209 mm. A2r: 61 lines commentary and headline surrounding text, 251 x 170 mm. Types: 14:104G, title; 16:112[A]R, text; 18:80[B]R, commentary, headlines. Initial spaces, with guide-letters.

Includes the commentary of Benvenutus Imolensis. This edition is undated; but because it is often found (as here) with Bevilacqua's 15 July

David R. Whitesell 79

1503 edition of Petrarca's *Opera*, it is presumed to date from the same year.

Initial spaces not filled in; without rubrication. Contemporary brown calf over reverse-bevelled wooden boards, rebacked; covers blind-tooled to a panel design, with gilt-tooled rosettes and title on front cover, remains of leather thongs nailed to back cover, brass latches on front cover; title in ink on top edges. MS inscriptions on title page, "15.09 Martini Lampeu[?] sum de [?]" at top, and "possessor est M. Sebastianus Sl[?] Canon. Wratl. 1548." at foot, also two effaced inscriptions; MS inscriptions on front pastedown, "Opitz Liegnitii 1779", "Oelsner. Vratisl. 1793", and "C.E. Norton. Cambridge, Mass. 1879". With this is bound the same printer's edition of Petrarca's *Opera* (15 July 1503).

HCR 12829; BM STC(I) p. 502; IGI 4:243; Goff P-370.

4 May 1905 – From the library of Charles Eliot Norton. *fIC.P447.B503l

BERNARDINUS VENETUS, DE VITALIBUS

(S1-2626e)   **Harmonius Marsus, Joannes:** Comoedia Stephanium. ca. 1503.

[For transcriptions see Reichling.] 4°. a-e⁴ f²; [22] leaves; 203 x 148 mm. a1v: 29 lines, 162 x 105 mm. Type: 3:111R. Woodcut initials on a2r, a3v; initial spaces.

For dating see BM STC(I).

Initial spaces not filled in; without rubrication. Recent half olive cloth and marbled boards, preserving old plain paper wrappers backed with gray paper. Some contemporary (non-authorial?) MS marginalia (cropped) and textual corrections. On the title page is a 12-line presentation inscription (cropped) from Harmonius Marsus to Philippus [?]. From the library of Richard Heber, with the "Bibliotheca Heberiana" stamp inside rear wrapper (no. 4595 in pt. 1 of the Sotheby sale catalogue of Heber's library, April 1834); later in the Britwell Court Library, with pencil note on front wrapper, "Britwell" (no. 544 in the Sotheby sale catalogue of books from the Christie-Miller library, July 1917).

R 933; Isaac 12738; BM STC(I) p. 323; IGI 4:44; Goff H-5.

29 March 1918 – Bought with the George Francis Parkman fund. *IC5. Ar555.503s

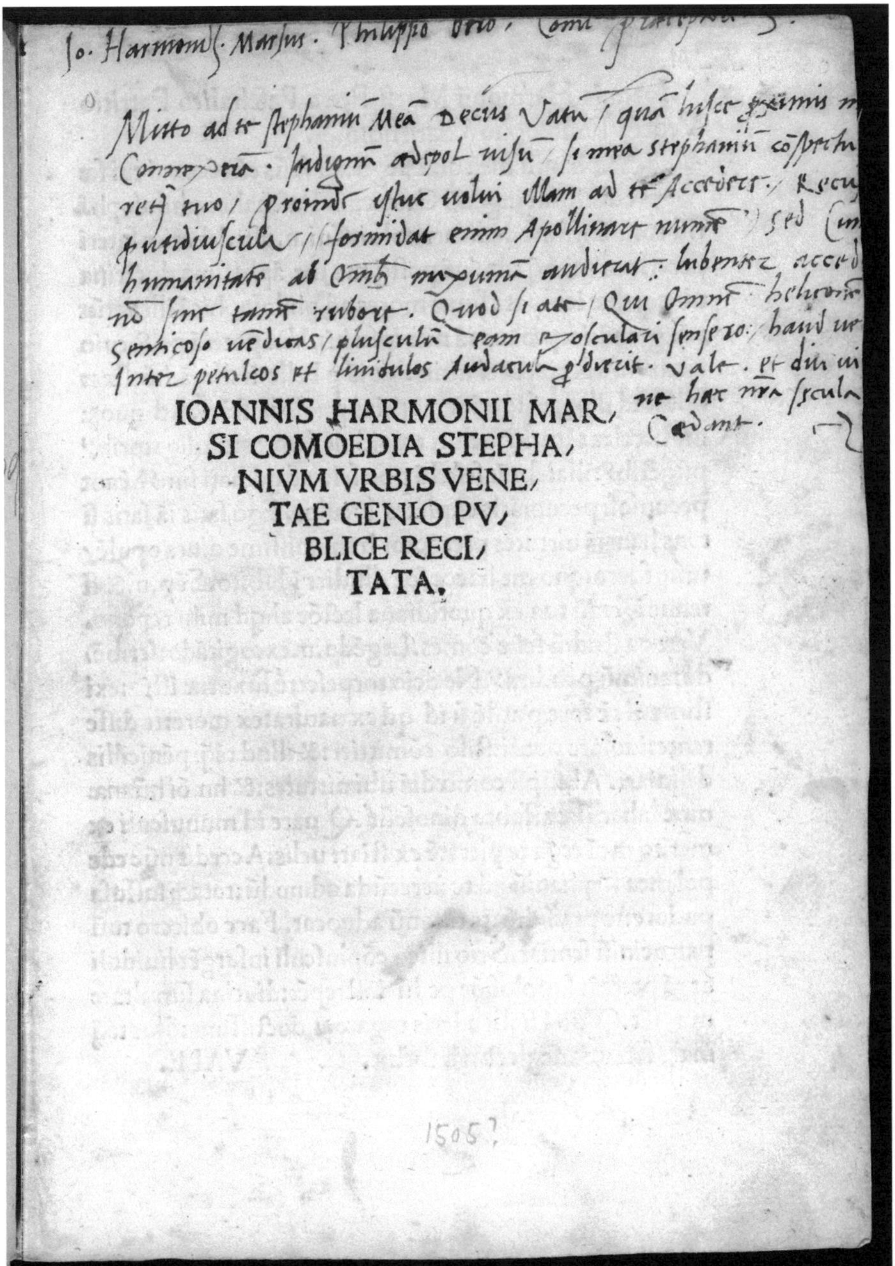

Jo. Harmoni̅ · Marsus · Philippo Deo, (omi̅ ...)

Mitto ad te stephaniu̅ mea̅ Decius Vata̅ / qua̅ hi̅s pri̅mis m Conn̅a̅si̅ta · Indigni̅ adspot nisu / si m̅ra stephaniu̅ co̅spechu re̅ tuo / proind̅ estuc uolui illam ad tt accersere / Recu futidiuscul̅ / sformidat enim Apollinare num̅) sed (m humanitate ab (omt̅) m̅opua̅ audirat : Inbenez accedi no sin̅e tame̅ rubore. Quod si ar̅ / Qui omne̅ helucro̅ senticoso uedicas / pinscula̅ eam osculari sense to. haud u Inter periuleos et limitulos Audacul̅ qi̅drecit. vale. et diu ui

ne hac n̅ra scula Cede̅nt.

IOANNIS HARMONII MAR,
SI COMOEDIA STEPHA,
NIVM VRBIS VENE,
TAE GENIO PV,
BLICE RECI,
TATA,

1505?

Figure 7. (S1-2626e): JOANNES HARMONIUS MARSUS *Comoedia Stephanium*
(Venice: Bernardinus Venetus, de Vitalibus, ca. 1503). Leaf a1 recto with author's presentation inscription.
(*IC5.Ar555.503s, Houghton Library, Harvard College Library)

ALDUS MANUTIUS, ROMANUS

S1-2645B **Theophrastus:** De historia plantarum [Greek]. 1 June 1497.

f°. A single leaf only. 301 x 201 mm.

In: Nicolas Barker, *Aldus Manutius and the Development of Greek Script & Type in the Fifteenth Century: With Original Leaves from the First Aldine Editions of Aristotle, 1497; Crastonus' Dictionarium Graecum, 1497; Euripides, 1503; and the Septuagint, 1518* (Sandy Hook, Conn.: Chiswick Book Shop, 1985).

The leaf is pppooo2 (fol. 114 (1st count)). Without rubrication. One of 200 copies. Original red cloth, in red cloth slipcase; the leaf is tipped in at end.

13 November 1985 – Bought with the Douglas W. Bryant fund. TypTS 970.85.194F

S1-2645C — Another copy. 300 x 200 mm.

In: Nicolas Barker, *Aldus Manutius and the Development of Greek Script & Type in the Fifteenth Century …* (Sandy Hook, Conn.: Chiswick Book Shop, 1985).

The leaf is eeeεεε3 (fol. 35 (1st count)). Without rubrication. One of 200 copies. Original red cloth, in red cloth slipcase; the leaf is tipped in at end.

Dumbarton Oaks Byzantine Library

S1-2645D — Another copy. 301 x 198 mm.

In: Nicolas Barker, *Aldus Manutius and the Development of Greek Script & Type in the Fifteenth Century …* (Sandy Hook, Conn.: Chiswick Book Shop, 1985).

The leaf is ααα6 (fol. 198 (1st count)). Without rubrication. One of 200 copies. Original red cloth, in red cloth slipcase; the leaf is tipped in at end.

Berenson Library, I Tatti

S1-2657A **Crastonus, Johannes:** Lexicon Graeco-Latinum. December 1497.

f°. A single leaf only. 295 x 214 mm.

In: Nicolas Barker, *Aldus Manutius and the Development of Greek Script & Type in the Fifteenth Century: With Original Leaves from the First Aldine Editions of Aristotle, 1497; Crastonus' Dictionarium Graecum, 1497; Euripides, 1503; and the Septuagint, 1518* (Sandy Hook, Conn.: Chiswick Book Shop, 1985).

The leaf is k8. Without rubrication. One of 200 copies. Original red cloth, in red cloth slipcase; the leaf is tipped in at end.

13 November 1985 – Bought with the Douglas W. Bryant fund. TypTS 970.85.194F

S1-2657B   — Another copy. 294 x 212 mm.

In: Nicolas Barker, *Aldus Manutius and the Development of Greek Script & Type in the Fifteenth Century ...* (Sandy Hook, Conn.: Chiswick Book Shop, 1985).

The leaf is c7. Without rubrication. One of 200 copies. Original red cloth, in red cloth slipcase; the leaf is tipped in at end.

Dumbarton Oaks Byzantine Library

S1-2657C   — Another copy. 295 x 213 mm.

In: Nicolas Barker, *Aldus Manutius and the Development of Greek Script & Type in the Fifteenth Century ...* (Sandy Hook, Conn.: Chiswick Book Shop, 1985).

The leaf is I6. Without rubrication. One of 200 copies. Original red cloth, in red cloth slipcase; the leaf is tipped in at end.

Berenson Library, I Tatti

S1-2686A   **Columna, Franciscus:** Hypnerotomachia Poliphili. December 1499.

f°. A single leaf only; ill.; 294 x 202 mm.

In: Theodore Low De Vinne, *Aldus Pius Manutius* (San Francisco: The Book Club of California, 1924).

The leaf is g6; with mimeographed slip describing the illustration on g6r. Woodcut uncolored; without rubrication. Copy no. 26 of 250 copies. Original half black cloth and decorated boards, printed label on front cover; the leaf is mounted on a stub following p. [6]. Booklabel of Joseph Halle Schaffner.

November 1972 – Bequest of Joseph Halle Schaffner. B 4452.322F*

JACOBUS PENTIUS, DE LEUCO

(S1-2702b)   **Persius Flaccus, Aulus:** Satirae. After 30 January 1501.

[For transcriptions see Reichling; but this copy has "Tabulā." instead of "Tabula." on leaf 25₆.] 4°. [1-24⁴ 25⁶]; 102 leaves; 193 x 145 mm. 1ᵣr: 39 lines of commentary and headline surrounding text, 170 x 122 mm. Types: 8:135G, title; 6:105R, text; 10:84R, commentary; 11:68G, commentary; some passages in Greek. Woodcut initials; initial spaces, with guide-letters.

Includes the commentary of Scipio Ferrarius. The privilege for this book was issued on 30 January 1501; cf. Rinaldo Fulin, "Documenti per servire alla storia della tipografia veneziana," *Archivio veneto* 23 (1882): 143, no. 109. Printer assignment from BM STC(I).

Initial spaces not filled in; without rubrication. Recent vellum. Bookplate of Morris H. Morgan.

R 671; BM STC(I) Suppl. p. 63; IGI 4:236; Goff P-352; Morgan (Persius) 56.

1 January 1910 – Gift of Morris H. Morgan. *OLC.P431.501b (A)

(S1-2702c)   — Another copy. 208 x 155 mm.

This copy has "Tabulā." instead of "Tabula." on leaf 25₆. Initial spaces not filled in; without rubrication. Old vellum; MS title written on bottom edges. From the library of Richard Ashhurst Bowie.

9 November 1908 – Gift of Mrs. E. D. Brandegee. *OLC.P431.501b (B)

GEORGIUS DE RUSCONIBUS

(S1-2750a)   **Portis, Leonardus de:** De sestertio pecuniis ponderibus et mensuris antiquis libri duo. ca. 1520.

A1r, TITLE: LEONARDI || DE PORTIS IVRISCONSVLTI VI ||

CENTINI DE SESTERTIO PE ‖ CVNIIS PONDERIBVS ET ‖ MENSVRIS ANTIQVIS ‖ LIBRI DVO. ‖ A2r: EGNATIVS LECTORI. ‖ (N³)IHIL Erat in oīl̄raria re noſtrati p[er]plexu[m] inno= ‖ lutũue magis: … ‖ … A3r: LEONARDI DE PORTIS IVRISCON= ‖ ſulti Vicentini de Seſtertio Pecuniis ponderibus ‖ & menſuris Antiquis, Liber Primus. ‖ (C¹⁰)OMMERCIA RERVM ‖ permutãdo cuiq[ue] ſuperflua & ne ‖ ceſſaria: … ‖ … I3v, line 3: quæ tamen & ipſa aliquãdo fortaſſe edentur ſi vita & otium ‖ ſuppetat. ‖ FINIS. ‖ Quæ abſente auctore librario[rum] in curia corrupta ſunt ſic corrigito. ‖ … I4v blank.

4°. A-I⁴; [36] leaves; 195 x 135 mm. A4r: 30 lines, 151 x 101 mm. Types: 240R (approx.), title; 100R, title and text; 72R, errata. Woodcut initials; woodcut diagram on I1r.

Edited by Giovanni Battista Cipelli. For dating and printer assignment, see BM STC(I).

Without rubrication. 19th-century half mottled sheep and decorated boards.

Isaac 13095; BM STC(I) p. 536; Goff P-943.

18 August 1966 – Received. Kress Library

DONINUS PINCIUS

(S1-2751a) **Hieronymus, Saint:** Epistolae. After 1500.

f°. [6], 390 (i.e. 392) leaves (323-324 repeated; 25, 71, 96, 139, 163, 186, 240, 298, 316, 334, 366, 390 misnumbered 52, 72, 69, 136, 263, 189, 220, 898, 315, 349, 266, and 903); 294 x 208 mm.

Includes Lupo de Olmeto's *Regula monachorum ex epistolis Hieronymi excerpta*. Printer assignment and date from Goff; this edition has also been assigned to Philippus Pincius.

Initial spaces not filled in; without rubrication. Contemporary limp vellum.

H 8564*; Polain 4436; GW 11:col. 56; IGI 4744; Goff H-177; Sack 1841; BSB-Ink H-256.

31 March 1931 – Received by exchange with the Newberry Library. *fMLC.H5325E.1505

NICOLÒ BRENTA

(S1-2751b) **Landinus, Christophorus:** Disputationum Camaldulensium libri IV. ca. 1507.

f°. [72] leaves; 295 x 205 mm.

Includes *De vita activa et contemplativa*, *De summo bono*, and *Allegoriae in Vergilium*. For printer assignment and dating see BM STC(I); IGI assigns this edition to Simon Bevilacqua.

Without rubrication. 19th-century sheep antique.

HCR 9851; Pr 5716; BMC 7:1209 (G.8972); BM STC(I) p. 368; IGI 3:217; Goff L-36; CIBN 2:153; BSB-Ink L-46.

31 March 1931 – Received by exchange with the Newberry Library. *fIC. L2346.481qb

Florence

NICOLAUS LAURENTII

S1-2854A **Dante Alighieri:** La Commedia. 30 August 1481.

f°. A single leaf only; ill.; 334 x 232 mm.

The leaf is b1, with the engraving for canto two of the *Inferno* on verso. Without rubrication.

9 November 1984 – Bequest of Philip Hofer. bTyp Inc 6120

BARTOLOMMEO DI LIBRI

S1-2915A **Savonarola, Hieronymus:** Dell'amore di Gesù. Before September 1495.

4°. A single leaf only; ill.; 177 x 127 mm.

The leaf is a1 (title page with woodcut). Without rubrication. Hinged to a sheet of white paper.

9 November 1984 – Bequest of Philip Hofer. bTyp Inc 6292

LORENZO MORGIANI,
IN PART WITH JOHANNES PETRI

S1-2998A   **Antoninus Florentinus:** Confessionale "Curam illius habe" [Italian]. 23 May 1493.

4°. A single leaf only; ill.; 208 x 138 mm.

The leaf is l4, containing the colophon on recto and woodcut on verso. Without rubrication.

9 November 1984 – Bequest of Philip Hofer. bTyp Inc 6355

ANTONIO TUBINI,
LORENZO DE ALOPA,
AND ANDREA GHIRLANDI

(S1-3033a)   **Savonarola, Hieronymus:** Expositio Orationis Dominicae [Italian] After 1500.

4°. [20] leaves; ill.; 214 x 143 mm.

Printer assignment from Goff; publication date from ISTC. BMC dates this edition to ca. 1510 and assigns it to Gian Stephano de Carlo. In this copy, the outer forme of sheet a3.4.5.6 has been misimposed, with the text of a4v misplaced on a5r, and a5r misplaced on a4v; line 1 of a4v begins, "facta quefta …".

Without rubrication. Modern gray wrappers.

C 5298; R 725; Pr 6428; BMC 7:1209 (C.70.e.18); BM STC(I) p. 393; IGI 5:41; Goff S-202; CIBN 2:549; Sander 6782; Kristeller 384c; ISTC is00202000.

17 May 1921 – From the Savonarola collection formed by Henry R. Newman. Bought with the Edward Henry Hall fund. *IC.Sa950E8. Ei510

(S1-3033b)   — Another copy. 194 x 140 mm.

In this copy, the outer forme of sheet a3.4.5.6 has been misimposed, with the text of a4v misplaced on a5r, and a5r misplaced on a4v; line 1 of a4v begins, "facta quefta …".

Without rubrication. Half modern dark brown morocco and brown cloth. With this is bound Savonarola's *Expositio in psalmum LXXIX: Qui regis Israel* [Italian] (Florence: Bartolommeo di Libri, ca. 1495).

17 May 1921 – From the Savonarola collection formed by Henry R. Newman. Bought with the Duplicate fund. Inc 6302

(S1-3033c)   — Another copy. 201 x 140 mm.

In this copy, bifolium a4.5 has been cancelled and replaced by a corrected bifolium with the text of a4r-5v completely reset and a4v-5r properly imposed; line 1 of a4v begins, "Dice adunche: ...".

Without rubrication. Modern gray wrappers.

17 May 1921 – From the Savonarola collection formed by Henry R. Newman. Bought with the Duplicate fund. *IC.Sa950E8.Ei510a

(S1-3033d)   **Savonarola, Hieronymus:** Expositio Orationis Dominicae. ca. 1505.

4°. [20] leaves; 206 x 134 mm.

Printer assignment from Goff; publication date from BMC. Rhodes dates this edition to ca. 1500.

Without rubrication. 19th-century half green sheep and marbled boards.

HR 14444; Pr 6427; BMC 7:1209 (845.e.29); BM STC(I) p. 393; IGI 5:41; Goff S-198; Rhodes (F) App. II, 38.

17 May 1921 – From the Savonarola collection formed by Henry R. Newman. Bought with the Edward Henry Hall fund. *IC.Sa950E8.1505

PRINTER OF PSEUDO-SAVONAROLA, *ESPOSIZIONE SOPRA IL SALMO VERBA MEA* (H 14410)

(S1-3033e)   **Pseudo-Savonarola:** Esposizione sopra il salmo Verba mea. ca. 1500.

4°. [10] leaves; 200 x 137 mm.

Variously attributed to Simone Cinozzi or Placido Cinozzi; see G. Cesare Olschki, "Un codice savonaroliano sconosciuto," *La Bibliofilia* 23 (1921): 152-65. For the printer assignment and date see ISTC.

Without rubrication. Contemporary MS inscription at top of a1r, "F. Simone Cinozi". Half modern black morocco and red cloth.

HCR 14410=H 14409?; Pr 6453 (unassigned); BMC 7:1209 (3905.dd.120); BM STC(I) p. 100; IGI 6:131; Goff S-203; CIBN S-151; Rhodes (F) 637.

17 May 1921 – From the Savonarola collection formed by Henry R. Newman. Bought with the Duplicate fund. *IC.Sa950.Az510e

(S1-3033f)   **Savonarola, Hieronymus:** Predica della renovatione della chiesa, fatta a di 13 di gennaio 1494. ca. 1500.

4°. [10] leaves; 208 x 134 mm.

For the printer assignment and date see CIBN.

Without rubrication. Modern gray boards.

HC(Add)R 14386; Pr 6452 (unassigned); BMC 7:1209 (3905.dd.117); BM STC(I) p. 614; IGI 8751; Goff S-242; CIBN S-119; BSB-Ink (S-160).

17 May 1921 – From the Savonarola collection formed by Henry R. Newman. Bought with the Edward Henry Hall fund. *IC.Sa950P.1505f

(S1-3033g)   **Savonarola, Hieronymus:** Predica fatta addì 18 di marzo 1497/8. ca. 1500.

[For transcriptions see Reichling; but this copy has "di" instead of "die" in line 2 of a1r.] 4°. a-b⁸; [16] leaves (16 blank); 202 x 134 mm. a4r: 37 lines, 165 x 92 mm. Type: 89R. Lombard initial on a1r.

For the printer assignment and date see BSB-Ink.

Without rubrication. Half modern brown calf and marbled boards. Blank leaf not present.

HC(Add)R 14397; Pr 6451 (unassigned); BMC 7:1209 (3905.dd.119); BM STC(I) p. 614; Isaac 13495; IGI 8765; Goff S-258; BSB-Ink (S-158); Rhodes (F) 673.

June 1963 – Bought with the Bennett Hubbard Nash fund. *IC. Sa950P.1505b

GIAN STEPHANO DI CARLO

(S1-3033h)   **Savonarola, Hieronymus:** Dell'amore di Gesù. ca. 1505?

4°. [22] leaves; ill.; 187 x 127 mm.

For the printer assignment and date see BM STC(I). Goff assigns this edition to Bartolommeo di Libri. Rhodes dates this edition to ca. 1500, without printer attribution.

Without rubrication. Modern stiff vellum, in a brown cloth slipcase. Gilt leather booklabel of Carl J. Ulmann; printed exhibition label pasted in, with added MS note attesting that this copy was loaned by Ulmann for display in "The Arts of the Book" exhibition at the Metropolitan Museum of Art, New York, May-September 1924.

H[not C] 14348*; Pr 6448 (unassigned); BMC 7:1209 (3832.df.13); BM STC(I) p. 612; IGI 8787; Goff S-172; CIBN 2:543; BSB-Ink (S-152); Rhodes (F) 693; Sander 6854; Kristeller 374e.

21 November 1952 – Gift of Harrison D. Horblit. Typ 525.10.771 (A)

(S1-3033i)   — Another copy. 212 x 140 mm.

Without rubrication. 19th century half brown calf and marbled boards. Imperfect: leaves c5-6 wanting; c1-2 remargined.

17 May 1921 – From the Savonarola collection formed by Henry R. Newman. Bought with the Edward Henry Hall fund. Typ 525.10.771 (B)

(S1-3033j)   **Savonarola, Hieronymus:** Dell'umiltà. ca. 1505?

[For transcriptions see Sander; Reichling omits a line division on a1r between "delli" and "predicatori".] 4°. a10; [10] leaves; ill.; 207 x 135 mm. a2r: 38 lines, 166 x 103 mm. Type: 87R. Woodcuts; woodcut initial on a1r; Lombards.

For the printer assignment and date see BM STC(I). Neither assigned nor dated by Goff.

Without rubrication. Red cloth.

HCR 14375; Pr 6447 (unassigned); BMC 7:1209 (3832.df.12); BM STC(I) p. 612; IGI 5:54; Goff S-281; CIBN 2:555; BSB-Ink (S-170); Rhodes (F) App. II, 40; Sander 6868; Kristeller 394c.

17 May 1921 – From the Savonarola collection formed by Henry R. Newman. Gift of J. P. Morgan. *IC.Sa950U.1505

(S1-3033k)   **Savonarola, Hieronymus:** Sermone dell'orazione. ca. 1505?

4°. [12] leaves; ill.; 207 x 132 mm.

For the printer assignment and date see BM STC(I). Neither assigned nor dated by Goff.

Without rubrication. Leaves foliated 64-75 in MS. Half modern black morocco and red cloth.

HCR 14403*; Pr 6446 (unassigned); BMC 7:1209 (3832.df.11); BM STC(I) p. 614; IGI 8776; Goff S-269; CIBN 2:553; BSB-Ink (S-166); Rhodes (F) 681; Sander 6837; Kristeller 382d.

17 May 1921 – From the Savonarola collection formed by Henry R. Newman. Bought with the Duplicate fund. *IC.Sa950P.1505e

(S1-3033l)   **Savonarola, Hieronymus:** Sermone sopra la natività. ca. 1505?

4°. [4] leaves; 208 x 139 mm.

In this edition, the caption title on a1r occupies three lines. For the printer assignment and date see BM STC(I). Neither assigned nor dated by Goff.

Without rubrication. Half modern green morocco and green cloth.

HCR 14402; Pr 6444 (unassigned); BMC 7:1209 (3901.ee.41); BM STC(I) p. 614; IGI 5:50; Goff S-263; CIBN 2:553.

17 May 1921 – From the Savonarola collection formed by Henry R. Newman. Bought with the Edward Henry Hall fund. *IC.Sa950P.1505c

(S1-3033m)   **Savonarola, Hieronymus:** Sermone sopra la natività. ca. 1505?

4°. [4] leaves; 201 x 140 mm.

In this edition, the caption title on a1r occupies four lines. For the printer assignment and date see BM STC(I). Neither assigned nor dated by Goff.

Without rubrication. Half modern red morocco and red cloth.

R 1383; Pr 6445 (unassigned); BMC 7:1209 (3901.ee.40); BM STC(I) p. 614;

IGI 5:50; Goff S-264; CIBN 2:553; BSB-Ink (S-167).

17 May 1921 – From the Savonarola collection formed by Henry R. Newman. Bought with the Edward Henry Hall fund. *IC.Sa950P.1505d

(S1-3033n)   **Nardus, Jacobus:** Comedia di Amicitia. ca. 1510.

[For transcriptions see Hain; but this copy has "FLO || RENTINO" on a3r and "CANTORONO" on c4r.] 4°. a-b⁸ c⁴; [20] leaves; 208 x 135 mm. a5r: 32 lines, 162 x 91 mm. Type: 102R. Initial space, with guide-letter, on a3r.

For the printer assignment and date see Rhodes. Goff assigns this to Lorenzo Morgiani and Johannes Petri and dates it ca. 1496-97.

Initial space, with guide-letter, not filled in; without rubrication. Half 19th-century brown sheep.

H 11673; BM STC(I) p. 461; Goff N-4; Rhodes (F) App. II, 32.

13 February 1937 – Bought with the Bennett Hubbard Nash fund. *IC5. N1663.510c

UNASSIGNED

(S1-3035f)   **Castellani, Castellano de':** Meditatione della morte. After 1500.

[For transcriptions see Sander.] 4°. a⁴; [4] leaves; ill.; 198 x 140 mm. 2 columns. a1v: 40 lines, 174 x 123 mm. Types: ca. 100R, caption title; 87R, text. Devices of Piero Pacini (Kristeller 51 [1-3]); Lombards.

Printed for Piero Pacini. Publication date from Goff.

Without rubrication. Recent half crimson morocco and marbled boards. Ownership stamp of Walter Ashburner in lower margin of leaf a4v. Imperfect: leaves a2-3 wanting; marginal repairs, with loss of a few letters on a1r-v.

Goff C-248; Sander 1777; Kristeller 91a.

April 1956 – Gift of Philip Hofer. Typ 525.10.261

(S1-3035g)   **Pulci, Luca:** Pistole in rima al Lorenzo de' Medici. ca. 1510.

[For transcriptions see Hain; but this copy has "pacini" on e6v.] 4°.

⁋Meditatione della morte cöpofta da Meffer Chaftellano de Ca,
lani cö due laude agiütoci dirietro / et diritta allo Speda,
lingo di fancta Maria nuoua .

⁋Sonetto   Vedete quanto fcherno
Ermate il paffo & rifguardate i fu Siuede hor di coftoro : fiche pêfate
fuperbi che nutrite il cor nel oro miferi chi noi fiamo / & chi uoi fia
guardate qual fö io / ql fö coftoro ⁋Sonetto   (te
quefti potenti & io uil feruo fu ⁋Cb guardi tu lettö ! cötêplo : & cb !
Quâti credon falir che uanno ingiu latua figura / eltuo felice ftato:
lepöpe / elregno / gliftati elthefiro de piangi pouerello il tuo peccato
fö oggi come alfuoco ü ̀ude alloro che ̀pfto ancor farai peggio c b me
che prefto fcoppia & nö fiuede piu Se te in piacere / de dimi chi tu fe !
Gia nufe pouerta tenere ftolto nol uedi : io fono ü corpo lacerato
hö p me fapre ilcielo puoi liferno che fu nel mondo come te creato
cofi fa il fructo chalbuö têpo e/colto uêne lamorte / & nö trouai merze.
Vn felice morire fa lhuomo eterno Ma fe laroza mia bructa figura
ftar feruo ü di p uiuer fêpre fciolto timuoue afofpirar piangi te fteffo
e un fermar laruota i fempiterno perche cofa creata alfin non dura.

                                                      a

Figure 8. (S1-3035f): CASTELLANO DE' CASTELLANI *Meditatione della morte*
(Florence: unassigned, after 1500). Leaf a1 recto.
(Typ 525.10.261, Department of Printing and Graphic Arts, Houghton Library, Harvard College Library)

David R. Whitesell 93

a-d⁸ e⁶; [38] leaves; 203 x 136 mm. a4r: 33 lines, 167 x 75 mm. Type: 101R. Devices of Piero Pacini (Kristeller 48, 51 [1, 3]); woodcuts; woodcut initial on a2r; Lombards.

Printed for Piero Pacini. The publication date is suggested by BM STC(I). Tura assigns the printing to Gianstefano di Carlo, ca. 1505.

Without rubrication. Recent brown diced calf, edges gilt; rebacked. Booklabels of Philip and Frances Hofer.

HC 13570*; Pr 6449; BMC 7:1209 (G.10737); BM STC(I) Suppl. p. 67; IGI 4:342; Goff P-1118; BSB-Ink P-882; Sander 6007; Kristeller 342c; Tura p. 100, no. 76.

24 July 1974 – Gift of Philip Hofer. Typ 525.05.716

Milan

ALEXANDER MINUTIANUS

(S1-3168a) **Picus de Mirandula, Johannes:** Hymni heroici tres cum commento. ca. 1507.

f°. [88] leaves; 278 x 196 mm.

Reichling's collation is incorrect; this edition collates: a-e⁶ f⁴ g-i⁶ K⁶ l-o⁶ p⁴ [q]². In some copies, leaf [q]2v is blank; in others, it bears a privilege, dated 11 September 1507, with imprint beneath, "Mediolani apud Alexandrum Minutianum". See Charles B. Schmitt, "A Note on the First Edition of Gianfrancesco Pico's 'Hymni Heroici Tres,'" *Papers of the Bibliographical Society of America* 59 (1965): 45-48.

This copy has the privilege and imprint on leaf [q]2v. Without rubrication. Old limp vellum, rehinged.

R 679; BM STC(I) p. 515; IGI 4:269; Goff P-641a.

September 1961 – Bought with the S.A.E. Morse fund. *fIC5.P5876.507h

GOTARDUS DA PONTE

(S1-3168b) **Sabellicus, Marcus Antonius:** Decades rerum Venetarum [Italian]. ca. 1510?

π1r, TITLE: [red-printed by letterpress, within white-on-black woodcut floriated border:] CRONICHE CHE TRACTANO DE LA ORI= ‖ GINE DE VENETI. E DEL PRINCIPIO DE ‖ LA CITA. E DE TVTTE LE GVERE DA ‖ MARE E TERRA FACTE IN ITALIA: ‖ DALMACIA: GRECIA: E CONTRA ‖ TVTI LI INFIDELI. COMPOSTE ‖ PER LO EXCELENTISIMO ME ‖ SERE MARCO ANTONIO SA ‖ BELLICO. E VOLGARIZA= ‖ TE PER MATHEO VE= ‖ SCONTE DE SAN= ‖ CTO CANCIANO. ‖ CON GRATIA ‖ ET PREVI ‖ LEGIO. ‖ [cross made from 5 cross types] ‖ π1v: La breue Tabula de quello che ſe contiene ne la preſenta Opera. ‖ … π8v, line 39: uore de Fiorentini. ‖ FINIS. ‖ a1r-v blank ‖ a2r: Matheo Viſconto da. s. Cantiã: a lingenioſo: e nobile Oldrado Lampu= ‖ gnano. Salute: e proſperita. ‖ … a5r: M. ANTONIO SABELLICO DE LORIGINE ‖ E FACTI VENETI DAL PRINCIPIO ‖ DE LA CITA FELICEMEN ‖ TE COMENZA. ‖ … V8r, line 18: Prouedadore Antonio Donato. Finis. ‖ Finiſcono le Deche del Facondiſſimo. M.A. Sabellico. E traducte de Lati= ‖ no in Volgare per Matheo Vesconte de. s. Canciano. Ad Instancia e ‖ Impenſa de Oldrato Lampugnano. Stampate cõ Gratia e Pri ‖ uilegii. … ‖ [cross] ‖ V8v: Mathei Vicecomitis. In funere. M.A.S. Sermocinatio breuis ad Doctos. ‖ … V9r, line 22: luget moderatorem optimum. ‖ Finis. ‖ [device of Gotardus da Ponte] ‖ V9v: REGISTRO DE LA PRESENTE OPERA. ‖ … V10r blank ‖ V10v: [within white-on-black floriated woodcut border, a red-printed woodcut block with text:] Deche De lorigine ‖ de Veneti e del princi ‖ pio de la cita fin a tem ‖ pi n[ost]ri de tute le guere ‖ da mar e terra i[n] Italia ‖ dalmatia grecia & ‖ contra tuti gli i[n]fideli ‖ cõpoſte p[er] lo ex° Me ‖ ſere Marcho Ant° Sa ‖ belico E uulgarizate ‖ per Matheo uiſcõte ‖ de san canzian.

f°. π⁸ a⁸ b-c⁶ d⁴ e-z⁶ [et]⁶ [con]⁶ [rum]⁶ A-C⁶ D⁸ E-T⁶ V¹⁰; [8], CCLXXXIII (i.e. CCLXXXI), [1] leaves (I blank; XXIIII-XXV omitted; XXXI, XCVI, CCXXXVIII misnumbered XXIX, XCVIII, and CCXXXVII); 286 x 210 mm. a6r: 40 lines and headline, 230 x 132 mm. (with side-notes, 230 x 161 mm). Type: 111R. Woodcut border, device, and title block; initial spaces, most with guide-letters.

Italian translation by Matheo Vesconte. Printed by da Ponte for Oldradus Lampugnanus. Dating from Goff.

Initial spaces not filled in; without rubrication. 18ᵗʰ-century mottled calf, edges stained red.

HC 14054; BM STC(I) p. 188; Isaac 13599; IGI 5:3; Goff S-5a; Sander 6650.

29 May 1962 – Gift of Ward M. Canaday. *fIC.Sa133.Ei507v

Bologna

BENEDICTUS HECTORIS FAELLI

(S1-3253a)   **Beroaldus, Philippus:** Declamatio philosophi, medici, oratoris et alia opuscula. After 1500.

[For transcriptions see Hain.] 4°. [1-12⁴]; LXXXXVI leaves (V, VII, XXIII, LXVIIII misnumbered Y, YIIII, XXII, and LXXIIII); 192 x 139 mm. 1,r: 28 lines, 159 x 93 mm. Type: 9:114R; some passages in Greek. Initial spaces.

The foliation is in signature position at the bottom of the page; there are no signatures. For dating and printer assignment see BSB-Ink.

Initial spaces not filled in; without rubrication. Half blue cloth and marbled boards.

H 2961*; GW 4:col. 27; IGI 1:205; Goff B-476; BSB-Ink B-378; Ballard 196.

Countway Library

(S1-3253b)   **Baptista Mantuanus:** Opera. 11 June 1502.

f°. [4], ccclxxxix, [1] leaves (4 and [ccclxxxx] blank; cc-ccxviii misnumbered c-cxviii); 304 x 193 mm.

Hain, describing an imperfect copy, considered this 15th-century printing.

Initial spaces, with guide-letters, not filled in; without rubrication. 18th-century blind-panelled calf. Ownership signature of Ethelbertus Burdetus on title page; autograph of Charles Eliot Norton on front pastedown. The two blank leaves not present.

H 2358; BM STC(I) p. 635; Pell 1758; GW 3:col. 314; Goff B-52.

4 May 1905 – From the library of Charles Eliot Norton. *fIC5.B2296. C5020

(S1-3253c)   **Pythagoras:** Symbola moraliter explicata a Philippo Beroaldo. 24 December 1503.

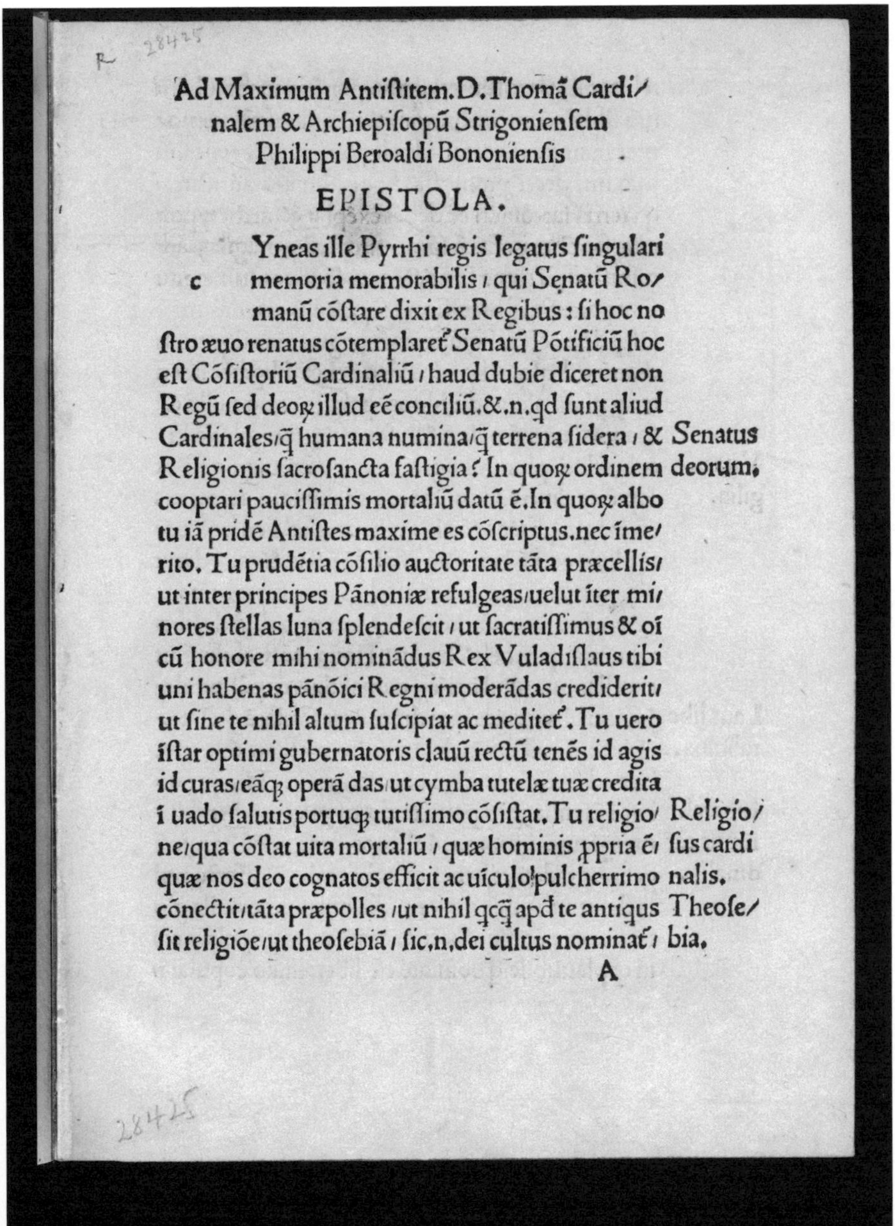

'Ad Maximum Antiftitem. D. Thomã Cardi∕
nalem & Archiepifcopũ Strigonienfem
Philippi Beroaldi Bononienfis

EPISTOLA.

c

Yneas ille Pyrrhi regis legatus fingulari
memoria memorabilis ∕ qui Senatũ Ro∕
manũ cóftare dixit ex Regibus : fi hoc no
ftro æuo renatus cótemplaret Senatũ Pótificiũ hoc
eft Cófiftoriũ Cardinaliũ ∕ haud dubie diceret non
Regũ fed deoȝ illud eé conciliũ.&.n.qd funt aliud
Cardinales∕q̃ humana numina∕q̃ terrena fidera ∕ & **Senatus**
Religionis facrofanǎa faftigia ? In quoȝ ordinem **deorum,**
cooptari pauciffimis mortaliũ datũ é. In quoȝ albo
tu iã pridé Antiftes maxime es cófcriptus. nec íme∕
rito. Tu prudétia cófilio auǎoritate tãta præcellis∕
ut inter principes Pãnoniæ refulgeas∕uelut íter mi∕
nores ftellas luna fplendefcit ∕ ut facratiffimus & oí
cũ honore mihi nominãdus Rex Vuladiflaus tibi
uni habenas pãnóici Regni moderãdas crediderit∕
ut fine te nihil altum fufcipiat ac meditet. Tu uero
iftar optimi gubernatoris clauũ reǎũ tenés id agis
id curas∕eãȝ operã das∕ut cymba tutelæ tuæ credita
i uado falutis portuȝ tutiffimo cófiftat. Tu religio∕ **Religio∕**
ne∕qua cóftat uita mortaliũ ∕ quæ hominis ꝓpria é∕ **fus cardi**
quæ nos deo cognatos efficit ac uiculo∕pulcherrimo **nalis.**
cóneǎit∕tãta præpolles ∕ut nihil qcq̃ apꝺ te antiqus **Theofe∕**
fit religióe∕ut theofebiã ∕ fic.n.dei cultus nominat∕ **bia,**

A

Figure 9. (S1-3253c): PYTHAGORAS *Symbola moraliter explicata a Philippo Beroaldo*
(Bologna: Benedictus Hectoris Faelli, 24 December 1503). Leaf A1 recto.
(*IC.B4584.503s, Houghton Library, Harvard College Library)

Aır: Ad Maximum Antiſtitem. D. Thomã Cardi/ || nalem & Archiepiſcopu[m] Strigonienſem || Philippi Beroaldi Bononienſis || EPISTOLA. || (c³)Yneas ille Pyrrhi regis legatus ſingulari || memoria memorabilis/ ... || A3r: SYMBOLA PYTHAGORAE A || PHILIPPO BEROALDO MO || RALITER EXPLICATA. || (d⁵)VO APVD VETERES || philoſopho[rum] genera fuiſſe tradu[n]tur || ... D4v, COLOPHON: FINIS. || Opuſculu[m] Philippi Beroaldi de Symbolis Pytha || goræ Impreſſum Bononiæ a Benedicto Hecto/ || ris. Anno ſalutis. M.D Tertio. Pridie Dominicu[m] || Natalem. || Regeſtum. ...

4°. A-C⁸ D⁴ [A1-4 signed 'A', 'Ai', 'Aii', 'Aiii']; [28] leaves; 201 x 142 mm. A4r: 27 lines and headline, 157 x 91 mm. Type: 6:112R. Initial spaces, with guide-letters.

Initial spaces not filled in; without rubrication. Recently bound in a vellum fragment from a MS choir book.

H 13624; BM STC(I) p. 89; Goff P-1147.

17 June 1949 – Bought with the George Schünemann Jackson fund. *IC. B4584.503s

(S1-3253d)   — Another copy. 189 x 140 mm.

Initial spaces not filled in; without rubrication. Recent decorated boards.

Countway Library

Verona

JOHANNES NICOLAI DE VERONA

S1-3370A   **Valturius, Robertus:** De re militari. 1472.

f°. A single leaf only; ill.; 315 x 223 mm.

The leaf is 21₂ (recto blank, full-page woodcut of an armed galley on verso). Woodcut uncolored; without rubrication. Trimmed, slightly affecting the woodcut.

9 November 1984 – Bequest of Philip Hofer. bTyp Inc 6912

Brescia

BONINUS DE BONINIS

S1-3403A **Dante Alighieri:** La Commedia. 31 May 1487.

f°. A single leaf only; ill.; 323 x 227 mm.

In: Philip J. Spartano, *The Brescia Dante* (Provo: Friends of Brigham Young University Library, 1975).

The leaf is bb2 (leaf [152]), containing part of Purgatorio, Canto II; full-page woodcut within white-on-black grotesque woodcut border on verso. Woodcut uncolored; without rubrication. Original illustrated red and white cloth; the leaf is tipped in following p. [x].

February 1976 – Bought with the John L. Warren fund. *fIC.D2358. S975b

ANGELUS AND JACOBUS BRITANNICUS

(S1-3425a) **Pylades, Johannes Franciscus Buccardus:** Genealogia deorum. After 1500.

a1r, TITLE: PYLADAE GENEALOGIA. ‖ a1v: Ad Lucam Tertium patritiorum Brixiæ Splēdorē: ‖ Et Mecoenatem fuum. ‖ Pylades. ‖ ... a2r: Deorum Genealogiæ a Pylade uerfibus Conclufæ. ‖ Liber primus. ‖ ... d6v, line 29: Qui nihil inuictum liquit in orbe ferox. ‖ FINIS.

4°. a-c⁸ d⁶; [b1 signed 'a iii']; [30] leaves; 181 x 130 mm. 28 lines (sig. d: 30-31 lines); a2r: 140 x 89 mm. Type: 102R. White-on-black woodcut initials.

Includes a poem by Lucas Tertius. Proctor assigned this edition to Brescia, without printer attribution or date; BMC and Goff date this after 1500; BM STC(I) assigns this to Venice, Johannes Rubeus, ca. 1508. Goff notes two variant "issues": in one, the poem on a1v has the heading "Ad Lucam Tertium patritiorum Brixiæ Splēdorē:"; in the other, the heading reads "Ad Lucam Tertiū patritiorū Brixiae Splēdorē". However, in comparing the Houghton copy (of the former "issue") with photocopies of the Folger Shakespeare Library copy (of the latter "issue"), it is obvious

Deorum Genealogiæ a Pylade uerſibus Concluſæ.
Liber primus.

Armine Cōcipimus Geneas cantare Deorū:
Quos pia gentiles turba uocare ſolet:
Quo nā qſꝗ patre:et q̄ ſit genitrice creatus:
Forſitan & clarum ſi quid in orbe dedit:
In quibus Aſcræi pars eſt non ultima uatis:
Multa etiam ſiculus quæ Diodorus agit.
Quicquid & aggeſſit quondam Certaldus in unum:
Aut ueteres ſcriptis nos docuere ſuis:
Melpomene aſſiſtas turba comitante ſororum.
Res & in hoc ſchedio ueſtra putatur agi.
Quem primum longæua deum Cōmenta uetuſtas
Dicitur:huic nomen Gorgonis illa dedit:
Quod neꝗ fas aperire foret:nec prodere cuiquam:
Hac uenerata ſuum relligione deum.
Hunc ſine principio:nulloꝗ autore parentem
Credidit in tenebris degere poſſe Chai.
Id chaos(ut perhibent)rudis atꝗ incondita rerum
Materies uno corpore iuncta fuit.
Cui neꝗ quam poſſet quiſquā dignoſcere formā:
Nec niſi pondus iners & graue:uultus erat.
Dicitur hanc deus is ſedem tenuiſſe profundam:
Hinc factum:ut nulli Cognitus ille foret:
Qui congeſta Chao diſcordia ferre tumultum
Semina concipiens intulit hiſce manum.
Litigium eduxit.primum id ſine matre profectum:
Panaꝗ:Tum Parcas exiliiſſe ferunt.   a ii

Figure 10. (S1-3425a): Johannes Franciscus Buccardus Pylades *Genealogia deorum*
(Brescia: Angelus and Jacobus Britannicus, after 1500). Leaf a2 recto.
(*IC.P6402.501g, Houghton Library, Harvard College Library)

that they are separate editions, one a page-for-page reprint of the other. The Folger copy is set in a roman type measuring 107 mm. per 20 lines. The Houghton copy is set in a roman type apparently identical to one (102R) used at Brescia by Jacobus Britannicus, who printed several other works by Pylades beginning in 1494. Because the references cited below presumably conflate the two editions, the Houghton copy is here given a full description.

In this copy, the heading on a1v reads "Ad Lucam Tertium patritiorum Brixiæ Splēdorē:". Without rubrication. 19th-century half brown sheep and marbled boards.

H 13617*; Pr 7049; BMC 7:1209; BM STC(I) p. 112; GW 5:col. 616; IGI 1:285; Goff P-1144; BSB-Ink B-953.

June 1975 – Bought with the George L. Lincoln fund. *IC.P6402.501g

Pavia

JOHANNES ANDREAS DE BOSCHO,
MICHAEL AND BERNARDINUS DE GARALDIS

S1-3472.5   **Mayno, Jason de:** Oratio in funere Hieronymi Torti habita. ca. 1495.

4°. [6] leaves; 208 x 145 mm.

Initial spaces, with guide-letters, not filled in; without rubrication. Recent marbled boards. No. 522 in the Christie's South Kensington sale catalogue, 18 November 2003 (unnamed, but library of Percy Barnevik).

H 10974*; IGI 6023; CIBN M-261; BSB-Ink M-61.

10 December 2003 – Bought with the Bayard Livingston Kilgour & Kate Gray Kilgour fund. Inc 7108.5

Oratio habita in funere excellétiffimi iurifcōfulti Hyeronim i
Torti tenentis primā catedraz in felici gymnafio Ticinenfi: p me
Jafoné de Mayno Mediolanenfem iurifutriufcz doctozem.

Tinam aliq me ad dicenduz occafio impu/
lifset: ꝗ vt in grauiz acerbo funere
Hyeronimi Torti iurifconfulti celebzis z pfumma
ti: laudatiua a me hodie habenda efset ozatio. Fue
rat mihi iādiu propofitum eius vitam ingeniuz ac
litteraturā fpaciofius z vberius propzijs z peculiaribus laudibus
exoznare: nō ꝙ cōmédationez mzaz illi expedire aut vfui foze im/
prudens mihi perfuaderem.fed vt fignuz aliquod grati in euz ani
mi aliquando proferrem. Naz cum eius fontibus quicquid in me
doctrinc efset exhaufifsem: z omnez ingenij mei cultuz inde fufce/
pifsem.ingratū me quodāmodo viuere exiftimabā: fi nō aliquo fal
té laudationis argumento: fuozuz in me meritoz z meç in illū ob
feruantiç perpetuaz recognitionez profiterer: quādoquidez maius
aliquid quod ei pftarez nō haberez.Iuuafset fcriptis in texere oēz
eius pcedétis vitç ferié:quibufue ftudioz gradibus ad tiñ doctri
ne, culmen efset euectus:vt fic a cūctis querēdus ac defiderādus
in exéplar eui pfentis trāfiret: mihi pcipue ꝗ illū z publice z pua/
tim ꝗ̃tū admirabar:tiñ diligebā z obferuabā. Propofuifsem ftu
dioz fuoz femitā tanꝗ fpeculū:quo viā ad fummū lraz apicez fpe
cularer.z fi nō tā alte fcandere vnꝗ poftez: at falté hifdez ꞏgradib⁹
inchoarez afcenfuz. Sz heu fati necefsitate ꝓpulfus:ꝗ ego hilarius
z exultātius dicere ꝑceperā: nūc fummifsius atꝗ moleftius i fune
brez meftaz fquallenté z oi ex ꝑte circūcifaz ozationem ꝑuertere.z
quafi epicedion deplozare ꝓpelloz. Nō omittaz tiñ fic vrgétib⁹ fa
tis.qn ea ꝗ letiozib⁹ z abfolutiozib⁹ vbis celebzāda fuerāt:bis re
mifsiozibus z hac parétali ozatóe ꝓplectar.   Uereri ét debui me
nō magnā hodie i dicédo expectatóez hfe: ꝙ nullū vos pres nouū
audituros.fz tiñ vetera i hoc viro recognituros exiftimetis: cui⁹ vi
te actióes z finguli ftudioz pgrefsus vobis iādiu inotefcūt: cū i ve/
ftris academijs verfat⁹:in veftris quoꝗ manibus creuerit.Sz eo
plus fidei me ꝓfecutuz fpero.qd ego vel in primis maxie defide/

Figure 11. S1-3472.5: Jason de Mayno *Oratio in funere Hieronymi Torti habita* (Pavia: Johannes Andreas
de Boscho, Michael and Bernardinus de Garaldis, ca. 1495). Leaf a1 verso.
(Inc 7108.5, Houghton Library, Harvard College Library)

Vicenza

LEONARDUS ACHATES

S1-3489A   **Herbarius**. 27 October 1491.

4°. Single leaf only; ill.; 195 x 137 mm.

In: Claus Nissen, *Herbals of Five Centuries: 50 Original Leaves from German, French, Dutch, English, Italian, and Swiss Herbals, With an Introduction and Bibliography* (Zurich: L'Art ancien, 1958).

The leaf is h4 (leaf LX), "Edera arborea". Half-page woodcut on recto with contemporary hand coloring; without rubrication. No. 12 of 100 copies. Tipped into a cream paper mat; in a cloth case. Possibly from an imperfect copy formerly owned by Dr. Karl Becher, Karlsbad.

Countway Library

S1-3489B   — Single leaf only; ill.; 195 x 140 mm.

In: Claus Nissen, *Herbals of Five Centuries* ... (Zurich: L'Art ancien, 1958).

The leaf is b4 (leaf XII), "Arthemisia". Half-page woodcut on recto with contemporary hand-coloring; without rubrication. No. 66 of 100 copies. Tipped into a cream paper mat; in a cloth case. Possibly from an imperfect copy formerly owned by Dr. Karl Becher, Karlsbad.

Dumbarton Oaks Garden Library

HENRICUS DE SANCTO URSIO

S1-3506.5   **Thienis, Gaietanus de:** Recollectae super libros Physicorum Aristotelis. 23 April 1487.

f°. [118] leaves (1 and 118 blank); 299 x 207 mm.

Initial spaces, a few with guide-letters, not filled in; without rubrication. Contemporary pasteboard, the boards covered with a vellum bifolium of Latin MS, written on one side only (probably Italian, early 15th century), comprising a portion of Sermon 60 of Pope Leo I; remains of tawed leather ties. Some contemporary MS marginalia, MS diagram on m1r;

David R. Whitesell 103

the leaves and columns have been numbered and folio references added to the table at end. Scored MS ownership notation, dated 1579, on a1r; later MS ownership notation on a2r, "Josephi Marchionis Trevisani"; old inscription on a1v, "C costo bologni. 40." Blank leaf p6 not present.

HC 15497*; Pr 7169; BMC 7:1046 (IB.31847); Pell 4945; Polain 1526; IGI 2349; Goff G-34; BSB-Ink C-41.

15 April 2004 – Bought with the Bayard Livingston Kilgour & Kate Gray Kilgour fund. Inc 7169

Colle di Valdelsa

BONUS GALLUS

S1-3534.8   **Oppianus:** Halieutica, sive De piscatu. 12 September 1478.

4°. [64] leaves; 207 x 137 mm.

Translated by Laurentius Lippius. Includes the *Disticha* of Lippius and a poem by Philippus Poscus. Quire h shows evidence of resetting: the catchwords given in the register for sheets h3.6 and h4.5 refer, not to the first lines on h3r and h4r, but to the last lines on h2v and h3v. In one BMC copy (IA.33514), d1 is unsigned and d8 is signed 'd1'; in the other BMC copy (IA.33513), d1 is correctly signed. In the Houghton Library copy, neither d1 nor d8 are signed, b2 is signed 'b3' (corrected in contemporary MS), b4 is signed 'biii', and a2 is unsigned.

This, the first printed book on fishing, has long been a Harvard desideratum, having been absent from the superb angling collections of John Bartlett (acquired in 1892) and Daniel B. Fearing (acquired in 1915); cf. Walsh 3: vii and 5: 28-29.

Initial spaces, with guide-letters, not filled in; without rubrication. Late 19th-century brown crushed morocco, flyleaves watermarked "1878". Some early MS annotations and marginal dashes. Inscription (17th-century?) on front flyleaf, "Oppiani Poeta De piscibus Liber". Bookplate removed from front pastedown. Lower outer corners trimmed diagonally.

HC 12015*; Pr 7242; BMC 7:1079 (IA.33513-14); IGI 7006; Goff O-65; CIBN O-30; BSB-Ink O-51.

26 June 2000 – Bought with the Faculty of Arts and Sciences fund, courtesy of the Harvard College Library. Inc 7242

FRANCE

Paris

JEAN BONHOMME

S1-3594.3   **Herbarius** [with French synonyms]. ca. 1486.

4°. A single leaf only; ill.; 202 x 144 mm.

The unsigned leaf contains a description of "Nasturciu[m] ortulanum", with half-page woodcut on recto. Woodcut uncolored; without rubrication. Contemporary MS annotations in Latin.

Pr 8050; BMC 8:13 (IA.39859); Pell 5745; GW 12272; Goff H-61.

9 November 1984 – Bequest of Philip Hofer. bTyp Inc 8050

ULRICH GERING

S1-3601.8   **Guillelmus Hilacensis:** Sermones super orationem dominicam. 1494.

8°. [264] leaves (264 blank); ill.; 138 x 98 mm.

Printed by Gering with Berthold Rembolt. Rembolt's full-page woodcut device (Renouard 955) appears on A1v in what may be its first use, possibly predating its appearance in Pr 8302 (16 December 1494).

Initial spaces not filled in; without rubrication. Modern vellum, edges gilt. A few early MS marginalia. Contemporary MS inscription (partly effaced) on title page, with later inscription, "aux Capucins D'aire". No. 83 in the Christie's South Kensington sale catalogue, 7 December 2004 (unnamed, but library of Percy Barnevik). Blank leaf not present.

HC 8219*; Pr 8301; BMC 8:29 (IA.40664); Polain 1805; GW 11904; Goff G-635; Sack 1711; BSB-Ink G-494.

2 February 2005 – Bought with the Edward and Bertha C. Rose Acquisition fund. Inc 8301

Figure 12. (S1-3605a): Pomponius Laetus *Romanae historiae compendium* (Paris: Jean Du Pre, 7 May 1501). Leaves A2 verso A3 recto. (*IC.L5691.499rd, Houghton Library, Harvard College Library)

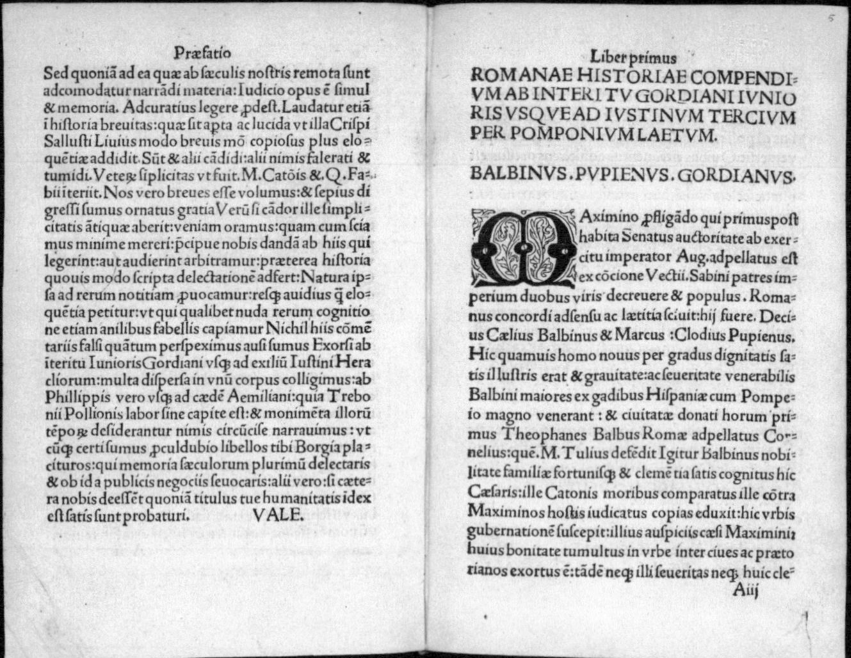

JEAN DU PRÉ

(S1-3605a)   **Laetus, Pomponius:** Romanae historiae compendium. 7 May 1501.

A1r, TITLE: Romanæ hiſtoriæ compendium: Ab interitu Gor= || diani Iunioris vſq[ue] ad Iuſtinum tertium. || Per Pomponium Lætum || [woodcut of a master and pupils, within border, 89 x [121+] mm.] || Laurea ſerta gerens/ muſiſq[ue] excultus amænis: || Gymnaſium Fauſtus pariſienſe polit. || A2r: Præfatio || FRANCISCO BORGIAE EPISCOPO || TEANEN. ET PONTIFICALIS ERARII || PRAEFECTO POMPONIVS LAETVS. || (S⁵)OLET quæri ab ſtudioſis viris vti || lis ne ſit hiſtoria. … || … A3r: Liber primus || ROMANAE HISTORIAE COMPENDI= || VM AB INTERITV GORDIANI IVNIO || RIS VSQVE AD IVSTINVM TERCIVM || PER POMPONIVM LAETVM. || BALBINVS. PVPIENVS. GORDIANVS. || (M⁴)Aximino p[ro]fligãdo qui primus poſt || habita Senatus auctoritate ab exer= || … K6v, COLOPHON: Finis || Romanæ hiſtoriæ compendiu[m] ab interitu gordiani iu || nioris vſq[ue] ad Iuſtinu[m] tertium a Pomponio læto cõ= || poſitum: & antiqua orthographia: ficuti auctor ipfe ‖ antiquitatis omnis diligentiffimus indagator affecta ‖ torq[ue] manu propria exfcripfit Impreffu[m] parifiis im= ‖ penfa Solertis viri Ioannis pratenfis. Anno a natali ‖ chriftiano M.ccccc. primo. Noñ. maii. ‖ K7r: Faufti poetæ regii. Ad fãctam euchariftiam Carmen ‖ (o²) Pia quæ facru[m] libamina pafcitis agnum: ‖ … K7v-8r blank ‖ K8v: [Du Pré's device] ‖ In vico sancti iacobi ad signum duorum cygnorum.

4°. A-K⁸; [62] leaves; ill.; 193 x 130 mm. A4r: 26 lines and headline, 154 x 97 mm. Type: 99R, leaded to 114 mm. on A3r-K7r. Device; woodcut initials; initial space, with guide-letter, on K7r.

The colophon date has sometimes been misinterpreted as 1500.

Initial space not filled in; without rubrication. 19th-century half green calf and marbled boards. Partly illegible contemporary inscription in French on A1v. Imperfect: woodcut on title page slightly cropped along right edge.

BM STC(F) p. 361; Goff L-27; Moreau 1501:84.

3 December 1907 – Bought with the Charles Eliot Norton fund. *IC. L5691.499rd

GUY MARCHANT

S1-3615.7   **Danse macabre** [Latin]. 15 October 1490.

f°. Two fragments only; ill.

Printed by Marchant for Geoffroy de Marnef. Edited by Pierre Desrey.

The fragments are: 1) top half of a2 (143 x 165 mm), containing woodcuts of a cleric seated before a reading desk (recto, lower margin cropped) and 4 figures of death playing musical instruments (verso); and 2) top half of a7 (129 x 174 mm), containing woodcuts of the canon and the merchant (recto) and the physician and the lover (verso). Woodcuts uncolored.

HC 10415; Pell 4107; Polain 4311; GW 7957; Goff D-21.

9 November 1984 – Bequest of Philip Hofer. bTyp Inc 7985.1

S1-3630.2   **Henricus de Herpf:** Directorium ad consequendam vitae perfectionem. ca. 1499.

8°. [12] leaves; 138 x 96 mm.

Includes the *De laude vitae solitariae* of Petrus Damiani (here ascribed to Basilius Magnus).

Paragraph marks, capital strokes, and underlinings added in red. 19th-century orange pastepaper boards. MS label with number "599" in upper left corner of front board. Recent bookseller's note on front flyleaf, "from collection of A.S. de Poorter, Brussels".

C 2940; Pr 8026; BMC 8:69 (IA.39729); Pell 5728; Polain 1863; GW 12224; Goff H-37a.

26 July 2000 – Bought with the Susan A.E. Morse fund. Inc 8026

S1-3630.8 **Pseudo-Augustinus:** De vita Christiana. 9 January 1500/01.

8°. [20] leaves; ill.; 130 x 87 mm.

Lombards. 18th-century mottled sheep, edges sprinkled red. Old signature on title page, "ABurel." Booklabel of Philip Hofer. With this is bound Pseudo-Augustinus, *Sermones ad heremitas* (Paris: Antoine Chappiel, 1500; see S1-3736B below).

GW 3047; Goff A-1361.

3 January 1939 – Gift of Philip Hofer. Typ Inc 8410

ANTOINE VÉRARD

S1-3632.4 **Lancelot du Lac:** La seconde partie de Lancelot. ca. 1494.

f°. A single leaf only; ill., 327 x 235 mm.

Parts one and three are dated 1 July and 30 April 1494; part two is undated.

The leaf is xx4. Large uncolored woodcut (224 x 172 mm) on verso, depicting mounted knights in battle, with a fortified town and spectators in two oversized windows in background. Initial added in red.

HC 9848; GW 12622; CIBN L-31; IDL 2883; Macf 35.

9 November 1984 – Bequest of Philip Hofer. pTyp Inc 8434.5

S1-3632.8 **Bueve de Hantone.** Between October 1499 and July 1503.

f°. [4], Cxxvi (i.e. Cxxii) leaves (lxxxvi-lxxxviiii omitted; xxiiii, lxxxv,

Cviiii misnumbered xiiii, xc, and Cvi); ill.; 274 x 197 mm.

Xylographic title; Lombards; calligraphic and grotesque initials. Modern red morocco by Devauchelle, covers and edges gilt. Some leaves remargined. Sheet c3.4 is of double thickness, consisting of two sheets pasted together.

IIC 3022; Pell 2259; GW 5712; IGI 2219; CIBN B-905; Macf 133.

7 July 1957 – Bought with the Amy Lowell fund. Inc 8458.1

PIERRE LEVET

(S1-3643a) **Gerardus de Vliederhoven:** Cordiale quattuor novissimorum. ca. 1502.

8°. [48] leaves; 131 x 89 mm.

Printed for Jean Petit, with his device (Renouard 881) on title page. GW attributes the printing to Pierre Levet. Dated by Moreau to ca. 1502 based on the state of Petit's device; GW and Goff date this edition to ca. 1499.

Lombards; without rubrication. Half modern red morocco and marbled boards, by Lobstein-Laurenchet. No. 469 in the Christie's South Kensington sale catalogue, 18 November 2003 (unnamed, but library of Percy Barnevik).

Pell 5082; Polain 1171; GW 7502; Goff (Suppl) C-894a; Moreau 1502:24.

29 January 2004 – Bought with the Bayard Livingston Kilgour & Kate Gray Kilgour fund. *NC.G3128C.1502

GEORG MITTELHUS

S1-3660.7 **Alphabetum sacerdotum.** ca. 1494-1495.

8°. [16] leaves; 129 x 88 mm.

Includes: S. Bonaventura, *De praeparatione ad missam*; Johannes de Peckham, *Meditatio de SS. Sacramento altaris*; and two Latin prayers. These additions, which comprise signature b, have been treated by incunabulists as a separate edition. However, because the title page (a1r) mentions both the *Alphabetum sacerdotum* and *De praeparatione ad missam*, the signing is continuous, and both signatures are typographically uniform, the tracts clearly constitute a single edition.

CIBN dates the S. Bonaventura to ca. 1496.

Initial spaces, with guide-letters, not filled in; without rubrication. Modern half vellum, boards covered with fragments from an unidentified early printed book. No. 415 in the Christie's South Kensington sale catalogue, 18 November 2003 (unnamed, but library of Percy Barnevik).

H 865*+3546*; Pell 2630 (S. Bonaventura); GW 1568+4682; CIBN B-663 (S. Bonaventura); BSB-Ink R-210+B-663.

10 December 2003 – Bought with the Bayard Livingston Kilgour & Kate Gray Kilgour fund. Inc 8115.5

JEAN MAURAND

S1-3702.6 **Anianus:** Computus cum commento. 20 December 1498.

4°. A single leaf only. 193 x 142 mm.

Maurand printed two issues, distinguished by variant devices and colophon wording: one for Pierre Regnault at Caen, another for Jean Petit at Paris.

The leaf is d5, of indeterminate issue. Without rubrication. Some 16th-century MS annotations in English and Latin. MS note by W.H. Allnutt, "From R. Smyth's Defense of the Masse 1546," i.e. removed from the binding on a copy of one of the three London, 1546 editions/issues of Richard Smith, *A Defence of the Blessed Masse, and the Sacrifice Therof* (STC 22820, 22820a, or 22821). Tipped onto fol. 40 of an album of printed fragments removed from bindings (presumably Oxford bindings of the late 16th-early 17th centuries) of books in the library formed by Hannibal Gamon Jr., later removed to Lanhydrock House, Cornwall. For additional provenance information, see S1-372.5. Late 19th-century half tan sheep and brown cloth. Marginal defects with minor text loss at top, dampstains.

C1733; Pell 781; GW 1976; Goff A-739a.

October 1963 – Bought with the Susan A.E. Morse fund. *fEC.A100. B659c

ANTOINE CHAPPIEL

S1-3736B   **Pseudo-Augustinus:** Sermones ad heremitas. 1500.

8°. Another copy. 130 x 87 mm.

In this copy, the first line of the title, Jaumar's device on the title page, and the heading on a3r are printed in black. Jaumar's device heightened in yellow. 18ᵗʰ-century mottled sheep, edges sprinkled red. Old signature on title page, "ABurel." Booklabel of Philip Hofer. With this is bound Pseudo-Augustinus, *De vita Christiana* (Paris: Guy Marchant, 9 January 1500/01; see S1-3630.8 above).

3 January 1939 – Gift of Philip Hofer. Typ Inc 8410

GASPARD PHILIPPE

(S1-3736b)   **Beroaldus, Philippus:** De felicitate. ca. 1501.

4°. [30] leaves; ill.; 178 x 127 mm.

Includes Beroaldus's *De optimo statu*. The two tracts historically have been treated as separate editions, with *De felicitate* considered a possible incunable; *De optimo statu* is dated 26 July 1501. However, the two parts were almost certainly issued together: they are typographically uniform, being page-for-page reprints of the Kerver editions of 1501 (GW 4136 and 4149), which were also issued together; *De optimo statu* begins with a caption title on Aa1r; the full-page woodcuts on A1v and Bb6v frame the two parts as a single publishing unit; the paper stocks of the Harvard copies are uniform in both parts; and the two parts are found bound together in both Harvard copies as well as in the British Library copy. Printed by Philippe for Denis Roce.

Without rubrication. Contemporary MS notation on Bb6v, now mostly illegible; some underlining in the text. Modern stiff vellum. No. 437 in the Christie's South Kensington sale catalogue, 18 November 2003 (unnamed, but library of Percy Barnevik).

C 1002 (*De felicitate*); BM STC(F) p. 50 (each tract separately listed); Pell 2222 (*De felicitate*); Polain 619 (*De felicitate*); GW 4137 (*De felicitate*); Goff B-486 (*De felicitate*); Moreau 1:15 (*De optimo statu*).

10 December 2003 – Bought with the Bayard Livingston Kilgour & Kate Gray Kilgour fund. Typ 515.01.203

(S1-3736c)   — Another copy. 195 x 132 mm.

Without rubrication. Modern flexible boards covered with a vellum leaf from a 15th-century Latin MS.

Countway Library

GUILLAUME EUSTACE

(S1-3736d) **Ordonnances sur les admortissemens des heritages nobles et roturières à gens d'eglise.** After 1500.

A1r, TITLE: Ordōnances ſur les admor= ‖ tiſſemens des heritaiges no ‖ bles et roturieres a ge[n]s degl'e ‖ [device (Renouard 309), 98 x 70 mm.] ‖ On les vend a la rue de la iuifrie a le[n]ſeigne des ‖ deux Sagittaires: ou au palais au troiziefme ‖ pillier. ‖ A2r: (P⁶)Our ce que les ordō ‖ nances royaulx faictes ſur le faict ‖ de rachat de rentes conſtituees ſur ‖ maiſons aſſiſes en la ville et faux ‖ bourgs de paris … ‖ … C8r, line 21: confiſcation: mais demeure a legliſe ſãs auſtre ſer= ‖ uice. ‖ ¶Finis. ‖ C8v: [device (Renouard 312), 145 x 90 mm.]

8°. A-C⁸; [24] leaves; 169 x 112 mm. A3r: 29 lines, 140 x 85 mm. Types: 150B (approx.), title; 96B, imprint, text. Woodcut devices of Guillaume Eustace, criblé initial on A2r.

Printing date from Goff.

Without rubrication. Recent vellum. Booklabel of George Dunn (no. 200 in pt. 1 of the Sotheby sale catalogue, February 1913).

Goff O-90.

15 March 1913 – Gift of the Alumni of the Harvard Law School. Law Library

BERTHOLD REMBOLT
AND JEAN PETIT

(S1-3736e) **Guillaume de Digulleville:** Le roman des trois pèlerinages. ca. 1517.

4°. [10], ccvi leaves (xxix-xxx, xxxiij-l, lv-lvj misnumbered xxxix-xl, xliij-lx, and lxv-lxvj); 198 x 132 mm.

Includes *Le pèlerinage de vie humaine, Le pèlerinage de l'âme,* and *Le pèlerinage de Jésus-Christ.* For dating see Moreau.

Without rubrication. 18th-century crimson morocco, edges gilt. From the library of Gabriel Cognacq.

HC 8326; BM STC(F) p. 130; Pell 4244; GW 10:col. 366; Goff G-641; Moreau 2:1596.

8 November 1955 – Gift of Hans Peter Kraus. *FC.G9455D.515v

UNASSIGNED

(S1-3736f)   **Persius Flaccus, Aulus:** Satirae. Between 1505 and 1513.

a1r, TITLE: P. Auli. Perfii. Flacci || Satyrarum opus. || [device of Jean Petit (Renouard 881)] || a1v: Auli Perfij Flacci Poete Satyrarū opus. || (n²)ec forte labra prolui caballino: || … c4r, line 5: Inuentus chryfippe tui finitor acerui. || ¶Auli Perfij/ Flacci Satyrarum finis. || ¶Vita Perfij. || (p²)Erfium argreffuro imprimis neceffarium || … c4v, line 19: fatyra explanata fufficiant. || Finis

4°. a-b⁶ c⁴; [16] leaves; 189 x 133 mm. A3r: 23 lines (leaded) and headline, 157 x 93 mm. Type: 102R. Device; initial spaces, with guide-letters.

Printed for Jean Petit. Dated on the basis of the state of Petit's device; cf. Goff Suppl.

Initial spaces not filled in; without rubrication. 19th-century half tan calf and marbled boards. Booklabel of Emory M. Wood; bookplate of Morris H. Morgan.

Goff P-338; Morgan (Persius) 49.

1 January 1910 – Gift of Morris H. Morgan. *OLC.P431.507

(S1-3736g)   **Dionysius Cartusianus:** Dialogus Christiani contra Sarracenum. ca. 1511/12.

[For transcriptions see Reichling; but this copy has "Christianus." in line 2 of a2r.] 4°. a-d⁸ e²; xxxv, [1] leaves; ill.; 172 x 119 mm. 2 columns. a2r: 42 lines and headline, 139 x 89 mm. Types: 140G (approx.), title; 115G, imprint on a1r; 80G, headlines and privilege; 63G, text. Devices of Guillaume Eustace (Renouard 309, 312); woodcut; woodcut initials.

Printed for Guillaume Eustace, probably by either Guillaume Desplains or Raoul Couturier. For dating and printer attributions, see ISTC. This copy has typographical features very similar to those of (S1-3736h)

Figure 13. (S1-3736d): *Ordonnances sur les admortissemens des heritages nobles et roturières à gens d'eglise* (Paris: Guillaume Eustace, after 1500). Leaf A1 recto. (Special Collections, Harvard Law Library)

P.Auli.Persii.Flacci
Satyrarumopus.

:IEHAN: PETIT:

Figure 14. (S1-3736f): Aulus Persius Flaccus *Satirae* (Paris: unassigned, between 1505 and 1513). Leaf a1 recto. (*OLC.P431.507, Houghton Library, Harvard College Library)

CNicolai Chappusij de mente et memo
ria libellus vtilissimus:ad Carolum Guil=
lardum Consiliariu regium :&
senatorij ordidinis pre
sidem dignissi
mum.

LE PELICAN

E   G

DE · MARNEF·

CVenum habes in vico sancti Iacobi sub intersignio
Pellicani.

Figure 15. (S1-3736j): NICOLAUS CHAPPUSIUS *De mente et memoria* (Paris: unassigned, ca. 1514?). Leaf A1
recto. (Ballard 760, Boston Medical Library in the Francis A. Countway Library of Medicine)

below, and the 17-line privilege in both editions is from the same setting of type.

Without rubrication. 19th-century vellum, edges stained red. From the library of Count Paul Riant.

CR 1991; BM STC(F) p. 107; GW 7:col. 451; IGI 2:158; Goff D-243a; ISTC id00243500.

28 December 1899 – Gift of J. Randolph Coolidge and Archibald Cary Coolidge. Asia 84.15*

(S1-3736h) **Samuel Maroccanus, Rabbi:** Epistola contra Iudaeorum errores. ca. 1511/12.

[For transcriptions see Reichling.] 4°. A⁸ B¹⁰; xvii, [1] leaves (xvi misnumbered xiiii); ill.; 172 x 119 mm. 2 columns. A2r: 41 lines and headline, 136 x 89 mm. Types: 115G title; 80G, headlines and privilege; 63G, text. Devices of Guillaume Eustace (Renouard 309, 312); woodcut; woodcut initials.

Translated by Alphonsus Boni Hominis. Printed for Guillaume Eustace, probably by either Guillaume Desplains or Raoul Couturier. For dating and printer attributions, see ISTC. This copy has typographical features very similar to those of (S1-3736g) above, and the 17-line privilege in both editions is from the same setting of type.

Without rubrication. 19th-century vellum, edges stained red. Gilt red leather booklabel of Count Paul Riant.

CR 5258; BM STC(F) p. 394; IGI 5:19; Goff S-115; ISTC is00115000.

26 February 1900 – Gift of John Harvey Treat. *SC.Sa495E.1510

(S1-3736i) **Turrecremata, Johannes de:** Contra principales errores Mahometi et Turcorum Sarracenorum. ca. 1511/12.

4°. lvi leaves; ill.; 171 x 115 mm.

Printed for Guillaume Eustace, probably by either Guillaume Desplains or Raoul Couturier. For dating and printer attributions, see ISTC.

Without rubrication. 19th-century vellum, edges stained red. Ownership inscription on title page, "Ex Biblioth. FF. Praedicat. Conv. Parisie[nsis] St. M. Annunciat. Ad S. Honor. 1664", and "Ex libris ff. Praedicatorum Parisiensum ad S. honoratum" on leaf A2r; a later inscription at foot of title page, "Ex libris G. Coiffeteau". Gilt red leather booklabel of Count Paul Riant.

HC 15746; BM STC(F) p. 429; IGI 5:238; Goff T-543a; CFM(F) 556; ISTC it00543500.

28 December 1899 – Gift of J. Randolph Coolidge and Archibald Cary Coolidge. C 809.7.30*

(S1-3736j)   **Chappusius, Nicolaus:** De mente et memoria. ca. 1514?

The Harvard copy is not the same as that described by Reichling, nor is it the same edition as the Edinburgh University Library copy described by Hargreaves, which has the device of Enguilbert, Jean, and Geoffroy de Marnef (Renouard 719). Since ISTC (and possibly Goff) conflate what in fact are at least two different and extremely rare editions, the Harvard copy is fully described here. For digital images of the National Library of Medicine copy, which conforms to the edition described by Reichling (possibly the same as Hargreaves's edition), see: http://visualiseur.bnf. fr/Visualiseur?Destination=Gallica&O=NUMM-52385.

A1r, TITLE: ¶Nicolai Chappufij de mente et memo || ria libellus vtiliffimus: ad Carolum Guil= || lardum Confiliariu[m] regium: & || fenatorij ordidinis prę || fidem digniffi || mum. || ∴ || ⋅⋅ ⋅⋅ || ⋅⋅ || [device] || ¶Venum habes in vico fancti Iacobi fub interfignio || Pellicani. || A1v: Pręfatio. || Magnifico ac prępotenti Domino Carolo Guillardo Confi= || liario Regio: & Senatorij Ordinis pręfidi ęquiffimo. Mœcena || ti Suo Nicolaus Chappufius. Fœlicitatem. || … A2r: De mente & Memoria. Fo. II. || Ad magnificum Excellentemq[ue] dominu[m] Carolum Guillar || du[m] ordinis fenatorij Pręsidem Nicolai Chappufij in libru[m] || fuum de mente & memoria. || Pręfatio/ || … C6v, line 17: exterminare. || FINIS.

4°. A-B⁴ C⁶; XIV leaves (XIII misnumbered VIII); 192 x 138 mm. A2r: 41 lines and headline, 169 x 95 mm. Types: 100G (approx.), first line of title; 80R, title, text, headlines; a few words in Greek. Device of Enguilbert and Geoffroy de Marnef (Renouard 720) on A1r; woodcut white-on-black criblé initials; Lombards.

Printed for Enguilbert and Geoffroy de Marnef. Date derived from the de Marnef device on the title page.

Without rubrication. Marbled boards.

[not R 1492]; GW 6:col. 424; IGI 2:60; Goff C-424; [not Hargreaves 40]; Ballard 760; ISTC ic00424000.

Countway Library

Lyons

JOHANNES SIBER

S1-3754A **Bertachinus, Johannes:** Repertorium iuris utriusque. ca. 1485/90.

f°. Three fragments only; 207 x 120 mm.

The fragments are all from vol. 3: xxx6 lower outer corner, lines 39-70; BBB3 upper outer corner, lines 1-38; BBB4 lower outer corner, lines 39-70. Removed from a binding. Initial letter added in red, paragraph marks added in red or blue. Stained and torn, with minor text loss. Formerly classified as Inc 25.6.

6 May 1929 – Transferred from the Law Library. bInc 8539.8

S1-3755A **Bartholomaeus Anglicus:** De proprietatibus rerum [French]. After 26 January 1486.

f°. Three fragments only; 76 x 129 mm.

The fragments, which have been removed from a binding, are all from leaf l8. Initial letters and capital strokes added in red. Dampstained.

29 March 1918 – Bought with the Charles Eliot Norton fund. bInc 8540

MICHEL TOPIÉ

S1-3782.5 **Eaux artificielles.** ca. 1494.

This edition was previously known only through an imperfect copy (wanting a1 and d4) at the Bibliothèque municipale, Lyons. The Harvard copy, cataloged as "N.p., ca. 1525" when acquired over 70 years ago, has now been properly identified through the good offices of Denise Hillard. It preserves the title leaf a1 but also lacks d4 as well as b3.4. The Lyons copy was described in detail by Claude Dalbanne in his article, "Trois éditions lyonnaises du *Traité des eaux artificielles*," *Gutenberg-Jahrbuch* (1932), 125-46, where a2r and d3v are reproduced in facsimile (fig. 12 and 11 respectively, mistakenly reversed in the bibliographical description on p. 146). Because both Dalbanne's description and GW contain minor errors and lacunae, a full description is given below.

A1r, TITLE: (L)Es || vertus et proprietes des eaues artificielles. Auec plu= || fieurs autres petis traictiez conuenables es corps hu= || mains. || a1v blank || a2r: Cy commence vng petit traictie des eaues || artificielles. et les vertus et proprietes di= || celles. lefquelles fôt prouffitables pour les || corps humains. || Prologue. || (I⁶)Ay voulu efcripre fe petit taictie. a la requefte de || ma trefnoble et redoubtee dame. ... || a8v, line 7: Cy fine vne petit traictie des || eaues artificielles et de leurs || proprietez fait a linftance et re || q[ue] fte de ma trefredoubtee dame || Madame la contesse de bou= || longne pour mediciner les po= || ures malades pour lamour de || dieu pour poffeder feliciter en || ce monde et en lautre. ... || b1r: Cy apres fenfuiuent plufieurs ver= || tus et proprietes de la meliffe. laquelle || eft expreffement requife et conuenable || pour conferuer [et] garder les corps hu= || mains. || ... b2r, line 4: Toutes ces precieufes vertus ont || efte côpofees par frere rogier vachon || de lordre de faint franfoysz || Cy apres enfuiuent plufieurs remeddes fou= || uerains. pour conseruer et garder la fante des || corps humains. || ... c2r: Cy commence vng autre petit traictie || pour faire feiguee fur tout le corps de lo[m]= || me humain. || ... c3r: Cy co[m]mence les vert[us] et proprietes || des herbes. ... || d3v, line 21: Cy finiffent les vertus et proprietes || des herbes faites par la difcretion du[n]g || docteur qui fappelloit Maiftre iehan || hymbres. et plufieurs autres maiftref || en medicine. Lefquelles herbes ilz ont || approuuees. || d4r-v wanting, blank?

4°. a⁸ b-c⁶ d⁴; signing a3 as 'a iij', b1 as 'b i', c1 as 'c', c3 as 'c iij', d1 as 'd'; [24] leaves (24 blank?); 175 x 110 mm. B1v: 37 lines, 140 x 93 mm. Type: 8:75B (measures 76 mm in the Harvard copy). Large woodcut calligraphic initial L (111 x 75 mm) on a1r; woodcut white-on-black floriated initials (20 x 20 mm) on a2r (I), b1r (O), c3r (L); Dalbanne records one more initial, presumably on bifolium b3.4; initial space, with guide-letter.

Dated by Dalbanne to ca. 1494 on the basis of the type. The large calligraphic initial L on a1r is reproduced in Hellmut Lehmann-Haupt, *Initials from French Incunabula* (New York, 1948), fig. 664. He notes that it was employed by Topié and his then-partner Jacques Heremberck in their 10 October 1490 edition of Raoul Lefèvre, *Recueil des histoires de Troyes* (Goff L-114), as well as by other Lyonnese printers such as Jacques Maillet (cf. Goff B-1055, 14 November 1494) and Martin Havard (two undated imprints ca. 1500). The initial is also found in Topié's edition of *Exposition de l'Ave Maria* (GW 9518, ca. 1490; cf. reproduction in CFM(F), no. 650). Includes tracts by Rogier Vachon (Roger Bacon?) and Jehan Hymbres; for detailed contents, cf. Dalbanne.

Initial space not filled in; without rubrication. Crimson cloth. Contemporary MS notation at foot of b5v; quires numbered 20-23 in MS (18th century?) on recto of first leaf at lower left corner. Imperfect:

bifolium b3.4 and leaf d4 wanting; d1 misbound following d3.

GW 9168; Parguez 405; ISTC ie00001100.

Countway Library

JACOBINUS SUIGUS AND
NICOLAUS DE BENEDICTIS

S1-3828.6   **Horae ad usum Romanum.** 20 March 1499.

8°. A single leaf only; ill.; 162 x 112 mm.

Printed for Boninus de Boninis.

The leaf is H5. Initial space not filled in; without rubrication.

HCR 11995; Pr 8662; BMC 7:324 (IA.42127-28); IGI 4863; Goff O-48; CIBN H-245; Bohatta(H) 99; Lacombe 501.

9 November 1984 – Bequest of Philip Hofer. bTyp Inc 8662

JOHANNES CLEIN

(S1-3838b)   **Pelbartus de Themeswar:** Stellarium coronae Beatae Mariae Virginis. ca. 1505.

4°. [202] leaves; 194 x 142 mm.

Printing date from BM STC(F).

Without rubrication. Recent vellum.

H 12564; BM STC(F) p. 343; IGI 6:252; CIBN 2:371; Baudrier 12:269.

June 1952 – Gift of Imrie de Vegh. *ZHC.P3620.496sp

JACOBUS SACON

(S1-3838c)   **Petrus Lombardus:** Sententiarum libri IV. 1510.

f°. 4 vols. and table (vol. 1: [146] leaves (140, 146 blank); vol. 2: [192] leaves;

vol. 3: [166] leaves; vol. 4: [192] leaves; table: [84] leaves (84 blank)); vols. 1-2: 307 x 220 mm., vols. 3-4: 315 x 220 mm., table: 313 x 212 mm.

With the commentary of St. Bonaventure; edited by Johannes Beckenhaub, who also compiled the table; with additions by him and by Nicolaus Tinctoris; includes *Articuli in Anglia et Parisius condemnati.* Printed for Anton Koberger.

A made-up set. Without rubrication. Volumes 1-2 bound together in contemporary blind-stamped brown leather over reverse-bevelled wooden boards, rebacked; brass clasp plates on front cover, latches on front, clasps and thongs gone; title in MS on top edges. Volumes 3-4 uniformly bound in contemporary half blind-stamped brown leather and reverse-bevelled beech boards; brass clasp plates on front cover, latches on front, clasps and thongs gone; title in MS on fore-edges. The table bound in contemporary blind-stamped light brown goatskin over reverse-bevelled beech boards, rebacked; brass latches on fore-edges, latches on top and lower edges gone; thongs gone; 1 brass corner boss remains on each cover, 3 other bosses now gone; edges stained red. The table is bound with Richardus de Mediavilla, *Quodlibeta* (Venice: Lazarus de Soardis, 10 July 1509). Old MS inscription on title page of vol. 1, "Ludouiçi a Gomez Rote Auditoris et. S. P. Regentis no 404", with "420" above (scored); ownership notation of the Cistercians of Langheim on title pages of vols. 3-4, "Langheim a[nno] 1641". Imperfect: title page of the table wanting.

R 72-3; IGI 4:255-56; Goff P-489; Sack 2808a; Baudrier 12:326.

Vols. 1-2: 7 May 1913 – Gift of Alain Campbell White; vols. 3-4: 1923 – From the philosophical library of William James; table: 2 October 1837 – Bought ("Cost 50 cents"). *fIC.B6407.491qf

Rouen

GUILLAUME LE TALLEUR

S1-3857A **Statham, Nicholas:** Abridgement of Cases. 1490.

f°. Another copy. 276 x 221 mm.

In this copy, the heading on z3r is printed; on q1r, bearer type consisting of the heading "Iustificaciõ" has been inked in error; blind impressions of bearer type are visible on several leaves; cf. BMC. Initial space on a1r not filled in; without rubrication. Foliated in MS; the index has been completed in MS with folio numbers. Modern blind-tooled brown morocco; old MS title, "Statham," at top of fore-edge. MS slip pasted inside front cover, "May. 23. 1690. p'tium li. 1-s. 5." Armorial bookplate ("Ioh. Mitford. Int. Temp. et. Hosp. Linc. Soc.") of John Freeman Mitford, 1ˢᵗ Baron Redesdale; from the Broxbourne Library of Albert Ehrman, with his armorial bookplate, Broxbourne Library booklabel, and "AE" stamp with added "R.810" (no. 544 in pt. 2 of the Sotheby sale catalogue of his library, 8 May 1978).

April 2001 – Bequest of Henry N. Ess. Law Library

Grenoble

UNASSIGNED

*(S1-3863a) **Statuta Delphinatus:** Libertates per principes delphinos Viennenses delphinalibus subditis concessae. After 4 March 1508.

π1r, TITLE: (L³)Ibertates per illuſtriſſimos princi || [red-printed:] pes delphinos viennenſes delphinalibus ſubdi= || tis conceſſe ſtatutaq[ue] [et] decreta ab eiſdem princi || pibus necnon magnificis delphinatus prefidibus quos || gubernatores dicunt [et] excelſum delphinalem ſenatu[m] edi || ta: quibus et forenſes [et] extraiudiciales cauſe facile dirimi || queant formis dudum emendatiſſime mandate: [red printing ends] vna cum || interinatione litteraru[mque] diſme[m]brationis comitatus Aſten || fis a ſenatu Mediolani. [et] adiunctionis dicti comitatus || inſigni curie parlame[n]ti delphinatus. Impenſa Franciſci || Pichati et Bartholomei Bertoleti grationopolitanoru[mque] || ciuium. || [woodcut arms of the Dauphin, 72 x 111 mm.] || ¶ [red-printed:] Venales habentur huiusmodi libelli grationopoli in || platea mali consilij apud Franciscum pichatu[mque]: et in vico || parlamenti apud Bartholomeum Bertoletum. || π1v blank || π2r: Tabula || ¶Rubrice statuto[rum] generaliu[mque] || ... π4v, col. 2, line 36: ¶Finis tabule. || a1r: De geneolo. Delphi. vie[n]nen. Fo. I || Geneologia delphi || norum viennen. || (N⁴)Otandum est [quod] || ... l7r, col. 2, line 29: Materonis. || l7v-l8v blank || aa1r: Statuta Delphinatus I || Quod custodian || tur paſſus. || (C⁴)Harles par la || grace de dieu Roy de frãce || ... ee7v, col. 2, line 27: I. robertet. || ee8r-v blank || A1r: ¶Littere regie [et] delphiñ. Cu[m] || earu[m] interinatione diſme[m]bra= || tione comitat[us] aſteñ. a ſena= || tu ſiue parlame[n]to mediolani || et adiunctione dicti comitat[us] || inſigni curie parlame[n]ti delphi || natis per modum in dictis lit || teris co[n]tentum. || ... A2v, col. 2, line 37: Actu[m] quarta martij. Anno d[omi]ni. M. || cccccviij. d[omi]ni Mu. Pu.

David R. Whitesell 123

Pal. Be. ra. || bo. mar. gal. [et] aduocatus.

4°. π⁴ a-l⁸, aa-ee⁸, A²; [4], LXXXVII, [1], XXXVII, [3] leaves ([LXXXVIII], [XXXVIII] blank); 238 x 167 mm. 2 columns. a1r: 45 lines and headline, 197 x 123 mm. Types: 140G (approx.), title, headlines; 105G, title; 83G, text. Woodcut arms of the Dauphin on π1r; initials.

Printed for François Pichat and Barthélemy Bertolet. The date 4 March 1508 appears in the text on leaf A2v. Printing ascribed by Maignien to the press of Jean Belon at Valence, though BM STF(F) and GW assign this edition to an unidentified Grenoble press.

Without rubrication. 19ᵗʰ-century crimson morocco, edges gilt, by Masson-Debonnelle, successors to Capé.

C 1922; BM STC(F) p. 129; GW 7:col. 327; Goff D-102; Maignien 4.

1936 – Received. Law Library

(S1-3863b) — Another copy. 246 x 168 mm.

Without rubrication. 19ᵗʰ-century vellum, title in MS on bottom edges. Contemporary MS marginalia. Contemporary signature, "Francoys Joubert" (scored), at foot of title page; later, partly illegible inscription beneath. Imperfect: wanting the last three leaves (ee8 (blank), A1-2).

1924 – Received. Law Library

NETHERLANDS

Delft

JACOB JACOBSZOON VAN DER MEER

S1-3869.7   **Horae** [Dutch]. 19 July 1484.

4°. A single leaf only. 214 x 143 mm.

The leaf is m5, with text incipit on recto, "Hier beghint des heylige[n] geest getide". Large initial on recto in red penwork and blue, with red penwork marginal extensions, heightened in green; other initials, paragraph mark, capital strokes, and underlinings added in red. Some faint offsetting on verso.

HC 7770*; Goff H-430; Camp 833; IDL 2372; CIBN H-266; BSB-Ink H-354; Bohatta(H) 1525.

9 November 1984 – Bequest of Philip Hofer. bTyp Inc 8872.1

Deventer

RICHARDUS PAFRAET
(FIRST PRESS)

S1-3882.5   **Agricola, Rodolphus:** Anna mater. April 1484.

4°. [10] leaves (1 blank); 198 x 138 mm.

Dated to 1485-88 by GW and Goff. However, in a letter of 7 April 1484 while on a visit to Deventer, Agricola wrote that he had given *Anna mater* to be printed; see F. Akkerman and A.J. Vanderjagt, ed., *Rodolphus Agricola Phrisius, 1444-1485* (Leiden, 1988), p. 319. Includes his *Mauricio comiti Spegelbergi epicedion, Epitaphium Maurici comitis Spegelbergensis*, and two *Epigrammata* ("Postera quid portet" and "Optima est vitae").

Initial spaces not filled in; without rubrication. Blind impressions of several lines of bearer type are visible at the foot of a10r. Modern half vellum. Contemporary MS marginalia in Latin on a1v-3r. On a1r, in red and black ink in a different contemporary hand, are a genealogical chart of St. Anne's children and two short Latin poems (the first with a MS gloss) on St. Anne (no. 1060 and 1067 in H. Walther, *Initia carminum ac versuum Medii Aevi posterioris Latinorum* (Göttingen, 1959)).

C 133; Pell 237; Polain 49; GW 484; Goff A-167; CIBN A-90; Camp 52; IDL 94.

6 September 2004 — Bought with the Bayard Livingston Kilgour & Kate Gray Kilgour fund. Inc 8950.5

Zwolle

PETER VAN OS

S1-3904.3   **Jacobus de Voragine:** Legenda aurea [Dutch]. 1 September-18 November 1490.

f°. A single leaf only; ill.; 282 x 206 mm.

Includes the *Martyrologium* of Usuardus in Dutch translation.

The leaf is a3 from pt. 1; half-page woodcut of the Circumcision on recto. Initial letter, paragraph marks, capital strokes, underlinings, and two highlights to the woodcut added in red.

C 6519; Pr 9137, 9136; BMC 9:86 (IB.48141-42); Polain 2221; Goff J-142; CIBN J-123; Camp 1766; IDL 2590.

9 November 1984 – Bequest of Philip Hofer. bTyp Inc 9137

BELGIUM

Oudenaarde

AREND DE KEYSERE

S1-3931.5   **Alexander de Villa Dei:** Doctrinale. ca. 1482.

4°. [22+] leaves; 200 x 135 mm. 15 lines, leaded, 144 x 83 mm. Types: 1:97B capitals; 2:102G (approx.) capitals, text; 4^A:97B, capitals. Initial spaces.

A fragment of a previously unrecorded edition, consisting of a single unsigned gathering of four leaves containing lines 503-619 from part I, chapter 4, without commentary. The text is divided as follows (per lineation in D. Reichling, *Das Doctrinale des Alexander de Villa-Dei* (Berlin, 1893)): leaf 1r, lines 503-517; 1v, 1 line inserted (not in Reichling), 518-531; 2r, 532-546; 2v, 547-561; 3r, 562-569, 1 line inserted (cf. Reichling's "varia lectio" for line 569), 570-575; 3v, 576-590; 4r, 591-603, 1 line inserted (not in Reichling), 604; 4v, 605-619. There are other variants from Reichling's text, some of which are not recorded in his apparatus. Presumably this edition, like nearly all preceding editions, comprised all 4 parts and some 2645 lines. If so, this fragment would constitute leaves 18 or 19 through 21 or 22 and gathering 5 or 6; the complete edition may have contained approximately 90 leaves.

The types clearly identify this fragment as the work of Arend de Keysere, probably printed at his first press in Oudenaarde. Except for the initial letter to each line, all text is set in de Keysere's type 2, known to the Hellingas only from its appearance in a single undated work (Campbell 586, Goff C-909, GW 7535), to which they assigned the date 1480-1481

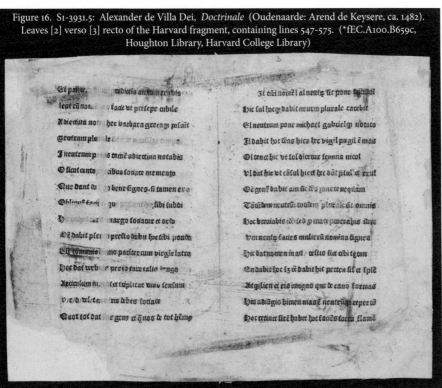

Figure 16. S1-3931.5: Alexander de Villa Dei, *Doctrinale* (Oudenaarde: Arend de Keysere, ca. 1482). Leaves [2] verso [3] recto of the Harvard fragment, containing lines 547-575. (*fEC.A100.B659c, Houghton Library, Harvard College Library)

(cf. W. & L. Hellinga, *The Fifteenth-Century Printing Types of the Low Countries* (Amsterdam, 1966), I, 56 and II, 442 and plates 122-126). The heavily leaded text and the absence of complete synopses for types 1 and 4 complicate the task of assigning each capital letter present in this fragment to its respective font. Of the variant letterforms to types 1 and 4 noted by the Hellingas (I, 57), the following are unique to type 1: N^1, P^1; the following are unique to type 4^A (simply a later state of type 1, in use by 1482): A^3, C^3, M^2, N^2, O^2, and P^2; and the following are also present: A^1, I^1, I^2, M^1, and O^1. It is not clear which, if any, forms also belong to type 2.

In a subsequent analysis of de Keysere's types, Jerome Machiels conflated types 1 and 4 into a single type 1; he also concluded that type 2 was introduced ca. 1481-1482 and "consists solely of a lower case, the capitals being taken from type 1" (English summary in J. Machiels, "Arend de Keysere, Master Printer 1480-1490," *Quaerendo* 4 (1974): 34-37; for full discussion, see J. Machiels, *Meester Arend de Keysere 1480-1490* (Ghent, 1974)). He also found that de Keysere employed type 2 at his second press at Ghent (1483-1490) in at least one work: a broadside dating to 1487 (GW 10475). Machiels identified four variant forms of capital letters which de Keysere began to use "as he was on the point of leaving for Ghent, or just after he arrived there [by April 1483]"; one of these, a capital H with a dotted counter, is present in this fragment. While types 1, 2, and 4^A have similar body sizes and could have been set together, one could perhaps argue that the fragment is set in a later state of type 2, employing capitals from types 1 and 4 cast on a larger body.

With the exception of a single capital letter, then, this fragment could be dated on typographical evidence to ca. 1482 or perhaps slightly earlier. The presence of a capital H with dotted counter does not rule out such a date—indeed, this fragment may prove its use at Oudenaarde. But absent other evidence, it could also be argued that this fragment was printed at de Keysere's second press at Ghent between 1483 and 1490.

There are two single-line initial spaces: leaf 1v, line 15 (Reichling 531), and leaf 3r, line 1 (Reichling 562). Bifolia 1.4 and 2.3 each contain a watermark running through the gutter, hence the edition was presumably printed in half sheets. The watermark depicts a unicorn (no close match in Briquet or Piccard; not found by Machiels in any other work printed by de Keysere).

Without rubrication. Extensive marginal restorations and other repairs, with slight text loss. Tipped onto fol. 33 of an album of printed fragments removed from bindings (presumably Oxford bindings of the late 16th-early 17th centuries) of books in the library formed by Hannibal Gamon Jr., later removed to Lanhydrock House, Cornwall. For additional provenance information, see S1-372.5. Late 19th-century half tan sheep and brown cloth.

October 1963 – Bought with the Susan A.E. Morse fund. *fEC.A100. B659c

Antwerp

GOVAERT BAC

S1-3941.5 **Boek der kerstenen salicheyt.** Between 1493 and 1511.

16°. [2+] leaves; ill.; 83 x 70 mm. 13 lines, 53 x 43 mm. Type: 3:81G, with Lombard A (4 mm). Initial spaces.

The Houghton fragment is a single bifolium purchased by Philip Hofer, in November 1950, from the London printsellers Craddock & Barnard, who described it as a fragment of Campbell 1499 (C 5219, IDL 3991, Inc

Ant 275), an edition printed by Govaert Bac in 1495. However, Ingrid Bouwens of the Museum Meermanno-Westreenianum has confirmed that the Harvard bifolium does not match the unique copy of Campbell 1499 in their possession. No other incunable or post-incunable edition of this text with the typographical features of our fragment appears to be known. Possibly Craddock & Barnard or other dealers dispersed similar fragments from the same misidentified copy. Oddly, while the Houghton bifolium is rubricated, with trimmed edges, there is no clear evidence of previous sewing; perhaps it was cut from an unused or waste sheet.

Govaert Bac's 1495 edition of this text, also printed in type 3 in 16° format, extends to 154 leaves and contains a series of 62 full-page woodcuts (cf. Clazina H.C.M. Kok, *De houtsneden in de incunabelen van de Lage Landen 1475-1500: inventarisatie en bibliografische analyse* (Amsterdam, 1994), v. 2, p. 655-658). Two of the woodcuts (Kok's 34.3:61, "Pinksteren", and 34.3:62, "H. Maria en H. Johannes geknield bij het gesloten graf") also appear in the Houghton fragment; while they are found on leaves q3r and q4v of the 1495 edition, here both woodcuts appear in the same order, but on versos. Kok identifies two other incunable editions printed by Bac (Campbell 706 and 829) which employ woodcuts from the same series, but neither matches our fragment.

Although the type in which this fragment is set was employed by two printers other than Govaert Bac (cf. W. & L. Hellinga, *The Fifteenth-Century Printing Types of the Low Countries* (Amsterdam, 1966), I, 96 and II, 390 and plates 271-273), the combination of type, text, and woodcut evidence strongly links this bifolium to Bac's press. Bac used type 3 from 1493 through 1511, but it has not yet been possible to date the fragment more precisely. The watermark, of which a small portion appears in one leaf, remains to be identified.

Imperfect: a single bifolium only, unsigned. Initials added in red. Tipped into a cream paper mat; remains of paper hinges from an earlier matting.

9 November 1984 – Bequest of Philip Hofer. bTyp Inc 9432.5

S1-3942.5 **Thomas de Erfordia:** De modis significandi. Between 3 July 1496 and 1499.

f°. [36] leaves; ill.; 199 x 140 mm.

Imperfect: leaves e1-4 only; wanting most of lines 30-36 and some other text on e4. Without rubrication.

Figure 17. S1-3941.5: *Boek der kerstenen salicheyt* (Antwerp: Govaert Bac, between 1493 and 1511). One side of the Harvard bifolium. (bTyp Inc 9432.5, Department of Printing and Graphic Arts, Houghton Library, Harvard College Library)

Figure 18. S1-3941.5: *Boek der kerstenen salicheyt* (Antwerp: Govaert Bac, between 1493 and 1511). Reverse side of the Harvard bifolium. (bTyp Inc 9432.5, Department of Printing and Graphic Arts, Houghton Library, Harvard College Library)

Tipped onto fol. 30 of an album of printed fragments removed from bindings (presumably Oxford bindings of the late 16th-early 17th centuries) of books in the library formed by Hannibal Gamon Jr., later removed to Lanhydrock House, Cornwall. For additional provenance information, see S1-372.5. Late 19th-century half tan sheep and brown cloth.

HC 424; Camp 74; Inv Ant 304; ISTC it00356930.

October 1963 – Bought with the Susan A.E. Morse fund. *fEC.A100. B659c

Unknown Town

PRINTER OF FLAVIUS JOSEPHUS

S1-3947B   **Valerius Maximus, Gaius:** Facta et dicta memorabilia [French]. Not after 1476.

f°. Two leaves only. 385 x 289 mm.

The leaves are: vol. 1, leaf 18_6 (beginning of Book III); and vol. 2, leaf 6_{10} (opening of Book VI). Each leaf contains a large miniature (ca. 150 x 175 mm) in brown ink and delicate watercolor; also a large penwork initial in red and blue, with marginal extension and red and blue infill; initials elsewhere added in red, paragraph marks in red or blue, capital strokes in yellow, underlinings in red, and headlines in red and blue. Formerly in the libraries of C. Czeczkowicka, Mario Uzielli, and Heinrich Eisemann. As of 1977, other leaves from this copy were in the possession of the Cleveland Museum of Art (beginning of Books VIII-IX); Dr. B. Solomons, London (beginning of Book V); and Bernard Quaritch Ltd. (beginning of Book IV; now in the Pierpont Morgan Library).

9 November 1984 – Bequest of Philip Hofer. pTyp Inc 9461.5

Figure 19. S1-3947B: GAIUS VALERIUS MAXIMUS *Facta et dicta memorabilia* [French] (Belgium: Printer of Flavius Josephus, not after 1476). Vol. 1, leaf 18₆ recto with miniature. (pTyp Inc 9461.5, Department of Printing and Graphic Arts, Houghton Library, Harvard College Library)

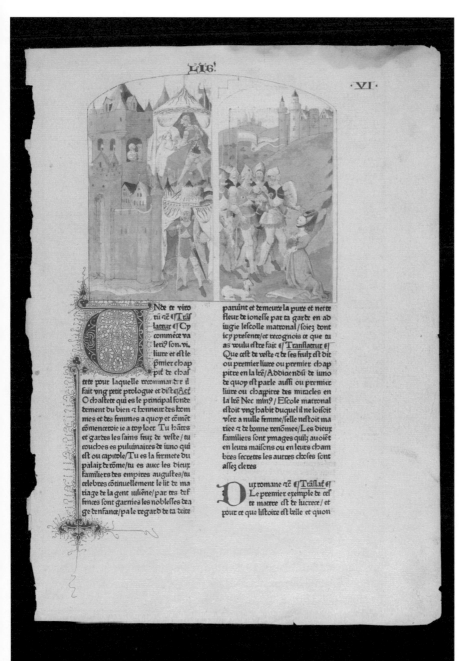

Nœ œ viro
tu aͦ e̅ Traͣ
lateur e̅ Cp
commeͤœ va
leri͛ ſon. vi.
liuœ et eſt le
p̅mier chap
pit œ chaſ
œœ pour laquelle œcom̅an̅œ il
fait vng petit p̅logue et diſtqＡｃｔ
O chaſteœ qui es le p̅incipal fonœ
tement du bien ꝗ honneur œs kom̅
mes et œs femmes a quoy et coͤmͤ
comenœwe ie a toy loer Tu haͤtes
et gaͣœs les ſains feuͥ œ veſte / tu
couches es puluinaires œ iuno qui
eſt ou capitole / Tu es la fermeœ du
palaiͥ œ rome / tu es auec les dieuͥ
familiers œs empiœs auguſtes / tu
celebres coͤtinuellement le lit œ ma
riaœ œ la gent iuliene / paͥ œs œf
fenœs ſont garnies les nobleſſes œ a
ge œnfanœ / pa le regaͥd œ ta œiœ

paruint et œmeuœ la puœ et netœ
fleur œ ioneſſe par ta garœ en ad
iugie leſcolle matronal / ſoieͣ œnt
icy p̅ſenœ / et reconois œ que tu
as wulu eſtœ fait e̅ Tranſlateur e̅
Que ceſt œ veſte ꝗ œ ſes feulͥ eſt dit
ou p̅emier liuœ ou p̅emier ch ap
pitre en la lꝛe̅ / Addiaꝺ̅u œ iuno
œ quoy eſt parle auſſi ou p̅emier
liuœ ou chappitœ œs miracles en
la lꝛe̅ Nec min͛ / Eſcole matronal
eſtoit vng habit duquel il ne loiſoit
vſer a nulle femme / ſelle neſtoit ma
rie ꝗ œ bonne renoͤmee / Les dieuͥ
familiers ſont ymages quilͣ auoiͤt
en leurs maiſons ou en leurs cham
bres ſecreœs les autres choſes ſont
aſſeͣ cleœs

Ou romane aͦ e̅ Traͣlat e̅
Le p̅emier exemple œ cel
œ matœe eſt œ lucreœ / et
pour œ que liſtoiœ eſt belle et quon

Figure 19. S1-3947B: Gaius Valerius Maximus *Facta et dicta memorabilia* [French] (Belgium: Printer
of Flavius Josephus, not after 1476). Vol. 2, leaf 6₁₀ recto with miniature. (pTyp Inc 9461.5, Department of
Printing and Graphic Arts, Houghton Library, Harvard College Library)

David R. Whitesell 133

SPAIN

Salamanca

PRINTER OF NEBRISSENSIS, *INTRODUCTIONES*

S1-3972.5 **Ovidius Naso, Publius:** Metamorphoses. ca. 1488.

4°. a-c¹⁰+; [30+] leaves; 190 x 143 mm. c1r: 28 lines, 160 x 97 mm. Types: 1:90G, signatures; 4:114R, text.

Imperfect: fragmentary bifolium c1.10 only. Without rubrication. This edition was previously known only through two fragmentary bifolia in the Bodleian Library (b4.7, c1.10) containing the text of Book I, lines 730-779, Book II, lines 115-167, 338-391, 841-875 and Book III, lines 1-17; the Harvard bifolium adds the text of Book II, lines 336-337 and 839-840. Books II-III are separated (leaf c10v) by a blank line, followed by a one-line incipit ("[...]eon liber tertius."). The extant bifolia indicate that Books I-II consisted of 30 leaves, quired in three gatherings of 10 leaves each, the second and third gatherings explicitly signed b and c. If this edition included Books I-XV of the *Metamorphoses*, it would have contained ca. 215 leaves of text. Kristian Jensen reports that the Bodleian bifolia "were extracted from the binding of *Passiones, Benedictiones, Lamentationes et reliquia* (Palencia: Didacus de Cordoba, 1536) ... purchased by Sir John Stainer ... in Seville in 1897 and presented by him to the Bodleian in the same year"; the Harvard bifolium has a different provenance (see below). The same printer also issued an edition of Ovid's *Amores* (IBE 4232), dated by IBE to ca. 1488, of which there is only one known copy: also a quarto set in Types 1 and 4, 28 lines per page, initial spaces, collating [a]⁸ b-e⁸ f⁶.

Tipped onto fol. 55 of an album of printed fragments removed from bindings (presumably Oxford bindings of the late 16th-early 17th centuries) of books in the library formed by Hannibal Gamon Jr., later removed to Lanhydrock House, Cornwall. For additional provenance information, see S1-372.5. Late 19th-century half tan sheep and brown cloth.

Pr 9562; Haeb(BI) 506; Vindel(A) 2:29:19; ISTC i000182700.

October 1963 – Bought with the Susan A.E. Morse fund. *fEC.A100. B659c

Burgos

"JUAN DE REI"

(S1-3983a) **Gómez, Fernán:** Centon epistolaris. ca. 1600.

4°. [2], 166 (i.e. 170) p. (25, 163-170 misnumbered 21 and 159-166); 193 x 139 mm.

The title page gives the imprint as Burgos, Juan de Rei, 1499, but this is clearly false: no other works by this printer are recorded, and the book bears every indication of having been printed well after 1500. Although the book was probably printed in Spain, the place and printer have yet to be identified. IBE dates this edition to ca. 1600.

Without rubrication. Old vellum.

H 7792; GW 6:col. 499; Goff G-321; BSB-Ink V-75; Haeb(BI) 148; IBE Post-incunables 78.

20 May 1921 – Bought with the Mary Osgood fund. Span 4740.5.5*

ENGLAND

Westminster

WILLIAM CAXTON

S1-3989.8 **Higden, Ranulphus:** Polycronicon [English]. After 2 July 1482.

f°. A single leaf only. 256 x 182 mm.

English translation by John Trevisa. With a continuation for the years 1387 to 1460 by William Caxton.

In: Benjamin P. Kurtz, *An Original Leaf from the Polycronicon Printed by William Caxton at Westminster in the Year 1482* (San Francisco: The Book Club of California, 1938).

The leaf is 21₁ (leaf CLxj). Without rubrication. Half linen and illustrated brown boards; leaf hinged onto the leaf following the title page.

HC 8659; Pr 9645; BL IB.55058-60; Polain 1959; GW 12468; Goff H-267; STC 13438; Duff 172; DeR(C) 49.

22 August 1938 – Bought with the Susan Green Dexter fund. B 4456.22F*

S1-3989.8A — Single leaf only. 256 x 181 mm.

In: Benjamin P. Kurtz, *An Original Leaf from the Polycronicon* … (San Francisco: The Book Club of California, 1938).

The leaf is 23₈ (leaf CLxxxiiij). Initial (on verso), paragraph marks and underlinings added in red. Half linen and illustrated brown boards; leaf hinged onto the leaf following the title page. Bookplate and signature, dated 1939, of Albert M. Bender.

15 April 1940 – Gift of Albert M. Bender. Typ 970.38.5050F

S1-3990.5 **Directorium sacerdotum ad usum Sarum.** ca. 1484.

f°. A single leaf only. In 2 fragments: lines 1-15 (113 x 152 mm), lines 24-33 (112 x 108 mm).

Includes *Defensorium Directorii* and *Tractatus Credi michi*. Edited by Clement Maydeston.

The leaf is k6. Without rubrication. Some 16th-century MS annotations in English and Latin. MS note by W.H. Allnutt, "From binding of Chrysostomi Javelli Logicae compendium 1573", i.e. removed from the binding on a copy of Chrysostomus Javellus, *Logicae compendium*, perhaps the 8° edition published Paris: Jacques Du Puys, 1573?

Tipped onto fol. 13 of an album of printed fragments removed from bindings (presumably Oxford bindings of the late 16th-early 17th centuries) of books in the library formed by Hannibal Gamon Jr., later removed to Lanhydrock House, Cornwall. For additional provenance information, see S1-372.5. Late 19th-century half tan sheep and brown cloth.

HC 6271; Pr 9669; BL IB.55114; GW 8456; STC 17720; Duff 290; DeR(C) 77; Bohatta(LB) 584=773; ISTC id00265200.

October 1963 – Bought with the Susan A.E. Morse fund. *fEC.A100. B659c

WYNKYN DE WORDE

S1-3994A   **Bartholomaeus Anglicus:** De proprietatibus rerum [English]. ca. 1495.

f°. A single leaf only. 305 x 204 mm.

In: *Three Lions and the Cross of Lorraine: Bartholomaeus Anglicus, John of Trevisa, John Tate, Wynkyn de Worde, and De Proprietatibus Rerum: A Leaf Book with Essays by Howell Heaney, Lotte Hellinga, Richard Hills* (Newtown, Pa.: Bird & Bull Press, 1992).

The leaf is e1. Without rubrication. Copy no. 105 of 138 copies. Original half red morocco; leaf laid in a mylar pocket at the end of the book.

2 November 1992 – Bought with the Rosamond B. Loring fund. *52L-881F

Oxford

THEODORICUS ROOD

S1-3999.8   **Lattebury, Johannes:** Liber moralium super threnis Ieremiae. 31 July 1482.

f°. A single leaf only. 111 x 142 mm.

The leaf is a fragment of O3, consisting of the outer column and right half of the inner column, containing lines 3-24 (recto) and lines 3-25 (verso). Without rubrication. Printed on vellum.

Tipped onto fol. 22 of an album of printed fragments removed from bindings (presumably Oxford bindings of the late 16th-early 17th centuries) of books in the library formed by Hannibal Gamon Jr., later removed to Lanhydrock House, Cornwall. For additional provenance information, see S1-372.5. Late 19th-century half tan sheep and brown cloth.

HC(+Add) 9928; Pr 9749; BL IB.55317-17c; Polain 2441; Goff L-75; STC 15297; Duff 238; Madan 1:1482 and 2:1482.9.

October 1963 – Bought with the Susan A.E. Morse fund. *fEC.A100.B659c

⚹ **S1-4000.8** **Logica.** ca. 1483.

f°. A single leaf only. 172 x 126 mm.

A collection of 19 treatises, including Roger Swineshede, *Insolubilia*; Thomas Bradwardinus, *De proportionibus*; and Albertus de Saxonia, *De velocitate*; with extracts from Paulus Venetus, *Logica parva*, and Johannes Buridanus, *Summulae*.

The leaf is F6. Without rubrication. MS note by W.H. Allnutt, "From the binding of J. Royard's Homiliae, Antverpiae MDXLIIII," i.e. removed from the binding on a copy of a work by Jean Royaerds, presumably either *Homiliae in evangelia ferarium quadragesime iuxta literam* or *Homiliae in omnes epistolas feriales quadragesimae iuxta literam*, both 8° editions published Antwerp: Joannes Steels, 1544.

Tipped onto fol. 48 of an album of printed fragments removed from bindings (presumably Oxford bindings of the late 16th-early 17th centuries) of books in the library formed by Hannibal Gamon Jr., later removed to Lanhydrock House, Cornwall. For additional provenance information, see S1-372.5. Late 19th-century half tan sheep and brown cloth.

Pr 9752; BL IB.55326; STC 16693; Duff 277; Madan 1:1483.3 and 2:1483.13.

October 1963 – Bought with the Susan A.E. Morse fund. *fEC.A100. B659c

London

JOHN LETTOU AND WILLIAM DE MACHLINIA

S1-4003A **Abbreviamentum statutorum.** ca. 1482.

f°. Another copy. 286 x 207 mm.

Duff and GW transcribe "vtlagerie" on N8v; this copy has "vtlagarie". Large penwork initial on A1r added in red with blue infill; initials elsewhere, paragraph marks, capital strokes, and underlinings added in red. Early 19th-century crimson blind- and gilt-stamped straight-grain morocco, edges gilt on the rough. Old inscription erased from H8v. From the library of the Dukes of Devonshire, with the Chatsworth bookplate ("Bookcase 1, Shelf E"); "10611" in MS on verso of front endleaf. Imperfect: leaf N8 mounted, lower outer corner wanting, with some text loss on recto and verso; outer margin of D8, N6-7 renewed, with slight text loss on D8.

April 2001 – Bequest of Henry N. Ess. Law Library

RICHARD PYNSON

S1-4017A **Abbreviamentum statutorum.** 9 October 1499.

8°. Another copy. 136 x 94 mm.

Woodcut initial on a1r; Lombards elsewhere. 18th-century blind-tooled calf; edges sprinkled red; rebacked and corners renewed with tan calf. Bookplate of William M. Fitzhugh, Jr.

April 2001 – Bequest of Henry N. Ess. Law Library

(S1-4021c) **Assises:** Liber assisarum. ca. 1502?

8°. Another copy. 123 x 92 mm.

19th-century gilt-stamped sprinkled calf, edges stained red, by W. Pratt. Cropped MS ownership notation on title page. With this is bound *Natura brevium* (London: Richard Tottel, 1584; STC 18402).

April 2001 – Bequest of Henry N. Ess. Law Library

SWEDEN

Stockholm

JOHANN SNELL

S1-4021.6 **Missale Upsalense.** ca. 1484.

f°. A single leaf only. 289 x 195 mm.

In: G. E. Klemming, *Sveriges äldre liturgiska literatur: bibliografi* (Stockholm: Kongl. Boktryckeriet, P. A. Norstedt & Söner, 1879).

The leaf, from the *Missae votivae, collectae et benedictiones*, is foliated "v vii" (leaf 24₇ (217) per Collijn's collation); small piece cut away from upper outer corner, affecting text. Printed on vellum. Lombard initials and rubrics printed in red. Initial spaces not filled in. Half brown cloth and printed gray boards; the leaf is inlaid and bound in following p. 2. For provenance and other information, see S1-813.8, with which this is bound.

C 4260; Pr 2647 (assigned to Lübeck, unidentified printer); BMC 2:562 (IB.56204); Goff M-730; CIBN M-483; Weale-Bohatta 1609; Collijn 1:29.

20 March 1902 – Bought with the Emil Christian Hammer fund. Inc 9828.50

BARTHOLOMAEUS GHOTAN

S1-4021.7   **Missale Strengnense.** 1487.

f°. A single leaf only. 288 x 191 mm.

In: G. E. Klemming, *Sveriges äldre liturgiska literatur: bibliografi* (Stockholm: Kongl. Boktryckeriet, P. A. Norstedt & Söner, 1879).

The leaf is A XIIII (leaf b6 (24) per Collijn's collation). Printed on vellum. Lombard initials, rubrics, and headlines printed in red; four-line floriated metalcut initial on recto printed in red, with added blue coloring; marginal extension added in blue on verso, additional rubrication in red. MS archival title dated 1574, from the leaf's prior use as a document wrapper, on verso. Half brown cloth and printed gray boards; the leaf is inlaid and bound in following p. 10. For provenance and other information, see S1-813.8, with which this is bound.

C 4234; Pr 2622 (assigned to Lübeck); BMC 2:553 (C.18.c.13); Goff M-722; CIBN M-475; Meyer-Baer 188; Weale-Bohatta 1486; Schr 4762a; Schramm 12:10; Collijn 1:69.

20 March 1902 – Bought with the Emil Christian Hammer fund. Inc 9828.50

JOHANN FABRI (SMEDH)

S1-4021.8   **Breviarium Strengnense.** 18 July 1495.

4°. A single leaf only. 189 x 133 mm.

In: G. E. Klemming, *Sveriges äldre liturgiska literatur: bibliografi* (Stockholm: Kongl. Boktryckeriet, P. A. Norstedt & Söner, 1879).

Collijn, GW, and Goff mistakenly call this an octavo; the horizontal chainlines prove the format to be quarto.

The leaf is unsigned. Lombard initials and rubrics printed in red. Half brown cloth and printed gray boards; the leaf is inlaid and bound in following p. 22. For provenance and other information, see S1-813.8, with which this is bound.

C 1318; Pr 9829; BL C.18.c.13; GW 5467; Goff B-1183; Bohatta(LB) 502; Collijn 1:138.

20 March 1902 – Bought with the Emil Christian Hammer fund. Inc 9828.50

JOHANN FABRI AND ANNA FABRI (SMEDH)

S1-4021.9   **Breviarium Upsalense.** 30 September 1496.

4°. A single leaf only. 174 x 122 mm.

In: G. E. Klemming, *Sveriges äldre liturgiska literatur: bibliografi* (Stockholm: Kongl. Boktryckeriet, P. A. Norstedt & Söner, 1879).

The colophon notes the death of Johann Fabri, and that printing was completed under the direction of his widow, Anna. Edited by Andreas Simonis.

The leaf is unsigned. Lombard initials and rubrics printed in red. Half brown cloth and printed gray boards; the leaf is inlaid and bound in following p. 24. For provenance and other information, see S1-813.8, with which this is bound.

HC(+Add) 3950; Pr 9830; BL C.18.c.13; Pell 2950; GW 5499; Goff B-1187; Bohatta(LB) 532; Schr 3627; Collijn 1:148.

20 March 1902 – Bought with the Emil Christian Hammer fund. Inc 9828.50

Hebraica

Soncino

JOSHUA SOLOMON BEN ISRAEL NATHAN SONCINO

S1-Heb-12A Biblia Hebraica: Nevi'im aharonim [Later Prophets]. 1485?

f°. Another copy. 243 x 174 mm.

Imperfect: pt. 2 only, 49 of 66 leaves, bound in order 7_{1-8}, 6_{1-8}, 4_8, 5_{2-8}, 4_{1-7}, 2_8, 3_{2-8}, 8_{1-10}; fore-edge margin of 8_1 mutilated, with some text loss. A portion of the missing text and commentary is supplied in old MS on four leaves bound in at front. Half modern sheep and decorated boards. Some MS inscriptions in Hebrew. From the library of Felix Friedmann of Amsterdam.

May 1987 – Bought with funds provided by a committee of donors. Judaica Division

S1-Heb-12.5 Jacob Ben Asher: Arba'ah turim [The four orders of the Hebrew code of law]. ca. 1490.

f°. 4 pts. (pt. 1: [94] leaves; pt. 2: [80] leaves; pt. 3: [50] leaves; pt. 4: [126] leaves).

Brown sheep. This copy was accessioned in 1961 and reported to Goff, but it cannot at present be located. Walsh lists it (5:473) among the incunabula "wrongly credited to [Harvard] by Goff," though it is not clear why he did so.

H 1880; Pr 7302; BMC 13:48 (C.50.d.5); IGI 5090 and E-77; Goff Heb-48; CIBN Heb-18; BSB-Ink I-1; Sander 3545; Adler 20-21; De Rossi p.114, no. 24; Freimann 21; Meyer 99; Offenberg (Census) 62; Steinschneider 5500, 2; Thes A 56.

1961 – Source unknown; transferred from Widener Library. *61-728F

References

I. Abbreviated References

Benzing, Köbel	Benzing, Josef. *Jakob Köbel zu Oppenheim, 1494-1533: Bibliographie seiner Drucke und Schriften.* Wiesbaden, 1962.
BM STC(I)	British Museum. *Short-Title Catalogue of Books Printed in Italy and of Italian Books Printed in Other Countries from 1465 to 1600 Now in the British Museum.* London, 1958.
Brüggemann	*Handbuch zur Kinder- und Jugendliteratur: vom Beginn des Buchdrucks bis 1570.* Hrsg. von Theodor Brüggemann, Otto Brunken. Stuttgart, 1987.
Campbell	Campbell, Tony. *The Earliest Printed Maps 1472-1500.* Berkeley, 1987.
Collijn	Collijn, Isak. *Sveriges bibliografi intill år 1600.* 3 vols. Uppsala, 1927–38. (Skrifter utgivna av Svenska litteratursällskapet, 10:5-18)
GW	The print version of the *Gesamtkatalog der Wiegendrucke* has been supplemented by an online version providing access, not only to published entries, but to drafts of unpublished entries. Available at: http://www.gesamtkatalogderwiegendrucke.de/
Haegen	Haegen, Pierre L. van der. *Basler Wiegendrucke: Verzeichnis der in Basel gedruckten Inkunabeln mit ausführlicher Beschreibung der in der Universitätsbibliothek Basel vorhandenen Exemplare.* Basel, 1998. (Schriften der Universitätsbibliothek Basel, Bd. 1)
Hargreaves	Hargreaves, Geoffrey D. *A Catalogue of Medical Incunabula in Edinburgh Libraries.* Edinburgh, 1976.
Heldenbuch	Heldenbuch. *Heldenbuch: nach dem ältesten Druck in Abbildung.* Hrsg. von Joachim Heinzle. 2 vols. Göppingen, 1981-87.
Hillard	Hillard, Denise. *Catalogues régionaux des incunables des bibliothèques publiques de France.* Vol.VI: *Bibliothèque Mazarine, Paris.* Bordeaux, 1989.
Hubay (Eichstätt)	Hubay, Ilona. *Incunabula Eichstätter Bibliotheken.* Wiesbaden, 1968.

ISTC   Incunabula Short-Title Catalogue, CD-ROM version: *The Illustrated ISTC on CD-ROM.* Edited by Martin Davies. 2nd ed. Reading, Eng., 1998.

         Updated version available at: http://www.bl.uk/catalogues/istc/index.html

Meltz   Meltz, C., "Die Drucke der Michaelisbrüder zu Rostock 1476 bis 1530." *Wissenschaftliche Zeitschrift der Universität Rostock,* 5 (1955/56), Sonderheft: 229-43.

Tura   *Edizioni fiorentine del Quattrocento e primo Cinquecento in Trivulziana.* Mostra curata da Adolfo Tura. Milano, 2001.

VE 15   Eisermann, Falk. *Verzeichnis der typographischen Einblattdrucke des 15. Jahrhunderts im Heiligen Römischen Reich Deutscher Nation: VE 15.* Bd. 1-2 in 3 vols. Wiesbaden, 2004.

II. Other References

[N.B. This list does not include personal library or sale catalogues.]

Campbell, Tony. "The Woodcut Map Considered as a Physical Object: a New Look at Erhard Etzlaub's *Rom Weg* Map of c.1500." *Imago Mundi* 30 (1978): 78-91.

Ciapponi, Lucia A. "Bartolomeo Fonzio e la prima centuria dei 'Miscellanea' del Poliziano." *Italia medioevale e umanistica* 23 (1980): 165-77.

Dalbanne, Claude. "Trois éditions lyonnaises du *Traité des eaux artificielles.*" *Gutenberg-Jahrbuch* (1932): 125-46.

Dane, Joseph A. "'Si vis archetypas habere nugas': Authorial Subscriptions in the Houghton Library and Huntington Library Copies of Politian, *Miscellanea* (Florence: Miscomini 1489)." *Harvard Library Bulletin,* n.s. 10, 2 (1999): 12-22.

Essling, Victor Masséna, prince d'. *Les livres à figures vénitiens de la fin du XVe. siècle et du commencement du XVIe.: études sur l'art de la gravure sur bois à Venise.* 3 pts. in 6 vols. Florence, 1907-14.

Fulin, Rinaldo. "Documenti per servire alla storia della tipografia veneziana." *Archivio veneto* 23 (1882): 84-212.

Gerritsen-Geywirtz, Gisela. "Zur Frühgeschichte der Harvarder Gutenberg-Bibel." *Gutenberg-Jahrbuch* (2000): 64-72.

Hobson, Anthony. "A German Student in Italy: His Books and Bindings." *Mélanges d'histoire de la reliure offerts à Georges Colin* (Brussels, 1998): 87-99.

Hobson, Anthony. *Humanists and Bookbinders: The Origins and Diffusion of the Humanistic Bookbinding 1459-1559*. Cambridge, Eng., 1989.

Ker, N.R. *Fragments of Medieval Manuscripts Used as Pastedowns in Oxford Bindings: With a Survey of Oxford Binding c.1515-1620*. Oxford, 1954. Reprinted with additions 2004.

Kofler, Walter. *Die Heldenbuch-Inkunabel von 1479: alle Exemplare und Fragmente in 350 Abbildungen*. CD-ROM. Göppingen: Kümmerle Verlag, 2003.

Kok, Clazina Helena Cornelia Maria. *De houtsneden in de incunabelen van de Lage Landen, 1475-1500: inventarisatie en bibliografische analyse*. 2 vols. Amsterdam, 1994.

Lehmann-Haupt, Hellmut. *Initials from French Incunabula*. New York, 1948.

Light, Laura. *Catalogue of Medieval and Renaissance Manuscripts in the Houghton Library*. Vol. 1. Binghamton, N.Y., 1995.

Machiels, Jerome. "Arend de Keysere, Master Printer 1480-1490." *Quaerendo* 4 (1974): 34-37.

—. *Meester Arend de Keysere 1480-1490*. Ghent, 1974.

Maignien, Edmond. *L'imprimerie, les imprimeurs et les libraires à Grenoble du XVe au XVIIIe siècle*. Grenoble, 1884.

Mazal, Otto. "Datierte gotische Einbände aus dem Augustiner Chorherrenstift Dürnstein a. d. Donau." *Gutenberg-Jahrbuch* (1961): 286-91.

Morris, Leslie A. *Rosenbach Abroad*. Philadelphia, 1988.

Olschki, G. Cesare. "Un codice savonaroliano sconosciuto." *La Bibliofilia* 23 (1921): 153-65.

Reichling, Dietrich. *Das Doctrinale des Alexander de Villa-Dei*. Berlin, 1893.

Rhodes, Dennis Everard. "An Unidentified 'Incunable' Printed at Augsburg Not Before 1502." *The Library*, 5th ser., 13 (1958): 54-56

Rodolphus Agricola Phrisius, 1444-1485. Ed. by F. Akkerman and A.J. Vanderjagt. Leiden, 1988.

Schmitt, Charles B. "A Note on the First Edition of Gianfrancesco Pico's 'Hymni Heroici Tres.'" *Papers of the Bibliographical Society of America* 59 (1965): 45-48.

Sheehan, William J. *Incunabula Bibliothecae apostolicae vaticanae.* 4 vols. Vatican City, 1997. (Studi e testi, 380-383)

Wagner, Bettina. "'Libri impressi Bibliothecae Monasterii Sancti Emmerammi': The Incunable Collection of St Emmeram, Regensburg, and Its Catalogue of 1501." *Incunabula and Their Readers: Printing, Selling and Using Books in the Fifteenth Century* (2003): 179-205.

Walther, Hans. *Initia carminum ac versuum Medii Aevi posterioris Latinorum.* Göttingen, 1959.

Way, Peter. "Jehan de Mouveaux's 'Primum Exemplar' (a Model Copy Made for Henri Estienne's 1512 Edition of Eusebius' *Chronicon*)." *Gutenberg-Jahrbuch* (2003): 93-118.

INDEXES

Venice, Bernhard Maler, Erhard Ratdolt, and Peter Löslein, 1477, S1-1729A

ASSISES
Liber assisarum
London, Richard Pynson, ca. 1502?, (S1-4021c)

AUGUSTINUS, AURELIUS, SAINT
De civitate Dei
Venice, Bonetus Locatellus, 9 February 1486/87, S1-2268.7
Epistolae
Strassburg, Johann Mentelin, not after 1471, S1-54.5

AUGUSTINUS, PSEUDO-
De vita Christiana
Paris, Guy Marchant, 9 January 1500/01, S1-3630.8
Sermo super orationem dominicam
Cologne, Ulrich Zell, ca. 1467, S1-315.5
Sermones ad heremitas
Venice, Bernardinus Rizus, 10 August 1490, S1-2181.5
Paris, Antoine Chappiel, 1500, S1-3736B

AVICENNA
Canon [Latin] (Lib. III)
Venice, Baptista de Tortis, 11 February 1492/93, S1-1934.2

BALBUS, JOHANNES
Catholicon
Strassburg, Printer of Jordanus, not after 1483, S1-218A

BAPTISTA MANTUANUS
Opera
Bologna, Benedictus Hectoris Faelli, 11 June 1502, (S1-3253b)

BARBARUS, HERMOLAUS
Oratio ad Fridericum III Imperatorem et Maximilianum I Regem Romanorum
Nuremberg, Peter Wagner, after 2 April 1490, S1-804.5

BARTHOLOMAEUS ANGLICUS
De proprietatibus rerum [English]
Westminster, Wynkyn de Worde, ca. 1495, S1-3994A
— [French]
Lyons, Johannes Siber, after 26 January 1486, S1-3755A

BERNARDUS CLARAVALLENSIS
Epistolae
Basel, Nicolaus Kesler, 1 December 1494, S1-1216.5
Sermones super Cantica canticorum
Rostock, Fratres Domus Horti Viridis ad S. Michaelem, 28 July 1481, S1-955.7

BEROALDUS, PHILIPPUS
De felicitate
Paris, Gaspard Philippe for Denis Roce, ca. 1501, (S1-3736b-c)
Declamatio philosophi, medici, oratoris et alia opuscula
Bologna, Benedictus Hectoris Faelli, after 1500, (S1-3253a)

BERTACHINUS, JOHANNES
Repertorium iuris utriusque
Lyons, Johannes Siber, ca. 1485/90, S1-3754A

BIBLIA [GERMAN]
Augsburg, Günther Zainer, not after 1474, S1-518.5
Nuremberg, Anton Koberger, 17 February 1483, S1-692A, S1-866.8

CASSIODORUS, MAGNUS AURELIUS
Expositio in Psalterium
    Basel, Johann Amerbach, 1491, S1-
1173A-B

CASTELLANI, CASTELLANO DE'
Meditatione della morte
    Florence, Unassigned, after 1500,
(S1-3035f)

CASUS PAPALES, EPISCOPALES ET
ABBATIALES
    Rome, Stephan Plannck, ca. 1492,
S1-1427.5

CAVICEUS, JACOBUS
Sex urbium dicta ad Maximilianum
Romanorum regem
    Venice, Printer of Caviceus, after 16
March 1491, S1-2192.8

CHAPPUSIUS, NICOLAUS
De mente et memoria
    Paris, Unassigned, ca. 1514, (S1-
3736j)

CICERO
Epistolae ad familiares
    Venice, Andreas Torresanus and
Bartholomaeus de Blavis, 31 January
1483/84, S1-1884A
Orationes
    Venice, Johannes de Gregoriis and
Jacobus Britannicus, 8 November 1483,
S1-1962.2

CLAUDIANUS, CLAUDIUS
De raptu Proserpinae
    Venice, Albertinus, Bartholomaeus,
and Johannes Rubeus, ca. 1505?, (S1-
2229d)

COLONNA, FRANCESCO see Columna,
Franciscus

COLUMNA, FRANCISCUS
Hypnerotomachia Poliphili
    Venice, Aldus Manutius, December
1499, S1-2686A

CONCILIUM BASILIENSE
Decretum de conceptione Beatae Mariae
Virginis
    Cologne, Johann Guldenschaff, ca.
1478, S1-415.3

CORPUS IURIS CIVILIS
Codex Justinianus
    Nuremberg, Johann Sensenschmidt,
24 June 1475, S1-664.5
Infortiatum
    Venice, Baptista de Tortis, 4
November 1495, S1-1938.5-.5A
Novellae etc.
    Venice, Jacobus Rubeus, 16 January
1477/78, S1-1657A

CRASTONUS, JOHANNES
Lexicon Graeco-Latinum
    Venice, Aldus Manutius, December
1497, S1-2657A-C

DANSE MACABRE [LATIN]
    Paris, Guy Marchant, 15 October
1490, S1-3615.7

DANTE ALIGHIERI
La Commedia
    Florence, Nicolaus Laurentii, 30
August 1481, S1-2854A
    Brescia, Boninus de Boninis, 31 May
1487, S1-3403A
    Venice, Petrus de Plasiis, 18
November 1491, S1-1777A

DENIS LE CHARTREUX see Dionysius
Cartusianus

DESTRUCTORIUM VITIORUM see

1487, S1-917.5-.5A
   Strassburg, Johann (Reinhard)
Grüninger, ca. 1489, S1-166A-B
   Augsburg, Johann Schönsperger, 13
May 1499, S1-608.5-.5A

Gebote
   Speyer, Peter Drach, ca. 1500, S1-
866.6

Gerardus de Vliederhoven
Cordiale quattuor novissimorum
   Paris, Pierre Levet, ca. 1502, (S1-
3643a)

Gerson, Johannes
De custodia linguae et corde bene
ruminanda
   Speyer, Johann and Conrad Hist, ca.
1483, S1-866.8

Gómez, Fernán
Centon epistolaris
   'Burgos, Juan de Rei, 1499' (i.e. ca.
1600), (S1-3983a)

Graduale Arosiense
   Lübeck, Steffen Arndes, ca. 1493, S1-
952.5

Guillaume de Digulleville
Le roman des trois pèlerinages
   Paris, Berthold Rembolt and Jean
Petit, ca. 1517, (S1-3736e)

Guillelmus Carthusiensis see
Guillelmus Hilacensis

Guillelmus Hilacensis
Sermones super orationem dominicam
   Paris, Ulrich Gering and Berthold
Rembolt, 1494, S1-3601.8

Harentals, Petrus de see Petrus de
Harentals

Harmonius Marsus, Joannes
Comoedia Stephanium
   Venice, Bernardinus Venetus, ca.
1503, (S1-2626e)

Heldenbuch
   Strassburg, Johann Prüss, ca. 1479,
S1-191.2

Henricus de Herpf
Directorium ad consequendam vitae
perfectionem
   Paris, Guy Marchant, ca. 1499, S1-
3630.2

Henricus de Vrimaria
Passio domini explanata
   Oppenheim, Jakob Köbel, ca. 1515,
(S1-1100b)

Herbarius
   Vicenza, Leonardus Achates, 27
October 1491, S1-3489A-B

Herbarius [with French Synonyms]
   Paris, Jean Bonhomme, ca. 1486, S1-
3594.3

Herbarius [with German Synonyms]
   Passau, Johann Petri, 1485, S1-997A-
B

Herpf, Henricus de see Henricus de
Herpf

Hieronymus, Saint
Commentaria in Bibliam
   Venice, Johannes and Gregorius de
Gregoriis, 1497-25 August 1498, S1-2033A
Epistolae
   Venice, Doninus Pincius, after 1500,
(S1-2751a)

Higden, Ranulphus
Polycronicon [English]

Disputationum Camaldulensium libri IV
Venice, Nicolò Brenta, ca. 1507, (S1-2751b)

LANGER, JOHANNES
De censibus
Mainz, Peter Schöffer, after 25 August 1489, S1-24.7

LATTEBURY, JOHANNES
Liber moralium super threnis Ieremiae
Oxford, Theodoricus Rood, 31 July 1482, S1-3999.8

LEGRAND, JACOBUS
Sophologium
Strassburg, Printer of Henricus Ariminensis, ca. 1476, S1-112.5

LOCHER, JACOBUS
Ludicrum drama de sene amatore
Strassburg, Unassigned, ca. 1503, (S1-310a)

LOGICA
Oxford, Theodoricus Rood, ca. 1483, S1-4000.8

LYRA, NICOLAUS DE see Nicolaus de Lyra

MAGNI, JACOBUS see Legrand, Jacobus

MAIORANIS, FRANCISCUS DE see Mayronis, Franciscus de

MANUALE PAROCHIALIUM SACERDOTUM
Cologne, Heinrich Quentell (second press), ca. 1492, S1-439.5

MARCHESINUS, JOHANNES
Mammotrectus super Bibliam
Strassburg, Georg Husner (first press), ca. 1476, S1-125.5

MAYNO, JASON DE
Oratio in funere Hieronymi Torti habita
Pavia, Johannes Andreas de Boscho, Michael and Bernardinus de Garaldis, ca. 1495, S1-3472.5

MAYRONIS, FRANCISCUS DE
Sermones de sanctis
Basel, Jacobus Wolff von Pforzheim, 1498, S1-1234.3

MEFFRET see Sermones Meffret De Tempore et De Sanctis

MELUSINA [GERMAN]
Basel, Bernhard Richel, ca. 1476, S1-1141.5

MISSALE ABOENSE
Lübeck, Bartholomaeus Ghotan, after 17 August 1488, S1-946.7

MISSALE SARESBERIENSE
Venice, Johannes Hamann, 1 September 1494, S1-2234.5

MISSALE STRENGNENSE
Stockholm, Bartholomaeus Ghotan, 1487, S1-4021.7
Stockholm, Johann Fabri (Smedh), 18 July 1495, S1-4021.8

MISSALE UPSALENSE
Stockholm, Johann Snell, ca. 1484, S1-4021.6

NARDUS, JACOBUS
Comedia di Amicitia
Florence, Gian Stephano di Carlo, ca. 1510, (S1-3033n)

NICOLAUS DE LYRA
Postilla super totam Bibliam
Rome, Conradus Sweynheym and Arnoldus Pannartz, 18 November 1471–

Pisis

PIUS II, POPE
Epistola ad Mahumetem
    Cologne, Ulrich Zell, ca. 1469/72,
S1-316.5
Epistolae familiares
    Cologne, Johann Koelhoff the Elder,
1478, S1-372.5

PLUTARCHUS
Vitae illustrium virorum
    Venice, Nicolaus Jenson, 2 January
1478, S1-1588A

POMPONIUS LAETUS, JULIUS *see* Laetus,
Pomponius

PORTIS, LEONARDUS DE
De sestertio pecuniis ponderibus et
mensuris antiquis libri duo
    Venice, Georgius de Rusconibus, ca.
1520, (S1-2750a)

PROGNOSTICON
Opusculum repertorii prognosticon in
mutationes aeris
    Venice, Erhard Ratdolt, before 4
November 1485, S1-1836A-B

PULCI, LUCA
Pistole in rima al Lorenzo de' Medici
    Florence, Unassigned, ca. 1510, (S1-
3035g)

PYLADES, JOHANNES FRANCISCUS
BUCCARDUS
Genealogia deorum
    Brescia, Angelus and Jacobus
Britannicus, after 1500, (S1-3425a)

PYTHAGORAS
Symbola moraliter explicata a Philippo
Beroaldo

Bologna, Benedictus Hectoris Faelli,
24 December 1503, (S1-3253c-d)

QUADRAGESIMALE VIATORIS
    Augsburg, Johann Bämler, 1479, S1-
547.5

RAINERIUS DE PISIS
Pantheologia
    Augsburg, Günther Zainer, 1474, S1-
516.8
    Nuremberg, Anton Koberger, 3
August 1474, S1-670A-B
    Nuremberg, Anton Koberger, 12
February 1477, S1-672.5

RETZA, FRANCISCUS DE
De generatione Christi, sive
Defensorium inviolatae castitatis B.V.M.
[Latin and German]
    Basel, Lienhart Ysenhut, ca. 1489-
1500, S1-1237.5

RHAZES, MUHAMMAD
Liber nonus ad Almansorem
    Venice, Bernardinus Stagninus, 12
November 1493, S1-2078.8

ROLEWINCK, WERNER
Fasciculus temporum
    Venice, Erhard Ratdolt, 24
November 1480, S1-1800A

SABELLICUS, MARCUS ANTONIUS
Decades rerum Venetarum [Italian]
    Milan, Gotardus da Ponte, ca. 1510?,
(S1-3168b)

Opera
    Venice, Albertinus Rubeus
Vercellensis, 24 December 1502, (S1-
2229c)

Augsburg, Johann Schönsperger, 1 February 1497, S1-601.7

SCHOTTUS, PETRUS
Lucubratiunculae
Strassburg, Martin Schott, 2 October 1498, S1-149.9

SEELEN-WURZGARTEN
Ulm, Conrad Dinckmut, 26 July 1483, S1-916.2

SERMONES MEFFRET DE TEMPORE ET DE SANCTIS
Basel, Nicolaus Kesler, not after 1483, S1-1202.7

SIXTUS IV, POPE
De sanguine Christi et De potentia Dei
Nuremberg, Friedrich Creussner, 1474, S1-766.5

SPECULUM HUMANAE SALVATIONIS [GERMAN]
Augsburg, Anton Sorg, S1-560.5

STATHAM, NICHOLAS
Abridgement of Cases
Rouen, Guillaume Le Tailleur, 1490, S1-3857A

STATUTA DELPHINATUS
Libertates per principes delphinos Viennenses delphinalibus subditis concessae
Grenoble, Unassigned, after 4 March 1508, (S1-3863a-b)

STATUTA SYNODALIA EYSTETTENSIA
Basel, Michael Furter, not after 1496, S1-1246.5

TEGLIATUS, STEPHANUS
Oratio coram Innocentio VIII pro die Pentecostes habita

Rome, Stephan Plannck, after 3 June 1487, S1-1404.8

TERASSE, PETRUS
Oratio de divina providentia
Rome, Stephan Plannck, after 9 March 1483, S1-1392.8

TEXTORIS, GUILLELMUS, PSEUDO-
Sermo de passione Christi
Strassburg, Printer of Jordanus, 11 February 1496, S1-258.5

THEGLIATUS, STEPHANUS see Tegliatus, Stephanus

THEMESWAR, PELBARTUS DE see Pelbartus de Themeswar

THEOPHRASTUS
De historia plantarum [Greek]
Venice, Aldus Manutius, 1 June 1497, S1-2645B-D

THIENIS, GAIETANUS DE
Recollectae super libros Physicorum Aristotelis
Vicenza, Henricus de Sancto Ursio, 23 April 1487, S1-3506.5

THOMAS AQUINAS
Commentaria in omnes Epistolas Sancti Pauli
Basel, Michael Furter, 16 October 1495, S1-1244A
Summae theologicae secundae partis pars secunda
Mainz, Peter Schöffer, 6 March 1467, S1-6.3
Super analytica posteriora et libros de interpretatione Aristotelis
Venice, Guillelmus Anima Mia, 16 November 1489, S1-2199A

PRINTERS AND PLACES

[Presses known by the title of a book are arranged in alphabetical order under "Printer of ..."]

ACHATES, LEONARDUS
Vicenza
S1-3489A-B

ALOPA, LORENZO DE (with TUBINI and GHIRLANDI)
Florence
(S1-3033a-c), (S1-3033d)

AMERBACH, JOHANN
Basel
S1-1159A, S1-1162A, S1-1163A-B,
S1-1173A-B, S1-1173.5, S1-1199.2-.2A

ANIMA MIA, GUILLELMUS
Venice
S1-2199A

Antwerp
S1-3941.5, S1-3942.5

ARNDES, STEFFEN
Lübeck
S1-952.5

Audenarde *see* **Oudenaarde**

Augsburg
S1-502A, S1-516.8, S1-518.5, S1-547.5,
S1-554A, S1-560.5, S1-561A,
S1-596.2-.2A, S1-596.4, S1-601.7,
S1-608.5-.5A, S1-609A, (S1-658c),
(S1-658d), (S1-658e)

BAC, GOVAERT
Antwerp
S1-3941.5, S1-3942.5

BÄMLER, JOHANN
Augsburg
S1-547.5

Basel
S1-1141.5, S1-1159A, S1-1162A,
S1-1163A-B, S1-1173A-B, S1-1173.5,
S1-1199.2-.2A, S1-1202.7,S1-1216.5,
S1-1227A-B, S1-1234.3, S1-1237.5,
S1-1244A, S1-1246.5, S1-1258A

Belgium (not assignable to any town)
S1-3947B

BENEDICTIS, NICOLAUS DE
Lyons
S1-3828.6

BERGMANN, JOHANN, DE OLPE
Basel
S1-1258A

BEVILACQUA, SIMON (Second press)
Venice
S1-2508.5, (S1-2544a)

Blaubeuren
S1-953.8

BÖTTIGER, GREGORIUS
Leipzig
S1-1037.5, S1-1043A

Bologna
(S1-3253a), (S1-3253b), (S1-3253c-d)

BONELLIS, MANFREDUS DE
Venice
S1-2482A

BONHOMME, JEAN
Paris
S1-3594.3

Boninis, Boninus de
Brescia
S1-3403A

Boscho, Johannes Andreas de
Pavia
S1-3472.5

Brenta, Nicolò
Venice
(S1-2751b)

Brescia
S1-3403A, (S1-3425a)

Britannicus, Jacobus (with
Gregoriis)
Venice
S1-1962.2

—(with Angelus)
Brescia
(S1-3425a)

Bulle, Johannes
Rome
S1-1381.5

Burgos
(S1-3983a)

Carlo, Gian Stephano di
Florence
(S1-3033h-i), (S1-3033j), (S1-3033k),
(S1-3033l), (S1-3033m), (S1-3033n)

Caxton, William
Westminster
S1-3989.8-.8A, S1-3990.5

Chappiel, Antoine
Paris
S1-3736B

Clein, Johannes
Lyons
(S1-3838b)

Colle di Valdelsa
S1-3534.8

Cologne
S1-315.5, S1-316.5, S1-343.5, S1-372.5,
S1-373.5, S1-415.3, S1-418.8, S1-424.5,
S1-427.5, S1-439.5, S1-457.2, (S1-478a),
(S1-491d)

Couturier, Raoul
Paris
(S1-3736g), (S1-3736h), (S1-3736i)

Cracow
(S1-1269a)

Creussner, Friedrich
Nuremberg
S1-766.5

Delft
S1-3869.7

Desplains, Guillaume
Paris
(S1-3736g), (S1-3736h), (S1-3736i)

Deventer
S1-3882.5

Dinckmut, Conrad
Ulm
S1-916.2, S1-917.5-.5A

Drach, Peter
Speyer
S1-835.8, S1-840A, S1-841A, S1-866.6

Du Pré, Jean
Paris
(S1-3605a)

EUSTACE, GUILLAUME
Paris
(S1-3736d)

FABRI, ANNA (with JOHANN FABRI)
Stockholm
S1-4021.9

FABRI, JOHANN (alone)
Stockholm
S1-4021.8

FABRI, JOHANN (with ANNA FABRI)
Stockholm
S1-4021.9

FAELLI, BENEDICTUS HECTORIS
Bologna
(S1-3253a), (S1-3253b), (S1-3253c-d)

Florence
S1-2854A, S1-2915A, S1-2998A,
(S1-3033a-c), (S1-3033d), (S1-3033e),
(S1-3033f), (S1-3033g), (S1-3033h-i),
(S1-3033j), (S1-3033k), (S1-3033l),
(S1-3033m), (S1-3033n), (S1-3035f),
(S1-3035g)

FRANKFORDIA, NICOLAUS DE (with
RENNER)
Venice
S1-1604.5-.5A, S1-1605.5

FRATRES DOMUS HORTI VIRIDIS AD S.
MICHAELEM
Rostock
S1-955.7

FROBEN, JOHANN
Basel
S1-1227A-B

FROSCHAUER, JOHANN
Augsburg
(S1-658c)

FURTER, MICHAEL
Basel
S1-1244A, S1-1246.5

GALLUS, BONUS
Colle di Valdelsa
S1-3534.8

GARALDIS, BERNARDINUS DE
Pavia
S1-3472.5

GARALDIS, MICHAEL DE
Pavia
S1-3472.5

GERING, ULRICH
Paris
S1-3601.8

GHIRLANDI, ANDREA
Florence
(S1-3033a-c), (S1-3033d)

GHOTAN, BARTHOLOMAEUS
Lübeck
S1-946.7

—Stockholm
S1-4021.7

GLOGKENDON, GEORG
Nuremberg
(S1-829a)

GREGORIIS, GREGORIUS DE
Venice
S1-2033A, (S1-2042b)

GREGORIIS, JOHANNES DE
Venice
S1-2033A

—(with BRITANNICUS)
Venice
S1-1962.2

Grenoble
(S1-3863a-b)

GRÜNINGER, JOHANN (REINHARD)
Strassburg
S1-166A-B, S1-171.5, S1-183A

GULDENSCHAFF, JOHANN
Cologne
S1-415.3, S1-418.8

HAMANN, JOHANNES
Venice
S1-2234.5

HECTORIS, BENEDICTUS *see* FAELLI,
BENEDICTUS HECTORIS

HIST, CONRAD
Speyer
S1-869.8
—with JOHANN HIST
Speyer
S1-866.8

HOCHFEDER, CASPAR
Nuremberg
(S1-829a)
—Cracow
(S1-1269a)

HUSNER, GEORG (First press)
Strassburg
S1-125.5

—(Second press)
Strassburg
(S1-304a)

see also Printer of the 1483 Jordanus de
Quedlinburg

JENSON, NICOLAUS
Venice
S1-1581A-B, S1-1584A, S1-1588A

KESLER, NICOLAUS
Basel
S1-1202.7, S1-1216.5

KEYSERE, AREND DE
Oudenaarde
S1-3931.5

KOBERGER, ANTON
Nuremberg
S1-670A-B, S1-672.5, S1-692A,
S1-714A, S1-732A-C, S1-751A,
S1-754.5-.5A, (S1-764a-b), S1-866.8

KÖBEL, JAKOB
Oppenheim
(S1-1100b)

KOELHOFF, JOHANN, THE ELDER
S1-372.5, S1-373.5

LAURENTII, NICOLAUS
Florence
S1-2854A

Leipzig
S1-1037.5, S1-1043A

LE TALLEUR, GUILLAUME
Rouen
S1-3857A

MORGIANI, LORENZO
Florence
S1-2998A

NICOLAI, JOHANNES, DE VERONA
Verona
S1-3370A

Nuremberg
S1-664.5, S1-670A-B, S1-672.5,
S1-692A, S1-714A, S1-732A-C,
S1-751A, S1-754.5-.5A, (S1-764a-b),
S1-766.5, S1-804.5, S1-813.8, S1-818.5,
(S1-829a), S1-866.8

Oppenheim
(S1-1100b)

OS, PETER VAN
Zwolle
S1-3904.3

OTMAR, JOHANN
Augsburg
(S1-658d), (S1-658e)

Oudenaarde
S1-3931.5

Oxford
S1-3999.8, S1-4000.8

PAFRAET, RICHARDUS (First press)
Deventer
S1-3882.5

PAGANINIS, PAGANINUS DE
Venice
S1-2359A-B

PANNARTZ, ARNOLDUS (with
SWEYNHEYM)
Rome
S1-1292.5, S1-1295A-B

Paris
3653, S1-3594.3, S1-3601.8, (S1-3605a),
S1-3615.7, S1-3630.2, S1-3630.8,
S1-3632.4, S1-3632.8, (S1-3643a),
S1-3660.7, S1-3702.6, S1-3736B,
(S1-3736b-c), (S1-3736d), (S1-3736e),
(S1-3736f), (S1-3736g), (S1-3736h),
(S1-3736i), (S1-3736j)

Passau
S1-997A-B

Pavia
S1-3472.5

PENTIUS, JACOBUS
Venice
(S1-2702b-c)

PETIT, JEAN
Paris
(S1-3736f)

PETRI, JOHANN
Passau
S1-997A-B

PETRI, JOHANNES
Florence
S1-2998A

PHILIPPE, GASPARD
Paris
(S1-3736b-c)

PIGOUCHET, PHILIPPE
Paris
3653

PINCIUS, DONINUS
Venice
(S1-2751a)

Pincius, Philippus
  Venice
    (S1-2473a)

Plannck, Stephan
  Rome
    S1-1392.8, S1-1404.8, S1-1427.5

Plasiis, Petrus de
  Venice
    S1-1777A

Ponte, Gotardus da
  Milan
    (S1-3168b)

Printer of:
  Caviceus
    Venice
      S1-2192.8
  'Darmstadt' Prognostication
    Mainz
      S1-30.7
  Flavius Josephus
    Belgium?
      S1-3947B
  Gesta Christi
    Speyer
      S1-833.8
  Henricus Ariminensis (Georg
  Reyser?)
    Strassburg
      S1-112.5
  Nebrissensis, Introductiones
    Salamanca
      S1-3972.5
  Pseudo-Savonarola, Esposizione
  sopra il salmo Verba mea
    Florence
      (S1-3033e), (S1-3033f),
      (S1-3033g)

the 1483 Jordanus de
Quedlinburg
  Strassburg
    S1-218A, S1-258.5
the 1483 Vitas patrum
  Strassburg
    S1-157A

Prüss, Johann
  Strassburg
    S1-191.2, S1-215.2, (S1-216c-e)

Pynson, Richard
  London
    S1-4017A, (S1-4021c)

Quentell, Heinrich (Second press)
  Cologne
    S1-427.5, S1-439.5, S1-457.2

R-Printer (Adolph Rusch)
  Strassburg
    S1-71.3, S1-79.7

Ratdolt, Erhard (with Maler and
Löslein)
  Venice
    S1-1729A

Ratdolt, Erhard (alone)
  Venice
    S1-1800A, S1-1818A, S1-1836A-B

'Rei, Juan de'
  Burgos
    (S1-3983a)

Rembolt, Berthold
  Paris
    S1-3601.8, (S1-3736e)

Renchen, Ludwig von
  Cologne
    S1-424.5

RENNER, FRANCISCUS (with
FRANKFORDIA)
Venice
S1-1604.5-.5A, S1-1605.5

REYSER, GEORG *see* Printer of Henricus
Ariminensis

RICHEL, BERNHARD
Basel
S1-1141.5

RIZUS, BERNARDINUS
Venice
S1-2174.5, S1-2181.5

Rome
S1-1292.5, S1-1295A-B, S1-1381.5, S1-
1392.8, S1-1404.8, S1-1427.5, (S1-1508a)

ROOD, THEODORICUS
Oxford
S1-3999.8, S1-4000.8

Rostock
S1-955.7

Rouen
S1-3857A

RUBEUS, ALBERTINUS
Venice
(S1-2229a-b), (S1-2229c), (S1-2229d)

RUBEUS, BARTHOLOMAEUS
Venice
(S1-2229d)

RUBEUS, JACOBUS
Venice
S1-1657A

RUBEUS, JOHANNES (Second press)
Venice
S1-2212A, (S1-2229d)

RUSCH, ADOLPH
Strassburg
S1-141A-B

see also R-Printer

RUSCONIBUS, GEORGIUS DE
Venice
(S1-2750a)

SACON, JACOBUS
Lyons
(S1-3838c)

Salamanca
S1-3972.5

SANCTO URSIO, HENRICUS DE
Vicenza
S1-3506.5

SCHÖFFER, PETER
Mainz
S1-6.3, S1-24A-B, S1-24.7

SCHÖNSPERGER, JOHANN
Augsburg
S1-596.2-.2A, S1-596.4, S1-601.7,
S1-608.5-.5A, S1-609A

SCHOTT, MARTIN
Strassburg
S1-149.9

SIBER, JOHANNES
Lyons
S1-3754A, S1-3755A

SMEDH, ANNA *see* FABRI, ANNA

SMEDH, JOHANN *see* FABRI, JOHANN

SNELL, JOHANN
Stockholm
S1-4021.6

S1-1581A-B, S1-1584A, S1-1588A,
S1-1604.5-.5A, S1-1605.5,
S1-1657A, S1-1729A, S1-1777A,
S1-1800A, S1-1818A, S1-1836A-B,
S1-1838.8, S1-1884A, S1-1934.2,
S1-1934.7, S1-1938.5-.5A,
S1-1962.2, S1-2033A, (S1-2042b),
S1-2078.8, S1-2174.5, S1-2181.5,
S1-2192.8, S1-2199A, S1-2212A,
(S1-2229a-b), (S1-2229c),
(S1-2229d), S1-2234.5, S1-2268.7,
S1-2359A-B, (S1-2473a),
S1-2482A, S1-2508.5, (S1-2544a),
(S1-2626e), S1-2645B-D,
S1-2657A-C, S1-2686A,
(S1-2702b-c), (S1-2750a),
(S1-2751a), (S1-2751b)

VÉRARD, ANTOINE
Paris
S1-3632.4, S1-3632.8

Verona
S1-3370A

Vicenza
S1-3489A-B, S1-3506.5

WAGNER, PETER
Nuremberg
S1-804.5

WERDEN, MARTIN VON
Cologne
(S1-478a)

Westminster
S1-3989.8-.8A, S1-3990.5, S1-3994A

WOLFF, JACOBUS, VON PFORZHEIM
Basel
S1-1234.3

WORDE, WYNKYN DE
Westminster
S1-3994A

YSENHUT, LIENHART
Basel
S1-1237.5

ZAINER, GÜNTHER
Augsburg
S1-502A, S1-516.8, S1-518.5

ZAINER, JOHANN, THE ELDER
Ulm
S1-907A, S1-911A

ZELL, ULRICH
Cologne
S1-315.5, S1-316.5, S1-343.5

ZIERIKZEE, CORNELIS DE
Cologne
(S1-491d)

Zwolle
S1-3904.3

Ege, Otto F. *Original Leaves from Famous Books: Eight Centuries, 1240 A.D.-1923 A.D.* [New York: Philip C. Duschnes, 1949]
S1-732C, S1-1777A, S1-1838.8

Hall, Edwin. *Sweynheym & Pannartz and the Origins of Printing in Italy: German Technology and Italian Humanism.* McMinnville, Oregon: Phillip J. Pirages, 1991.
S1-1295A-B

Jackson, Donald. *Johann Amerbach.* Iowa City, Iowa: Prairie Press, 1956.
S1-1163A-B

Klemming, Gustav Edvard. *Sveriges äldre liturgiska literatur: bibliografi.* Stockholm: Kongl. Boktryckeriet, P. A. Norstedt & Söner, 1879.
S1-813.8, S1-818.5, S1-946.7, S1-952.5, S1-4021.6, S1-4021.7, S1-4021.8, S1-4021.9

Kurtz, Benjamin P. *An Original Leaf from the Polycronicon Printed by William Caxton at Westminster in the Year 1482.* San Francisco: The Book Club of California, 1938.
S1-3989.8-.8A

A Leaf From the Letters of St. Jerome, First Printed by Sixtus Reissinger, Rome, c. 1466-1467: With an Historical Essay by Jeremy duQuesnay Adams and a Bibliographical Essay by John L. Sharpe III, Edited by Bennett Gilbert. Los Angeles: Zeitlin & Ver Brugge, 1981.
1318A

Monumenta Germaniae et Italiae Typographica: deutsche und italienische Inkunabeln in getreuen Nachbildungen. 12 pts. in 3 vols. Berlin: Reichsdruckerei, 1892-1913.
S1-141A, S1-516.8, S1-664.5, S1-670B, S1-840A, S1-955.7, S1-1729A

Nissen, Claus. *Herbals of Five Centuries: 50 Original Leaves from German, French, Dutch, English, Italian, and Swiss Herbals, With an Introduction and Bibliography.* Zurich: L'Art ancien, 1958.
S1-24A-B, S1-40A-B, S1-166A-B, (S1-216d-e), S1-596.2-.2A, S1-608.5-.5A, S1-917.5-.5A, S1-997A-B, S1-3489A-B

Nissen, Claus. *Tierbücher aus fünf Jahrhunderten: sechzig originalgraphische Tafeln aus deutschen, französischen, niederländischen, englischen, italienischen und schweizerischen Prachtwerken, 1491-1966, mit einer Einführung in die Geschichte der Zoologie.* Zurich: L'Art ancien, 1968.
S1-40C

S1-911A

WAY, PETER S1-1818A

WERTHER S1-1141.5

WESPACH, JOHANNES, OF ULM 556, 1210

WESSBACH, JOHANN, OF ULM *delete; see*
    WESPACH, JOHANNES, OF ULM

WESTON, CHARLES DIMICK (H '36, B.
    1914) S1-1244A

WESTON, GEORGE BENSON (H 1897, B.
    1874) S1-1244A

WHARTON, EDITH (1862-1937) S1-1962.2

WHEATLAND, DAVID PINGREE (H '22,
    1898–1993) S1-502A, S1-1836A-B

WHITE, ALAIN CAMPBELL (H '02, 1880–
    1951) (S1-3838c)

WINSHIP, GEORGE PARKER (H 1893,
    1871–1952) S1-1588A

WIPACHER, TOBIAS (1593) 2537

WITTOCK, MICHEL S1-1884A

WOLFFRAMI, VITUS (D. 1508) S1-216.5

WOOD, EMORY M. (S1-3736f)

WYNNE-FINCH, HENEAGE S1-149.9

ZABRISKIE, CHRISTIAN A. (S1-310a)

ZWICKAU. RATSSCHULBIBLIOTHEK
    (S1-310a)

ZYSSENHEIM, JOHANNES 216, (S1-304a)

Index of Incunabula Containing Manuscripts

S1-24.7, S1-30.7, S1-258.5, S1-804.5, S1-911A, S1-1292.5, S1-1836A, S1-2181.5, S1-2268.7, (S1-3253c), (S1-3736c), S1-3882.5

Index of Incunabula with Identified Bindings

Augsburg. Ambrosius Keller (Kyriss shop 49) 496
Basel. Jakob Spindler (Kyriss shop 64) S1-1135.3
Dürnstein (Lower Austria) Augustinian Canons (B.M.V.) S1-1584A
Ellwangen. Johannes Meifoge (Kyriss shop 68) 1119
Heilsbronn. Johannes Moyses (Kyriss shop 72) 1946
Memmingen. Unidentified binder (Kyriss shop 111) 707
Tübingen. Johannes Meifogl *delete; see* Ellwangen. Johannes Meifoge
Valentius (?) *delete; see* Memmingen. Unidentified binder

POINTS OF BIBLIOGRAPHICAL INTEREST

Author's presentation inscription (S1-2626e)

Bearers 159, 270, 293, 294, 467, 545, 554, 563-565, 568, 1003, 1008, 1045, 1247, 1914, 2529, 2551, 2605, S1-216.5, S1-258.5, S1-457.2, S1-554A, S1-1043A, S1-3857A, S1-3882.5

Broadsides (S1-829a), S1-866.6

Dance of Death woodcuts S1-3615.7

Foliation in lower margin (S1-3253a)

Leaf books 5, S1-24A-B, S1-40A-B, S1-40C, S1-125.5, S1-141A-B, S1-166A-B, (S1-216c), (S1-216d-e), S1-516.8, S1-547.5, S1-596.2-.2A, S1-601.7, S1-608.5-.5A, S1-664.5, S1-670B, S1-692A, S1-732A-B, S1-732C, S1-754.5-.5A, S1-813.8, S1-818.5, S1-840A, S1-907A, S1-917.5-.5A, S1-946.7, S1-952.5, S1-955.7, S1-997A-B, S1-1163A-B, S1-1173A-B, S1-1227A-B, S1-1295A-B, S1-1581A-B, S1-1588A, S1-1604.5-.5A, S1-1729A, S1-1777A, S1-1800A, S1-1838.8, S1-1938.5-.5A, S1-2359A-B, S1-2645B-D, S1-2657A-C, S1-2686A, S1-3403A, S1-3489A-B, S1-3989.8-.8A, S1-3994A, S1-4021.6, S1-4021.7, S1-4021.8, S1-4021.9

Maps (S1-829a)

Miniatures S1-191.2, S1-216.5, S1-3947B

Misimposition (S1-3033a-b)

Model copy S1-1818A

Music, Printed S1-952.5, S1-1135.3, S1-2234.5

Proof sheets S1-6.3, S1-596.4, S1-953A, S1-1037.5

Purchase notes, Early S1-216.5

Rubricator's date 655, S1-216.5

Rubricator's name S1-216.5

Setting copy S1-1818A

Type, Flat impression of 3994

Unrecorded editions S1-596.4, S1-953A, S1-3931.5, S1-3941.5

Vellum, Books printed on S1-6.3, S1-946.7, S1-952.5, S1-3999.8, S1-4021.6, S1-4021.7

CONCORDANCES

Hain/HUL

[Walsh numbers for incunabula duplicated in this Supplement are repeated here.]

H	HUL	H	HUL	H	HUL
450	S1-372.5	1988	S1-315.5	3171	S1-754.5-.5A
350	2482, S1-2482A	1991	S1-315.5	3173	139-41, S1-141A-B
412	S1-457.2	2003	S1-2181.5	3174	2359, S1-2359A-B
424	S1-3942.5	2055	S1-2268.7	3175	S1-1199.2-.2A
437	907, S1-907A	2210	1932, S1-1934.2	3540	714, S1-714A
469a	S1-343.5	2252	218, S1-218A	3546	S1-3660.7
528	(S1-491d)	2358	(S1-3253b)	3746	1258, S1-1258A
652	751, S1-751A	2419	S1-804.5	3770	1043, S1-1043A
865	S1-3660.7	2513	3755, S1-3755A	3852	S1-813.8
900	561, S1-561A	2856	S1-955.7	3938	S1-818.5
1140	S1-258.5	2872	S1-1216.5	3950	S1-4021.9
1214	2998, S1-2998A	2909	S1-258.5	3993	1159, S1-1159A
1254	S1-1604.5-.5A	2961	(S1-3253a)	4574	1173, S1-1173A-B
1256	S1-835.8	2980	3754, S1-3754A	4805	S1-2192.8
1307	1726-29, S1-1729A	3022	S1-3632.8	5125	S1-1962.2
1339	1244, S1-1244A	3034	S1-71.3	5190	1884, S1-1884A
1459	S1-6.3	3051	S1-1292.5	5501	2685-86, S1-2686A
1493a	2199, S1-2199A	3054	S1-1605.5	5535	1162, S1-1162A
1599	841, S1-841A	3061	1581, S1-1581A-B	5537	1162, S1-1162A
1657(4)	2645-45A, S1-2645B-D	3118	1227, S1-1227A-B	5946	2851-54, S1-2854A
		3133	S1-518.5	5948	3403, S1-3403A
1880	S1-Heb-12.5	3137	692, S1-692A, S1-866.8	5950	1777, S1-1777A
1966-67	S1-54.5			6081	S1-869.8

H	HUL	H	HUL	H	HUL
6086	S1-1237.5	8659	S1-3989.8-.8A	10532	S1-1234.3
6112	(S1-658c)	8898	182-83, S1-183A	10551	S1-125.5
6140	S1-30.7	8943	(216b), (S1-216c-e)	10729	S1-439.5
6151	2655-57, S1-2657A-C	8944	34-40, S1-40A-C	10974	S1-3472.5
6271	S1-3990.5	8946	S1-166A-B	11063	S1-1141.5
6515	S1-1934.7	8948	23-24, S1-24A-B	11253	S1-946.7
6620	(S1-658e)	8949	S1-596.2-.2A	11422	S1-2234.5
6677	(S1-478a)	8952	S1-917.5-.5A	11461	S1-171.5
6717	1817-18, S1-1818A	8956	S1-608.5-.5A	11673	(S1-3033n)
6926	1800, S1-1800A	9003	S1-216.5	11995	S1-3828.6
7001	S1-427.5	9091	911, S1-911A	12015	S1-3534.8
7123	(S1-1100b)	9126	2212, S1-2212A	12022	S1-1381.5
7428	(S1-2473a)	9302	501-02, S1-502A	12310	1584, S1-1584A
7530	840, S1-840A	9339	S1-1037.5	12315	1163, S1-1163A-B
7633	S1-1173.5	9574	S1-1938.5-.5A	12553	(S1-658d)
7686	S1-866.8	9599	S1-664.5	12564	(S1-3838b)
7770	S1-3869.7	9624	1657, S1-1657A	12829	(S1-2544a)
7792	(S1-3983a)	9848	S1-3632.4	13016	S1-516.8
8219	S1-3601.8	9851	(S1-2751b)	13017	670, S1-670A-B
8326	(S1-3736e)	9892	S1-24.7	13018	S1-672.5
8365	S1-418.8	9893	S1-24.7	13127	1588, S1-1588A
8419	S1-191.2	9928	S1-3999.8	13393	1834-36, S1-1836A-B
8445	997, S1-997A-B	10158	(S1-310a)	13410	Heb-11-12, S1-Heb-12A
8451	3487-89, S1-3489A-B	10363	1295, S1-1295A-B		
8564	(S1-2751a)	10415	S1-3615.7	13570	(S1-3035g)
8581	2032-33, S1-2033A	10469	S1-112.5	13617	(S1-3425a)
				13624	(S1-3253c-d)

H	HUL	H	HUL	H	HUL
13868	609, S1-609A	14402	(S1-3033l)	15031	S1-1246.5
13899	S1-2078.8	14403	(S1-3033k)	15092	3855-57, S1-3857A
14054	(S1-3168b)	14410	(S1-3033e)	15369	S1-1392.8
14134	554, S1-554A	14444	(S1-3033d)	15456	S1-1404.8
14153	S1-373.5	14508	726-32, S1-732A-C	15497	S1-3506.5
14348	(S1-3033h-i)	14509	S1-601.7	15720	S1-833.8
14375	(S1-3033j)	14524	S1-149.9	15723	S1-833.8
14386	(S1-3033f)	14798	S1-766.5	15746	(S1-3736i)
14397	(S1-3033g)	14942	S1-560.5	15847	3369-70, S1-3370A

Proctor/HUL

Proctor	HUL	Proctor	HUL	Proctor	HUL
83	S1-6.3	1340	S1-457.2	2245	S1-804.5
123	23-24, S1-24A-B	1413	S1-439.5	2271	S1-813.8
128	S1-24.7	1448	(216b), (S1-216c-e)	2282	S1-818.5
153	S1-30.7	1494	(S1-491d)	2317	S1-833.8
160	34-40, S1-40A-C	1533	501-02, S1-502A	2336	841, S1-841A
208	S1-54.5	1543	S1-516.8	2342	840, S1-840A
234	S1-71.3	1577	S1-518.5	2403	S1-866.8
253	S1-79.7	1624	S1-547.5	2447	S1-869.8
299	139-41, S-141A-B	1636	554, S1-554A	2532	907, S1-907A
329	S1-112.5	1648	561, S1-561A	2548	911, S1-911A
409	S1-149.9	1763	S1-596.2-.2A	2561	S1-916.2
419	157, S1-157A	1767	S1-916.2	2622	S1-4021.7
463	S1-171.5	1786	S1-601.7	2623	S1-946.7
485	182-83, S1-183A	1801	609, S1-609A	2644	S1-952.5
572A	S1-215.2	1852	(S1-658c)	2647	S1-4021.6
632	218, S1-218A	1967	670, S1-670A-B	2749	S1-1246.5
633A	S1-216.5	1972	S1-672.5	2829	997, S1-997A-B
641	S1-258.5	2028	692,S1-692A,S1-866.8	3022	1043, S1-1043A
811	S1-315.5	2068	714, S1-714A	3023	S1-1037.5
818	S1-316.5	2084	726-32, S1-732A-C	3316	S1-1292.5
1037	S1-372.5	2111	751, S1-751A	3321-25	1295, S1-1295A-B
1053	S1-373.5	2115	S1-754.5-.5A	3617	S1-1381.5
1219	S1-415.3	2128	S1-766.5	3636	S1-1392.8
1262-63	S1-424.5	2198	S1-664.5	3676	S1-1404.8

Proctor	HUL	Proctor	HUL	Proctor	HUL
4100	1581, S1-1581A-B	6428	(S1-3033a-c)	7637	S1-1173.5
4105-11	1584, S1-1584A	6444	(S1-3033l)	7686	S1-1216.5
4113	1588, S1-1588A	6445	(S1-3033m)	7706	S1-1234.3
4160	S1-1604.5-.5A	6446	(S1-3033k)	7717	S1-1237.5
4163	S1-1605.5	6447	(S1-3033j)	7727	1244, S1-1244A
4248	1657, S1-1657A	6448	(S1-3033h-i)	7760	1227, S1-1227A-B
4367-68	1726-29, S1-1729A	6449	(S1-3035g)	7776	1258, S1-1258A
4379	1800, S1-1800A	6451	(S1-3033g)	8026	S1-3630.2
4390	1817-18, S1-1818A	6452	(S1-3033f)	8050	S1-3594.3
4401	1834-36, S1-1836A-B	6453	(S1-3033e)	8301	S1-3601.8
4482	1777, S1-1777A	6912	3369-70, S1-3370A	8410	3736, S1-3736B
4503	S1-1962.2	6973	3403, S1-3403A	8540	3755, S1-3755A
4558	2032-33, S1-2033A	7049	(S1-3425a)	8662	S1-3828.6
4699	1884, S1-1884A	7131	3487-89, S1-3489A-B	8768	3855-57, S1-3857A
4956	S1-2181.5	7158	delete	9136-37	S1-3904.3
5124	2212, S1-2212A	7160	3503	9467	(S1-1269a)
5170	2359, S1-2359A-B	7169	S1-3506.5	9562	S1-3972.5
5194	S1-2234.5	7242	S1-3534.8	9645	S1-3989.8-.8A
5556	2645-45A, S1-2645B-D	7299	Heb-11-12, S1-Heb-12A	9669	S1-3990.5
5561	2655-57, S1-2657A-C			9725	3994, S1-3994A
5574	2685-86, S1-2686A	7302	S1-Heb-12.5	9749	S1-3999.8
5716	(S1-2751b)	7374	S1-2192.8	9752	S1-4000.8
6091	(S1-2229d)	7572	1162, S1-1162A	9760	4003, S1-4003A
6120	2851-54, S1-2854A	7573-76	1163, S1-1163A-B	9795	4017, S1-4017A
6292	2915, S1-2915A	7591	1173, S1-1173A-B	9829	S1-4021.8
6355	2998, S1-2998A	7613	S1-1199.2-.2A	9830	S1-4021.9
6427	(S1-3033d)	7615	1159, S1-1159A		

Gesamtkatalog/HUL

[GW numbers from Bd. X, Lfg. 1-Bd. XI, Lfg. 2 (1992-2003), published too late for inclusion in the concordance in Walsh vol. 5, have been added below with reference to the relevant Walsh entries.]

GW	HUL	GW	HUL	GW	HUL
3	4003, S1-4003A	2743	(4021a), (S1-4021c)	4283	2359, S1-2359A-B
4	4017, S1-4017A	2882	S1-2268.7	4285	S1-1199.2-.2A
434	2482, S1-2482A	2905	S1-54.5	4294	S1-754.5-.5A
484	S1-3882.5	2995	S1-315.5	4298	S1-518.5
563	S1-457.2	3004	S1-2181.5	4303	692, S1-692A, S1-866.8
600	907, S1-907A	3008	3736, S1-3736B		
655	(S1-491d)	3047	S1-3630.8	4682	S1-3660.7
773	S1-343.5	3124	1932, S1-1934.2	5054	1258, S1-1258A
861	(S1-2229a-b)	3186	218, S1-218A	5088	1043, S1-1043A
866	delete	3346	S1-804.5	5373	S1-813.8
86	751 [incorrectly recorded as GW 866], S1-751A	3414	3994, S1-3994A	5458	S1-818.5
		3418	3755, S1-3755A	5467	S1-4021.8
		3926	S1-1216.5	5499	S1-4021.9
1561	S1-1173.5	3934	S1-955.7	5712	S1-3632.8
1568	S1-3660.7	4137	(S1-3736b-c)	6102	S1-2174.5
1602	561, S1-561A	4157	3754, S1-3754A	6163	1173, S1-1173A-B
1976	S1-3702.6	4209	S1-71.3	6195	S1-1427.5
2079	2998, S1-2998A	4210	S1-1292.5	6433	S1-2192.8
2195	S1-1604.5-.5A	4216	S1-1605.5	6763	S1-1962.2
2197	S1-835.8	4222	1581, S1-1581A-B	6838	1884, S1-1884A
2290	1726-29, S1-1729A	4275	1227, S1-1227A-B	7223	2685-86, S1-2686A
2334(4)	2645-45A, S1-2645B-D	4282	139-41, S141A-B	7502	(S1-3643a)
				7723	S1-664.5

GW	HUL	GW	HUL	GW	HUL
7502	(S1-3643aA)	10691	476	10950	426
7723	S1-664.5	10698	1178	10983	S1-952.5
7814	2655-57, S1-2657A-C	10710	1448	11307	1417
7957	S1-3615.7	10714	164-65	11309	2994
7966	2851-54, S1-2854A	10716	812-13	11328	1505
7968	3403, S1-3403A	10731	365	11335	939
7970	1777, S1-1777A	10736	936	11341	2047
8648	840, S1-840A	10738	585	11345	1476
9159	S1-1934.7	10750	349	11349	787
9168	S1-3782.5	10762	S1-866.8	11351	87
9268	609, S1-609A	10772	352	11353	9-10
9433	1817-18, S1-1818A	10800	339	11354	1574
9835	S1-427.5	10815	929	11355	1334
10275	S1-1237.5	10818	425	11356	1141
10505	841, S1-841A	10825	328	11357	1587
10566	1436	10841	S1-415.3	11358	1318
10567	S1-866.6	10870	460	11361	1741
10596	1744	10879	208	11362	1128
10598	2370	10888	3924	11363	1130
10644	1092	10894	146	11366	694
10647	1093-94	10896	163	11368	161
10653	1481	10899	737	11370	1906
10655	383	10902	265-66	11371	1133
10664	1537	10943	1007	11373	167
10671	354	10944	943	11375	2125
10674	452	10945	905-06	11376	2170

GW	HUL	GW	HUL	GW	HUL
11377	1225	11466	689	11711	S-195A
11378	2131	11475	2072	11714	1091
11379	733	11476	1907	11715	264
11380	1911	11478	2356	11728	613
11382a	1940	11489	1938	11822	289
11385	1900	11495	1950	11835	3826-27
11396	586	11501	1954	11862	815
11401	2365	11502	1229	11863	520
11405	539	11506	2610	11867	1224
11409	1681	11512	290	11871	892
11417	41	11539	887	11878	3883
11420	408	11553	811	11895	450
11422	2153	11563	130	11902	2311
11431	396	11570	828	11904	S1-3601.8
11432	1361	11575	829	11905	3791-92
11434	1218	11580	3446	11908	3791-92
11436	3419	11591	1763A	11910	3794-95
11447	1246	11594	2773	11912	244-45
11450	85	11595	2763	11916	3796-97
11451	12-13	11596	2766	11917	992
11453	1332	11597	S-1068A	11918	3663
11456	1123	11684	1631	11937	964
11460	1866	11691	1401	11971	724
11463	1129	11696	2350	11978	3901
11464	1773	11697	2729	12049	1114, S-1114A
11465	1875	11707	2354	12056	2360

GW	HUL	GW	HUL	GW	HUL
12091	1480	12272	S1-3594.3	12429	3360-61
12102	3984	12275	999	12431	1214
12109	3300, S-3300A	12276	3487-89, S-3487	12432	2090
12114	Heb-18-19	12278	2540-41	12433	1216
12116	2187	12302	S-473A	12436	1221
12117	1829	12310	3291-93	12437	2785-86, S-2786A
12187	262, S-262A	12312	1793	12451	503-14
12188	214, S-214A	12313	2477	12468	S1-3989.8-.8A
12189	S-209A-B	12314	2599	12471	227
12193	104-05	12318	1496	12477	2898
12219	932	12319	3210	12479	1483
12220	930	12321	1645-46	12482	1429
12224	S1-3630.2	12322	1359	12522	3944
12225	851	12323	1991-93	12622	S1-3632.4
12228	1228	12325	2404-06	12656	S1-1141.5
12232	588	12344	965	12659	192
12233	114-16	12374	279	12667	3193
12255	981-82	12409	2800-01	12699	3938
12256	399	12411	1498	12753	868
12262	477	12419	2032-33, S1-2033A	12756	975
12265	3721	12420	1318A	12763	S-450A
12269	867	12422	52-53	12789	386
12270	997, S1-997A-B	12426	1721	12809	387

Goff/HUL

Goff	HUL	Goff	HUL	Goff	HUL
A-3	4003, S1-4003A	A-1320	3736, S1-3736B	B-63	2692, S1-692A, S1-866.8
A-4	4017, S1-4017A	A-1361	S1-3630.8		
A-153	2482, S1-2482A	A-1427	1932, S1 1934.2	B-1038	(S1-2042h)
A-167	S1-3882.5	B-24	218, S1-218A	B-1086	1258, S1-1258A
A-209	S1-457.2	B-52	(S1-3253b)	B-1107	1043, S1-1043A
A-235	907, S1-907A	B-106	S1-804.5	B-1164	S1-813.8
A-265	(S1-491d)	B-143	3994, S1-3994A	B-1179	S1-818.5
A-329	S1-343.5	B-146	3755, S1-3755A	B-1183	S1-4021.8
A-387a	(S1-2229a-b)	B-386	S1-1216.5	B-1187	S1-4021.9
A-393	751, S1-751A	B-427	S1-955.7	C-156	S1-2174.5
A-528	S1-1173.5	B-476	(S1-3253a)	C-236	1173, S1-1173A-B
A-554	561, S1-561A	B-486	(S1-3736b-c)	C-248	(S1-3035f)
A-739a	S1-3702.6	B-534	S1-71.3	C-355	S1-2192.8
A-785	2998, S1-2998A	B-535	S1-1292.5	C-424	(S1-3736j)
A-867	S1-1604.5-.5A	B-541	S1-1605.5	C-524	1884, S1-1884A
A-869	S1-835.8	B-547	1581, S1-1581A-B	C-545a	S1-1962.2
A-928	1726-29, S1-1729A	B-598	1227, S1-1227A-B	C-708	(S1-2229d)
A-959(4)	2645-45A, S1-2645B-D	B-605	(S1-764a-b)	C-767	2685-86, S1-2686A
		B-607	139-41, S141A-B	C-894a	(S1-3643a)
A-1156	(4021a), (S1-4021c)	B-608	2359, S1-2359A-B	C-960	2655-57, S1-2657A-C
A-1238	S1-2268.7	B-610	S1-1199.2-.2A		
A-1267	S1-54.5	B-619	S1-754.5-.5A	D-21	S1-3615.7
A-1302	S1-315.5	B-627	S1-518.5	D-29	2851-54, S1-2854A
A-1316	S1-2181.5			D-31	3403, S1-3403A

Goff	HUL	Goff	HUL	Goff	HUL
D-33	1777, S1-1777A	G-641	(S1-3736e)	J-142	S1-3904.3
D-102	(S1-3863a-b)	H-5	(S1-2626e)	J-171	S1-424.5
D-158	(S1-658c)	H-37a	S1-3630.2	J-260	1159, S1-1159A
D 162	S1 30.7	H-51	(S1-1100b)	J-575	S1-664.5
D-243a	(S1-3736g)	H-61	S1-3594.3	J-592	1657, S1-1657A
D-311	840, S1-840A	H-64	997, S1-997A-B	L-27	(S1-3605a)
D-452	S1-1934.7	H-68	3487-89, S-3487, S1-3489A-B	L-36	(S1-2751b)
E-20	609, S1-609A			L-58	S1-24.7
E-48	(S1-658e)	H-129	S1-1381.5	L-75	S1-3999.8
E-117	1817-18, S1-1818A	H-160	2032-33, S1-2033A	L-262	(S1-310a)
F-129	S1-427.5	H-177	(S1-2751a)	M-42	S1-112.5
G-34	S1-3506.5	H-267	S1-3989.8-.8A	M-94	S1-1234.3
G-39	(S1-2473a)	H-430	S1-3869.7	M-221	S1-439.5
G-51	841, S1-841A	H-461	182-83, S1-183A	M-237	S1-125.5
G-87	469	H-486	34-40, S1-40A-C	M-440	S1-1202.7
G-97	23-24, S1-24A-B	H-489	(216b), (S1-216c-e)	M-476	S1-1141.5
G-98	S1-596.2-.2A	H-509	S1-216.5	M-644	S1-946.7
G-103	S1-917.5-.5A	Heb-24	Heb-11-12, S1-Heb-12A	M-722	S1-4021.7
G-107	S1-608.5-.5A			M-730	S1-4021.6
G-108	S1-166A-B	Heb-48	S1-Heb-12.5	N-4	(S1-3033n)
G-114	S1-866.6	I-13	911, S1-911A	N-131	1295, S1-1295A-B
G-217	S1-415.3	I-45	2212, S1-2212A [incorrectly recorded as I-54]	O-48	S1-3828.6
G-220	S1-866.8			O-65	S1-3534.8
G-321	(S1-3983a)	I-54	*delete*	P-46	1584, S1-1584A
G-333	S1-952.5	I-191	501-02, S1-502A	P-51	1163, S1-1163A-B
G-635	S1-3601.8	J-28	S1-1037.5	P-253	(S1-658d)
		J-95	S1-1838.8		

Goff	HUL	Goff	HUL	Goff	HUL
P-338	(S1-3736f)	R-7	670, S1-670A-B	S-281	(S1-3033j)
P-352	(S1-2702b-c)	R-8	S1-672.5	S-307	726-32, S1-732A-C
P-370	(S1-2544a)	R-153	S1-1237.5	S-308	S1-601.7
P-465	1162, S1-1162A	R-180	S1-2078.8	S-321	S1-149.9
P-467	(S1-304a)	R-261	1800, S1-1800A	S-364	S1-916.2
P-472	S1-418.8	S-4	(S1-2229c)	S-581	S1-766.5
P-486	714, S1-714A	S-5a	(S1-3168b)	S-663	S1-560.5
P-489	(S1-3838c)	S-17	(S1-1508a)	S-689	3855-57, S1-3857A
P-501	S1-2508.5	S-21	554, S1-554A	S-735	S1-1246.5
P-519	157, S1-157A	S-39	S1-171.5	T-62	S1-1392.8
P-641a	(S1-3168a)	S-115	(S1-3736h)	T-122	S1-258.5
P-698	S1-316.5	S-169	2915, S1-2915A	T-123	S1-1404.8
P-832	1588, S1-1588A	S-172	(S1-3033h-i)	T-209	S1-6.3
P-943	(S1-2750a)	S-198	(S1-3033d)	T-234	1244, S1-1244A
P-1006	1834-36, S1-1836A-B	S-202	(S1-3033a-c)	T-254	2199, S1-2199A
		S-203	(S1-3033e)	T-535	S1-833.8
P-1118	(S1-3035g)	S-242	(S1-3033f)	T-543a	(S1-3736i)
P-1144	(S1-3425a)	S-258	(S1-3033g)	V-44	3947A, S1-3947B
P-1147	(S1-3253c-d)	S-263	(S1-3033l)	V-88	3369-70, S1-3370A
Q-2	S1-547.5	S-264	(S1-3033m)	V-278	S1-79.7
R-6	S1-516.8	S-269	(S1-3033k)	W-24	S1-869.8

Not in Goff

HUL

3653

S1-191.2

S1-215.2

S1-372.5

S1-373.5

(S1-478a)

S1-596.4

(S1-829a)

S1-953.8

S1-1135.3

(S1-1269a)

S1-1427.5

S1-1938.5-.5A

S1-2234.5

S1-3472.5

S1-3632.4

S1-3632.8

S1-3660.7

S1-3754A

S1-3782.5

S1-3931.5

S1-3941.5

S1-3942.5

S1-3972.5

S1-3990.5

S1-3999.8

S1-4000.8

Wrongly credited to HarvCL, Harv(DO)L, Harv(L)L, or PH by Goff

D-215

F-322

F-323

I-54

L-28

V-114